The Bedside
Guardian
41

The Bedside Guardian *41*

A selection from

The **Guardian** 1991–92

edited by John Course

and introduced

by Michael White

FOURTH ESTATE · *London*

First published in Great Britain in 1992 by
Fourth Estate Limited
289 Westbourne Grove
London W11 2QA

A catalogue record for this book is available from
the British Library.

ISBN 1–85702–057–X

Typeset by York House Typographic Ltd, London
Printed in Great Britain by Clays Ltd, St Ives plc

Contents

Nice to be back

Exit Gorby, stage right

Other worldly matters

Contents

Contents

Introduction

Michael White

Cancel the subscription, dammit

Every so often I shudder at my newspaper bill and decide to prune it. But which papers should be cancelled? Can't do without the *Daily Mail*, it gets my blood pressure pumping over breakfast, a role performed by the *Sunday Times* at the weekend. Got to keep an eye on *The Times* and the *Indy*. The *Torygraph* is full of nuggets and the *FT* is so interesting these days.

How about cancelling the *Guardian*, then? In moments of rage, say twice a week, there comes the desire to chop off the hand that feeds me. How could they have led the paper on that ridiculous story? How humiliating that the sub-editors have allowed one of my spelling mistakes to creep into print again. And why have they carried another letter from that idiot?

I know others share such thoughts because I am in regular receipt of long letters from a gentleman in Bayswater attacking the bias and incompetence of myself and my colleagues in some detail. I write back, urging Furious of Bayswater to try another newspaper. But he won't.

You may know how he feels. In newspaper reading – and employment – as elsewhere in life, many are wanderers, but others are creatures of habit. Or rather, as I prefer to see it, loyal to our chosen tribe, despite everything, warts and all. One can get addicted to warts in Bayswater.

The *Guardian* tribe is much mocked by its rivals, for wishy-washy liberalism, for dangerous leftism, for muesli-eating and for 'wimmins' issues, for priggery and for naïve idealism, not to mention dropping 'Manchester' from the title in 1959.

Boisterous caricature, long out-of-date, or badges of honour? All of the above. While bits of the image are true, other bits are hilariously untrue. There are, for example, still not enough women in senior positions at the *Guardian*, and the managing director, Jim Markwick, once stood as a Conservative candidate against Stan Orme in Salford East. 'Too good for those Salford Tories, Michael,' Stan later confided.

In short, the position is confused, as befits a paper of progressive outlook. But never mind. One of the perks of working for the paper is the perceptible shudder that the very mention of its name raises among well-bred folk in the Home Counties whose acquaintance is confined to summaries of the *Guardian*'s views provided by the *Telegraph*.

For new members of the tribe seeking further enlightenment and warts, I still recommend Michael Frayn's early novel, *Towards the End of the Morning*, not least for its opening sequence's description of the generic *Guardian* editor furtively hoping not to be noticed around the office.

Or they can read this edition of *The Bedside Guardian*, for enduring evidence of *Guardian* qualities that still appeal to me apart from good writing, which is a fuddy-duddy *Guardian* tradition that other newspapers now embrace: a mixture of humour and irony, passion and outrage (not enough of it!), plus tolerance to leaven the pervasive under-doggery, which I happen to like best of all.

It's tempting to name names, but everyone has their own favourites. Besides, the thing about a newspaper is that, while some get the bylines and the journalistic prizes, the product (as we call it in marketing circles) is a team effort. Subs (who not only edit the nightly flow of unmanageable words but write the headlines we reporters get blamed for), advertising salesfolk, printers, circulation reps, even the management, play their parts. And, since the *Guardian* is owned by a non-dividend-paying trust (chairman: H. Young, whom you will read in a moment), a grateful nod is also due to the rest of the Guardian and Manchester Evening News group whose profits help sustain the enterprise in a world of global media empires.

Sufficient to say that the first battered edition of the *Bedside Guardian* on my shelf, Number 2 in the series, contains the word teenager in cautious quotation marks and, in one of Alistair Cooke's pieces, reference to a 'coloured maid' at Harry Truman's retirement party in 1953. Much has changed and the pace is more measured, the prose more consciously erudite. But No. 2 is the recognisable ancestor of No. 41 and contains 8 bylines of people I knew personally or know, including Cooke – who writes me letters, far more charming and occasional than Furious of Bayswater's, politely correcting errors of fact or grammar. Continuity of institutions is another deplorable *Guardian* vice I endorse.

A generation after the elegant Cooke stopped writing for the paper he remains one of my *Guardian* heroes, along with the late Mark Arnold-Forster, intensely modest, and, less modest, the late Peter Jenkins (who left the tribe). Along with shy Nancy Banks-Smith who nightly socks it to the telly and fierce Melanie Phillips who daily socks it to us all.

Along with the reticent Martin Woollacott, the voluble Frank Keating, and Matt Engel, the Middlesex all-rounder who realised that John Major was going to become Prime Minister (and got himself good odds at the bookies) long before Hugo did, or I did, or Ian Aitken. Ian waited 20 years to get into the *Bedside Guardian* because he was not one of those fancy writers who get more than their share in these volumes, but that indispensable man, the hard news reporter. There, I have named names and not managed to include that black-bearded anarcho-giant, Steve Bell. But he can look after himself. Meanwhile, columnist Aitken is in John Course's selection again this year. I'm not, dammit. There's another reason to cancel the subscription.

Cabbages and kings

February 6, 1992: leader

Forty years on

Forty is usually a pretty miserable, in-between sort of birthday: and the Queen's 40 years on the throne, celebrated today, offers only an in-between sort of opportunity for a party. The tributes to diligence and duty are, of course, sincerely meant. The Queen has achieved a great deal of which she can be completely proud. But this time the arriving anniversary has been used more as an excuse for looking at problems than as a reason for ringing bells. Take a few of those difficulties. There is the question of taxes, and whether the Queen should pay them. There is the question of publicity and the propensity of young royals to do stupid things. There is the question of popularity (and visibility) slipping in advanced middle age. There is the question of how long Prince Charles will grey and linger in the waiting-room of public life. These are tedious and gritty matters; and they can easily be built into a dirge of discontent and doom.

That's much overdone. Some of the pains are, in isolation, pure confection. There is, for instance, no reason for anyone with a sense of history to expect some early transfer of the Throne as though it were the presidency of a local rotary club. Of course the Queen will go on and on: that's how she, and we, understand the job. But one thing can get tangled with another. Because, for instance, the royal family wallowed for much of the 1980s in the soapy glamour of beautifully groomed young people doing expensive things, it's natural that audience and critics alike somehow expect the soap stars to change in real life, as they do on the screen. And the ostentation of the spending – the Dallas touch to the dynasty – in turn triggers the taxation charge.

But such interweaving of issues also points towards a solution. Start with cash. In an article which drew quiet Palace endorsement, the *Economist* argues that the Queen isn't remotely as rich as inflated and muddled legend pretends: indeed, that she has been eating into private capital over the years to keep some of the peripheral royals in reasonable style. This suggests an obvious answer: let the peripherals do more of their own eating. And here, indeed, is the rub. The royal family, thanks to some now unfashionable fertility, has become obviously too big for its own good: too many dukes and duchesses performing too few public chores, but lacking any real role – or indeed any eventual relevance. (It's one of the saddest sights of recent years to see a Sarah Ferguson who wanted to keep on working for a living turned into a drifting partygoer by a system that allows men to have some kind of armed service life, but condemns women to wait at home and cut ribbons and open fêtes).

One thing, in fact, goes with another across the Queen's 40 years. There is the end of Empire and the inevitable shrinking of the Commonwealth. There is the ever closer integration of Britain with Europe; together with the ever

February 6, 1992: Steve Bell·

clearer requirement that the British royals, like the Euro-royals, should become more informal and everyday members of society. That is what the House of Windsor has always been good at: managed change. Now the change to be managed is one to a smaller, cheaper family with a continuing place in national life but without too much grandiose apparatus that simply doesn't fit any longer. It is a necessary course adjustment. It may be difficult for the Queen because she has thrown so much of her life into the Commonwealth. It will need some rather shrewder and more powerful Palace advisers than currently seem to exist. But it can and will be done: and there will surely be a 50th birthday with rather less agonising in the background.

March 21, 1992: Melanie Phillips

The royal one-parent family

Pity our poor dear Queen. She finds herself increasingly the head of not so much the royal family as the royal one-parent family. She remains constant but her nearest and dearest are disintegrating around her. Who next? she must be thinking with dread. The possibilities have closed in to a critical point. Her sister's marriage has collapsed, her daughter's marriage has collapsed, now her second son's marriage has collapsed, while her youngest son appears to have decided not even to attempt this increasingly remote goal of a stable royal marriage.

These, however, are all bit part actors. The big one is Prince Charles, Hamlet to Prince Andrew's Bottom. The pressure on the Prince and Princess of Wales is now overwhelming. If they were to separate, say many commentators, it would be catastrophic for the Windsor dynasty. All failed marriages are sad, and all failed royal marriages are significant and sad, but the only marriages that must remain inviolate at all costs are those of the monarch and her heir. The Wales marriage fuels an unstoppable stream of speculation that it is in trouble. But Prince Charles appears to suffer from a more serious problem than the state of his marriage, judging from his own utterances and behaviour.

He appears to be searching fruitlessly for a worthwhile role to play and a meaning to his life, giving an impression of crankiness, unpredictable mood swings and a distinct absence of stiff upper lip. So the real message for Her Majesty as she surveys the fresh wreckage of minor royal lives is stark. She can never abdicate. She and her mother are the only constants in the family firm to embody unquestioning, undeviating, unchanging duty.

Duty lies at the heart of the furore over Fergie and explains why this family breakdown is more serious than previous ones. It's another pointer to the growing crisis for the British monarchy in sustaining its role as an icon for the nation. It is surely no coincidence that the Queen Mother deliberately put her health on the line this week on a parade ground in Berlin. The Queen Mother is the embodiment of that quasi-mystical sense of royal duty, dignity and changelessness. At 91 she is a national institution. She was ill last week with a chill she couldn't shake off. Yet she stood shivering for 35 minutes on a rain-soaked parade ground in Berlin. Why?

John Barnes, a lecturer in government at the London School of Economics, says he is certain she did it to reassert the permanence of the royal sense of duty precisely because the Duchess of York was in spectacular revolt against it. The Queen Mother was presenting the St Patrick's Day shamrock to the Irish Guards. 'It was done deliberately on the Queen Mother's part,' he says. 'She was ill but performed her role as a symbolic figure. She must have been risking her life. She went and did something totally unselfish, laying down her life to protect the monarchy.'

It is such values that the royals feel are so threatened by the Duchess of York's behaviour. When Princess Margaret was divorced it didn't matter that much because she was only the Queen's sister. When Princess Anne separated from Captain Phillips, it still didn't matter that much because, although the marriage had collapsed, the Princess Royal so completely embodied the notion of royal duty that her royal role remained utterly intact. But the Duchess of York has rebelled against the doctrine.

Royals have always led lives of hypocrisy and humbug on the basis that whatever the peccadilloes behind palace walls, the pretence of serenity must be maintained to retain the mystique of the royal family. The Duchess of York appears to have refused to tolerate the humbug and play the game according to the rules. That's why Buckingham Palace has turned on her. Being stripped of all her royal duties from midday on Thursday was reminiscent of the treatment meted out to Mrs Simpson when Edward VIII married her. Fergie appears to be about to become a royal un-person.

Despite yesterday's apology by the Queen's hapless press secretary, Charles Anson, it is true that the royal family is furious with the Duchess. They feel, as Mr Anson faithfully reported, that she's long been out of control with all the high jinks and unwise friendships. Her offence was to have stripped the mystery from the monarchy and refused to toe the party line. That's why Prince Andrew is hardly even being talked about even though, as the Duchess is reported to have remarked bitterly, it takes two to make or break a marriage. Real people's lives are not the issue here. The issue is the symbolism and mystery of the monarchy.

People want the royal family to be both real and unreal,

to be both accessible and remote, to be like them but better than them. The fact that marriage breakdown is now a commonplace isn't the point. The royal family serves as a symbol for The Family. This is because the part they play is not to be like us but to stand for us. On a rational level, of course, their constitutional functions are negligible. Much of what they do is a kind of make-work; hence the existential angst of the heir to the throne, desperately trying to turn a symbolic role into a practical job. And on the same rational level, it is obviously true that the royals will suffer similar matrimonial problems to the rest of us. But as Vernon Bogdanor, reader in government at Oxford University, argues, the monarchy works not on a rational but a powerful emotional level. It embodies the ideal of The Family, which is why separations hurt.

The royal family is a national obsession reflected and deepened by the media. It has been turned into a soap opera by the tabloid press, with most of the quality press pretending to be more cerebral and maybe even disdainful, but just as hooked. When Prince Andrew's engagement to Sarah Ferguson was announced six years ago, Alexander Chancellor pointed out in the *Sunday Telegraph* the assumption by the media that nothing else was of such consuming interest to the British public. He wrote: 'Are we right, or are we mad? If we are right, are you then mad? Or are we all equally mad? A friend of mine walking down Piccadilly on the day the engagement was announced saw three middle-aged ladies burst into tears of joy as they read the news in the evening paper.' What are they feeling now, those three middle-aged ladies, one wonders?

There are those who harbour suspicions that the *Daily Mail* broke the story this week because it knew that overwhelming interest in this drama would divert public attention away from the Government's continuing difficulties in the election campaign. The question is whether the soap opera is now beginning to make people impatient or even angry.

There are two possible reactions to the fragmentation of the royal family. Either people feel everyone should be much more tolerant now of family breakdown, or they feel it shouldn't happen because it damages the essence of monarchy.

Sometimes people hold both opinions at once. The reason for the paradox is that although people may identify to some extent, the royal family are *not* like us. Professor Maurice Bloch, an anthropologist at the London School of Economics, points out: 'Their family organisation is totally different from everyone else. The royal family is more like those primitive families, the clans and lineages that have to continue through time. That's the reason for a lot of the fascination with them. The fact that European families don't have this continuity is felt intensely as a problem. People feel that their own little corner is continually breaking up.' So as our own families break up, maybe there's even more need for the iconic family to remain intact.

The importance of that family is enshrined in the constitution. Royal marriages and divorces are decided by the Queen on the advice of the Cabinet. These relationships are not private matters but public property. As Bogdanor says: 'Maybe Fergie couldn't stand that tension between public and private. But as long as it doesn't affect the Queen or Prince Charles it's not a total disaster.'

European royal families suffer these tensions too, although at a less advanced stage. In Spain King Juan Carlos is hugely popular because he brought about the restoration of democracy, so the fact that he gave himself a very limited constitutional role doesn't matter. Everyone knows it all wouldn't be there but for him. Nevertheless he's got problems with his son, Prince Felipe, who's attached to a commoner, Isabel Sartorius. The convention is that the Spanish royal family doesn't marry commoners.

Queen Sofia is insisting that unless the monarchy sticks by
the old rules it will be ruined. Certainly, in the British
royal family it is marriages with commoners which have
come unstuck. Antony Armstrong-Jones, Mark Phillips and
now Sarah Ferguson have all showed in various ways they
were not prepared to put up with the demands of the
unreal royal life. But the supposition that only other royals
can stand the heat of the Windsor kitchen doesn't quite
hold up since the Queen Mother, embodiment of the
royal ethos, was also a commoner once.

Other European monarchs are more informal. They
tend to go round on bicycles, and the Swedish King Carl
Gustav XVI, who's been deprived of all constitutional
functions, is sometimes seen shopping in high-street
stores. Would a similar informality solve the problems of
the British monarchy? No, says Bogdanor, it wouldn't suit
the British temperament, which wants to feel deferential
and likes ceremonial flummery. 'No Labour government
has ever dared attack the monarchy because they know
how popular it is among the working class. It's notable
that John Smith made a point that he wasn't proposing to
do anything about the Civil List. It's an emotional commitment which began with Queen Victoria. Before that the
monarchy was held in low esteem but in the 19th century
it associated itself with the development of the franchise
and so became inextricably involved with parliamentary
democracy.'

So how damaging is the rumpus over the Yorks? 'It's
desperately damaging to the monarchy,' says the LSE's
John Barnes. 'The feeling of sympathy may conceal that.
The monarchy stands for everything you want to be. You
want to have children you can be proud of; then something like this happens. It's not just that they're getting
divorced, but she turns out to want to carry on with doing
the job but doesn't want the burdens of it. The reality of
Fergie comes up smack against the ideal of the Queen.
She's betrayed the ideal. So the defence mechanism goes

into action, that she should never have been allowed to marry him in the first place.

'The fragmenting of the royal family is a trauma. As long as the Queen is around we can cope with it. My worry is the effect 10 or 20 years on if the Queen herself is gone, the person who is utterly immune to all this criticism, and replaced by a guy who isn't ideal . . . I would say the monarchy is a god until the Queen dies or abdicates. So the practical effect is that she must never abdicate. When she dies there will be no image or icon against which to set off any bad behaviour.' The only solution to this predicament, Barnes suggests, comes in the form of the Princess of Wales. Already, he says, she is shaping herself into the mould of the Queen Mother. 'They are very similar in many ways: both originally commoners, both remarkable beauties, both in emotionally distant if not actually unhappy marriages.'

It appears that whatever difficulties there may be with the Wales marriage, the Princess is determined to put duty first and adapt. If not, if that marriage were to collapse or if the Princess stopped going among Mother Theresa and Aids victims and kicked over the gilded cage that encloses her, Barnes foretells disaster for the monarchy. 'If that were to happen, if the Princess does not fill that role, then the pressure to abolish the monarchy and become a republic would become unstoppable. But God knows how you'd do it.'

June 6, 1992: leader

The royal dogs of war

Some eighteen months ago the combined forces of the British press agreed a new Code of Conduct for the industry, established and funded an independent Press

Complaints Commission, and vowed to clean up their act. That was not high-minded altruism. It had become absolutely necessary because public contempt for much newspaper conduct was spilling over into the House of Commons. Fresh laws curbing the freedom of journalists to report and investigate stood poised. A committee under David Calcutt QC had clearly put the press on probation.

The first year of PCC probation, as the Commission noted a few weeks ago, proved a tentative success. The number of complaints about press behaviour was more limited than lurid legend portended. The distinguished lay members of the body worked well alongside the editors. There was a tolerable feeling of progress and, at the margins, of increased restraint. Self-regulation in matters of freedom is always better than the galumphings of a legal system which (as Captain Robert Maxwell might have observed, had he still been with us) offers rather more protection to rich rogues than it does to Joe Public.

One area of press reporting through the eighteen months has not, however, improved. The House of Windsor has never had it so bad. Yesterday's *Daily Mail* banner headline – Princess Diana 'tried to take her own life' – is the nadir for the moment. But tomorrow, bringing the first episodes from a new royal book with attendant hype, is another day: the start of another week.

Take just a few of the solemnly agreed clauses from the Code of Conduct. Clause One (after the reference to 'a substantial element of self-restraint by editors and journalists') reads: 'Newspapers and periodicals should take care not to publish inaccurate, misleading or distorted material.' Clause Three reads: 'Newspapers, whilst free to be partisan, should distinguish clearly between comment, conjecture and fact.' Clause Seven states: 'Unless their inquiries are in the public interest, journalists should not photograph individuals on private property without their consent.' And there is much, much more, prefaced by the injunction that 'all members of the press have a duty to maintain the highest professional and ethical standards'.

Fine words (and some concomitant actions). But where, remotely, do they apply to current coverage of the royal family?

They don't. The royals are open house. They sue not, neither do they complain to the Commission. We shall see, in what remains of 1992, a swathe of books and tales detailing the sexual activities of Marlene Dietrich. That is because she is dead. She cannot sue for libel. The royals are the living dead of British society.

In fact, almost clinically, the institution of the Press Complaints Commission has made the predicament of the Windsors worse. They are the only area left off limits, where almost anything may be said or written without fear of retribution.

Examine, for example, yesterday's *Daily Mail* exercise. It is a spoiler, a pre-emptive strike before tomorrow's *Sunday Times* serialisation of a book by Andrew Morton. But it summons up the full talents of its front-page author, Nigel Dempster.

Mr Dempster's work depends upon the work of a second author – 'the writer Nicholas Davies'. This gent is our old friend Nick Davies, last heard of leaving Captain Maxwell's *Mirror* employment in a mild tiff over the 'professional and ethical standards' of journalists peddling arms. Inside the *Mail* we learn more of how Davies, through 'nearly a year of research, slowly gained the confidence of those close to Prince Charles'. We hear how, in the autumn of 1991, he went to an 'expensive restaurant' – as opposed to a transport caff – in the West End, where an 'uneasy royal confidant' told him of an incident six years before where the Princess of Wales had taken an unspecified dose of paracetamol. It was never, Davies explained, 'a full-blooded attempt to kill herself'. It was 'a terrible cry for help'. So much for the lead headline. A straight case of inaccuracy under Clause One. And where

– as a 'senior reporting team' ploughs in to 'check out Davies's amazing story', finding rumours, backstairs gossip and finally someone referred to as 'another source', are we under Clause Four: Privacy? Are we 'detecting or exposing crime'? Are we 'protecting public health and safety'?

Tomorrow, the *Sunday Times*, with a £250,000 or so serialisation investment to protect, offers Andrew Morton's 'main course' – the words of the paper's editor, rather gleefully hinting yesterday that 'not once, but several times' the Princess was in deep despair 'and there were cries for help which she probably now regrets'. Mr Morton, a former royal scribe for the *Daily Star* and *News of the World*, stands to make a million or so from his book. Its special selling point is either that it has direct access to the Princess: or not. Mr Morton himself says merely the Princess 'did not co-operate with the book in any way'. He did not interview her. She did not read the text. According to the editor of the *Sunday Times*, some of the stuff came from her 'best pals' – though why such dear chums should spill beans about 'cries for help she probably now regrets' is obscure.

There are two issues here, with some intermingling. One is the health of the royal family. That has had its ups and downs through history: and this is one of the downs. A particular conjunction of young royals and rocky marriages – ballooned into a real-life version of *Dynasty* – has lowered respect, esteem and a public readiness to go on funding the show. This is, as yet, very far from the 'threat to survival' posed by Nigel Dempster yesterday. But the institution itself has problems and is not making a very good fist of sorting them out. The calibre of advice it seems able to call on is feeble.

But – and here comes the intermingling – the tabloid, and now the broadsheet, press have become an oppressive part of the new reality. The Princess of Wales, last month, could not take a private swim in a private pool without telephoto lenses intruding. Clause Seven of the Code. And how, in the reaches of Clause Eleven, which seeks to protect young children from hurt or harassment, are we to assess the impact of the paracetamol yarn on Princes William and Harry, two forgotten kids? Is it possible for children in such circumstances to grow up to be normal, balanced human beings? Or is the current flaking under pressure merely accelerating cause and effect?

This newspaper, for the most part, is monarchically agnostic. The institution, like many others, is there for as long as it serves a popular purpose. But this debate is not about institutions: it is about people and what is tolerable.

We find 'the writer Nicholas Davies' and the *Daily Mail* pretty intolerable. We find Andrew Morton's coming millions intolerable. We find intolerable the editor of the *Sunday Times*'s oleaginous sympathy for the 'deep despair' of the Princess. We find the sales-drumming confections between the papers of News International hard to tolerate. We gag over one phrase from one of them yesterday. 'A courtier told the *Sun* . . . ' We find the 'best pals' and 'confidants' and 'Palace insiders' and 'the friends of Diana' – enough vinegary tomato sources to drown a plate of chips – contemptible.

Is there 'a story' in there somewhere? Who can tell? There may be. But it is buried beneath the garbage and the rivalries and the cash within a narrow industry of royal manufacturers. And the excavation has gone too far: from uncovering the story to being the story.

May 20, 1992: Peter Lennon

Sins of the fathers

When the news came over the radio that Eamonn Casey, the Bishop of Galway and Kilmacduagh, Apostolic Administrator of Kilfenora, had fathered a child by an American woman called Annie Murphy, a man stopped his car on an Irish motorway and burst into tears. 'What will I tell my son now?' he wailed.

On a radio talk-in, a woman demanded crossly: 'How can I explain this to my mother?'

First there was bewilderment. Then as the days unchastely unveiled stories of love nests on the Kerry coast and kissing in the back seat of a car, while the chauffeur (Monsignor John O'Keeffe) kept his eyes off the rear mirror, the airways and roadways, tea shops and church yards, the very ether of sunny windy Southern Ireland was vibrant with distress calls.

The priests, as is their wont, were on hand to minister on air and in the press: a tactful presence, restrained as always in the early excesses of grief; an understanding companion holding out hope of healing and forgiveness. For long hallucinatory hours last week you were convinced that it was the laity who had done something awful and not the clergy.

What the clergy were engaged in was one of their most challenging missionary tasks in its history: reconverting, in a hurry, the Irish population back to its normal state of sacerdotal gullibility. Those soft, canonical brogues, which so often carry a hint of hysteria and repressed violence, were reasserting the power of a state within a state: the Irish Catholic, Apostolic, ironclad, reactionary Church.

It is a body accountable to nobody in Ireland, in practice also immune from civil law, as we saw last week when laymen and churchmen tacitly agreed to make light of the bishop's 'borrowing' £70,000 from church funds to give to Annie Murphy. (The bishop had 'made amends', was the general judgment, although Eamonn Casey, in fact, had not returned any money; it was returned for him by anonymous 'friends'.)

The Irish Catholic Church was finally being brought down, was the judgment of outsiders as the Church reeled before this uncontrollable cacophony of outrage and distress. But a closer scrutiny of what went on demonstrated that the Church will neither be immediately brought down nor substantially lose its moral authority over this affair. However, Annie Murphy has produced a Peter over which the Irish hierarchy stumbles badly and which inevitably will be one of the rocks that will destroy the power of the Church in Ireland. But it could be some time – a decade perhaps.

For the hierarchy the Casey affair is a matter not of substance but of volume. Despite the public babble of astonishment, the Irish have long lived in tolerant knowledge of their whiskey priests, and the furtive erotic collisions of lusty countrymen in reversed collars with girls in search of super solace were normally a matter of pity and tact. Since this was a vintage catastrophe, the Irish, who like to give good value, were suitably loquacious about it. In fact it was no huge step to accept the misdemeanours of a bishop, particularly one already known for reckless ways with the bottle and motor car. It was the sound being turned up for the neighbours to hear, to a degree that no pretence could be maintained, which was the problem.

The Irish Catholic Church has two powerful foundations: the practical one of being socially and politically an autonomous structure and the more significant one of being woven into the heart and psyche of the people. No one in Southern Ireland, no matter how apparently complete his or her personal rupture with the Church, is unaffected by Catholic thinking. An *Irish Times* columnist,

John Waters, aged 36, told me that it is common to find the new generation of radical lay critics of the Church using the Church's own vocabulary in attacking it: they use terms such as 'sin'. A non-practising Catholic, he would never, he said, describe himself as 'non-Catholic'.

Sprinkled with obedience at birth, saturated to the roots of their imagination all their young learning life (from the birth of the Republic the State readily relinquished education to the Church), in moments of crisis the critics are essentially thinking *within* an Irish Catholic framework. In the end most accept with varying degrees of restlessness and rebellion the most grotesque relationships and most pitiless edicts of the hierarchy. The vast majority accept having their lives policed by people, often of low intelligence, wilfully rejecting normal relationships for themselves but imposing their bizarre and furtive understanding of sexual matters on others. (It must be said that the priest himself is also a victim of this conditioning.)

This relationship between priest and people was one which originated in Penal times when the priest hid in the ditches with the peasants and brought them outlawed education. So the priest in Ireland is not just a reticent pastor: he is your brother and father; your, often amusing, uncle; your family doctor on mental problems; your sometimes drinking and always sporting companion, particularly for games such as hurling, so long wedded to bigoted nationalism.

To betray the priest, to abandon him to dispassionate outside judgment is as great a trauma as betraying one of your own family; indeed, more difficult, since there is also a subtle distance in the intimacy that protects the priest from an accumulation of those luscious fermenting family detestations which often lead households to the most exuberant kind of internecine betrayals.

The nature of this relationship means that it is the lay victims who will, for the moment, prevent disintegration.

Women, who so elaborately suffer from the Church's edicts, were last week often the most uncharitable about Annie Murphy; the most forgiving of the bishop's lapse.

If the outsider is misled into overestimating the seriousness of Irish outrage in these matters, the Irish themselves have been overestimating for decades the intellectual and sexual freedom they have achieved. At one point in the 1960s, Ireland was taken by the wave of anti-authoritarian, liberal thinking that swamped the Western world. The Irish learned to talk openly about condoms instead of sniggering about 'French letters'; young people asserted their freedom of conscience and right to express their sexuality without guilt.

The chief result of this was that it reduced the incidence of knee-wobbling in lanes; young people could have sex in comfort. (It is quite untrue that the Irish were inveterate virgins; they were spectacularly dissolute in damp erotic discomfort; experts in 'safe' sex.) The social stigma on a woman having sex before marriage has largely gone. A women's movement, concerned with better pay and better provision for deserted wives, developed from 1969, at first representing no threat to Catholic values.

A whole new generation of sexually at ease young people appeared to have arrived. But when these young people settled into marriage, traditionally early, they immediately reverted to the old ways and ensured that their children were sent through the process of Catholic education, even the most radical hedging their bets 'for the child's sake'. The children were sent to Mass and expected to go to confession.

Contraception clinics were opened in Dublin, Cork, Limerick and Galway, although 63 per cent of the population was still opposed to the sale of contraceptives. The Church, bending a little before the liberal forces, assumed a position described by Professor J. H. Whyte in *Church and State in Modern Ireland* as 'disclaiming any suggestion that the State was obliged to defend by legislation the moral teaching of the Catholic Church'.

Then, in 1972, Ireland appeared to take another leap into the 20th century when, following a referendum, Article 44 of the constitution was repealed: Ireland no longer recognised the 'special position' of the Catholic Church.

The stated purpose was to reassure the Protestants of Northern Ireland. The Unionists were not fooled; they totally discounted the importance of this step. They were right. In the following decade a series of referenda established that the country was solid behind the Church's rejection of not only abortion and contraception but also divorce. True, in the latter case the Church could not rely simply on reminders of the inviolability of the sacrament of marriage; it had to adulterate its spiritual message with a whisper across the country that if divorce came in, the women would run off with half of the farms of Ireland.

Both the Primate of Ireland, Cahal Daly, and Bishop Casey are known outside Ireland as liberal clerics. Daly for his outspoken stand against the paramilitary, IRA or Loyalist; Casey, former chairman of Shelter in Britain, for his undisputed splendid work for the homeless in Britain and the poor of his diocese in Connaught. Eamonn Casey also took a sensational public stand against American policy in El Salvador when he refused to meet President Reagan on a visit to Ireland.

This apparent liberality makes them all the more effective. Undoubtedly sincere as these stands are, both Daly and Casey are inflexible theological conservatives. (Indeed one priest in Ireland publicly made the point in Casey's favour that at least he did not consider using contraceptives.)

By the 1990s the Irish Church had built a dam against some very turbulent waters. The fall in vocations and incidence of priests abandoning their vows reached critical proportions. The distress of these ex-priests became increasingly public as counselling centres were set up. But until last week there was no such service for the women who often form the other half of these tragic relationships.

At one point last week when the full tragedy of a liberal bishop disgraced by a sexual indiscretion became known, it seemed impossible that the hierarchy could duck a debate on the issue of celibacy. Indeed the president of the Conference of Priests declared on radio: 'There is a lot of debate already among priests themselves. A debate must be good because if we have values we believe the Church must not be afraid to come out and defend those values.'

He must have missed the reaction of the Primate of Ireland a few hours before to a journalist who suggested that 'the Church was having a particular problem at the moment with priests who are having difficulty in remaining celibate'. 'It is grossly irresponsible to create absolutely unsubstantiated rumours of that kind,' fumed his Eminence. (Cognescenti got the impression that the Primate was actually responding to rumours that there was another bishop, as yet unmasked, in the same plight.)

The spokesman for the Irish hierarchy in Dublin made a fine Jesuitical distinction when I put the issue to him. 'Regardless of celibacy or not,' he said, 'the woman was divorced, that is married, and she wasn't free really to do what they did. Celibacy is not an issue in this particular case.'

But despite Cardinal Daly, ecclesiastical celibacy and its associated painful dilemmas became a hot issue the next day. Fr Pat Buckley, a priest who had been relieved of his functions because of his stand on celibacy and now practises independently in Northern Ireland – 'The nearest thing you'll get to a freelance priest in Ireland,' he remarked – took up the challenge. He offered to help set up a counselling group for Irish women who have had relationships with priests. When I rang him that night he said he had already had contact from seven women.

'All seven have had relationships with ordinary priests,' he said, 'and two have had children by priests. One of the ladies from Cork wanted to set up such a group and asked five priests in Cork to assist her, but they all refused. The cardinal yesterday foolishly said that it was all only rumour-mongering and that annoyed one of the ladies. There are women who have been involved for up to 20 years with priests and then been dumped.'

Fr Buckley, aged 42, once worked in the notorious Divis flats in Belfast and now performs the marriage ceremony for ex-priests (the Church refuses to perform such ceremonies). 'They won't let anyone out of the priesthood now unless the priest gets a certificate saying he is insane or a pervert.'

How does Fr Buckley escape pressure from the Church? 'I've had my problems but I am protected by a million Protestants who are watching up here; the good old Protestant ethos of the North. So for PR reasons they are not doing too much to me. I was offered a parish in America but refused.'

How will it all end? John Waters of the *Irish Times* made a comparison with the endless scandals that beset the Charles Haughey regime and finally brought him down: 'There were all those things which really stretched the credulity and tolerance of the people and yet Haughey went on for another decade. But he was finally brought down by the same events.'

Haughey, Waters claims, survived because he created a scapegoat in Sean Doherty, the minister involved in a phone-tapping affair which finally also brought down Haughey. Waters believes the same thing will happen with the Church, Bishop Casey being, for the moment, the convenient scapegoat. 'The church will bandage up the wounds and go on,' he said.

There is no one else to bandage the wounds. From its

inception the Republic explicitly handed over the moral leadership of the country to the clergy. Thirteen years ago Professor Liam Ryan defined the Church role as 'the conscience of society'. Now there is not a single political leader that one could imagine capable of taking a lead or any kind of moral initiative in this crisis.

If you looked in rural areas last week you could see the process of 'bandaging' – recuperation – well under way, a proof that whatever liberality there is in Ireland is confined to the urban areas. The classical image of the laity and churchmen working in tandem was evident.

For the *Western People*, serving Bishop Casey's diocese, the lead story of the week was 'Archbishop dedicates Knock apparition chapel', with a picture of a happy Archbishop of Tuam. Inside, a five-paragraph leader grappled with the Casey affair, emphasising that the clergy's 'goodness outweighs their frailties' and reminding, if not actually warning, readers that the Almighty was 'the only one to judge'. A columnist relegated the affair to his third item, pointing out that Bishop Casey's really grievous sin was to entertain the Pope so well on his visit to Ireland that he came late to the Knock shrine and 'deprived many thousands of expectant pilgrims of the opportunity of seeing him close up'. So with solemnity and flippancy the faithful were directed to let the matter drop.

The safety valve for pent-up feelings was provided by local radio, in a programme, *Faith Alive*, fronted by priests. 'There was great support for Bishop Casey,' presenter Fr Brendan Hoban told me. 'The older men and women blamed the woman. And it came through strongly that he didn't get any money out of it. It wasn't for his own personal gain.' But it was to solve his personal problem? 'Well, I suppose so.'

Did Fr Hoban actually discuss the issues with the listeners? 'No, we allow people to make statements. Or we would reply on a point of information.' Such as what? 'Is it a sin to do this, or wrong to do that. That sort of thing.'

Shortly after, a lusty voice spoke up in support of Bishop Casey: the secretary of Galway Gaelic Athletic Association Hurling Board, Phelim Murphy. 'We made the statement because the Bishop was getting a lot of flak and we are thanking him for the support he gave to Galway,' he said.

Support? 'He was a great hurling supporter and was always at our functions in victory or defeat.'

Would the fact that the Bishop had 'borrowed' from the parish funds not make them hesitate? 'Oh, we wouldn't get involved in that aspect of it. He was always at our functions, win or lose, victory or defeat.'

March 7, 1992: Dave Hill

A hole in his soul

Like the rest of us, Robert is not always right on top of the game of life. Sometimes, as he'll tell you, the whole thing seems to spin out of control, leaving Robert bewildered and exhausted. The situation is hardly eased by the fact that Robert plays by a different set of rules to most of the London humanity that passes blankly before his eyes each day. But Robert is not defeated. He's got his system of survival. He has his priorities worked out.

'Number one, that's me dog.'

His dog is Lady. Lady Muck. Lady is still a pup, a silky black collie cross with eyes that ooze enthusiasm and a nose that gets everywhere. When Robert is on the move he keeps Lady on the end of a rope. But when he's working his pitch, selling *The Big Issue* magazine outside the Body Shop in Victoria Street, she curls up on his rucksack, good as gold. And when at night Robert beds down in the doorway of a nearby building society, Lady's protective presence ensures that he doesn't have to sleep, in his own words, 'with one eye open'.

Priority number two is Robert's little pleasures. He likes his Benson and Hedges, his knuckle's-worth of draw (though he's vowed to give that up) and, most of all, he likes his beer. There's a pub on his patch, not far from Victoria station, where staff and patrons alike welcome him as a regular. And why not? He's always friendly, swapping pleasantries while he waits for his light-and-lager. And unlike a lot of men who can put pints and pints away, Robert settles himself quietly in the corner with Lady at his feet and doesn't force himself on anyone.

Food, perhaps surprisingly, makes it only to priority three. Robert eats regularly but unevenly, that is to say, when he goes to *The Big Issue*'s office (upstairs at the West London homeless drop-in centre in Marylebone) in the mornings to help with distribution, he polishes off all the fried breakfast he can handle. Otherwise, his intake is frugal.

The reasons for this are various. Robert gets paid a modest sum for his *Big Issue* distribution work and makes a little more from selling his quota of magazines. So his eating habits are not straightforwardly the result of penury. There are other reasons and these concern related matters of habit and circumstance.

In the evenings, for example, the kind of cheap, unfussy places where Robert might eat by day – such as sandwich bars or greasy spoon cafés – tend to be shut. Robert's appetite has therefore been obliged to adapt to the strictures of his lifestyle. The other factor in this dietary equation is beer. When your stomach is filled with six pints, maybe ten, maybe more, there isn't really room for anything else. And if, as the witching hour slips by, the steady ache of hunger intrudes upon Robert's sleep, he can always depend on the benevolence of Lady Muck.

'Dog biscuits. They're a lot more nutritious than ordinary biscuits.' Robert, in the pub, sniggered at this, and took another gulp from his glass. 'A few Shapes, they soon fill you up!'

Robert has been living on the streets for four-and-a-half years. He was 16 when he walked out of his parents' home in one of south London's least glamorous suburbs, because he was forever falling out with his dad. He can't explain why the situation was so bad. He just knows it was always that way. The position is less fraught with his mother, whom he visits quite frequently. But the whole question of Robert's relationships with his family is clouded with profound and palpable anxiety.

It was perfectly understandable that he wanted to keep the identities of his family secret from anyone who might read this article and work out who they are. But the surface equanimity with which a deal on this matter was struck could not conceal Robert's inner turmoil.

His staccato south London accent always demands full concentration, but probing his past domestic pain – especially when he hasn't had a drink – can set waves of stress sweeping through his enunciation. Once, over the phone, I asked if I could meet his mum.

'Why d'you want that?'

I had thought it might help people understand Robert's own story better.

'But what's the good of it?' Robert's final refusal was delivered with incongruously formal politeness, as if he feared that his panic might be taken for rudeness.

'No thank you . . . '

'Fair enough. It's OK, honestly.'

'No thank you . . . '

In general, when Robert talks about his early life, he sticks to the edited highlights. One of the earliest and best came when, at the age of nine, he and a friend sneaked away from their boys' special boarding school (long since closed) in Southwark and walked and walked until they'd crossed over London Bridge. It was eight o'clock at night before the police rounded them up and sent them back.

Special school was all right, Robert says. He hadn't been able to handle it at an ordinary primary because he kept getting into fights. But at special school the kids and the teachers were cool and there were pillow fights in the dorms. Once, they went on a week's holiday in Cornwall, living on a barge on a canal. What Robert remembers best was going on a scrumping spree and getting caught up an apple tree.

Such delinquencies paled compared with his next anecdote. When Robert was 13, 'they' – tellingly, perhaps, it was never quite established who 'they' were – took him out of special school and sent him to a standard state secondary. It was a disaster. One day, Robert's younger brother had some of his belongings stolen. Robert knew who'd done it and took unilateral action: 'I was in a fight with these six geezers. One of them got concussion.'

Expulsion was inevitable. Robert had lasted just three months. He saw out his secondary education at a different special boarding school, then entered the world of work as a tyre and exhaust fitter through the Youth Training Scheme. He did well enough and went on to full-status employment in the trade.

For more than a year Robert was bringing in a wage, sporadically at times, but sometimes well over £200 a week. He had bank accounts, saving accounts and credit accounts to his name and moved into his girlfriend's flat. They had a baby daughter. Robert seems to have thrown himself into the traditional role of provider with unquestioning gusto.

'I got a TV, video, fridge-freezer, microwave, radio, Hoover, everything.' But domestic appliances did not bring contentment, not like in the ads. Robert rowed with his girlfriend and he was in and out of work. He moved for a while to a bedsit but his debts were building up and he couldn't pay the rent. Some of the money he spent came from what he describes, without much elaboration, as 'dodgy dealings', and a lot of it went, of course, on beer, consumed from the end of work until chucking out time.

Robert found himself evicted, pursued by creditors and at odds with the family home. He needed to escape to a place where he wouldn't need much money and where he couldn't be traced. And he wanted to be left alone. It was at that point that Robert upped and vanished into the twilight world of the streets. There are various kinds of people sleeping rough: at one extreme are the haggard gentleman veterans, whiskery reminders of a time when homelessness was a footnote to the political agenda (some would argue it still is) and human dereliction was sufficiently scarce for comedy sketch writers to make wise winos and crafty tramps the butt of their wit without causing national offence. At the other is a younger breed, some of them girls, from materially comfortable homes who are inclined to describe themselves as poets, who try their hand at life in the subways and go back home within a week.

Somewhere between these polarities lies Robert. Disaffected enough to have disowned mainstream life, yet young enough to still crave rehabilitation, the pattern of his more recent personal history comprises an earnest struggle for self-improvement punctuated with demoralising lapses.

Most of the time, he personifies the successes of *The Big Issue* magazine, vindicating the import of its slogan: 'Helping the homeless to help themselves.' Since getting involved with the magazine, Robert has really progressed. He used to be an out-and-out beggar, but now he has a Halifax account and is trusted with the office petty cash. He has his own tent as well which, until recently, he pitched alongside other homeless people on Lincoln's Inn Field. He used to sleep in car parks or on trains. One way or another Robert has been one of British Rail's more grateful patrons. He and some friends used to make their home aboard rolling stock in a siding in Selhurst.

Another time Robert would catch his sleep on the Victoria to Gatwick express, commuting from London to Sussex and back several times in the course of a night. On one occasion he climbed drunkenly into a stationary carriage and woke up, with a shock, in Sevenoaks.

Today, Robert routinely discusses this possibility or that of finding a flat or a room to rent. But the struggle is now in his mind and Robert still has some mountains to climb.

A few weeks ago he cancelled what would have been our second interview date. A problem had come up but he didn't want to discuss it. We remade our appointment but when I turned up Robert wasn't around. I went to the pub, where the staff explained he had left the night before 'really pissed'.

I found him in Victoria Street, working his usual pitch, but with his look of wide-boy bravado usurped by the pinched cheeks of apprehension. A bandage clung loosely to his right hand. I'd made him a tape of Little Richard and Marvin Gaye, but Robert explained it wasn't much use to him now as his tape player was broken: 'I smashed it over this geezer's head.'

Robert looked at the ground when he said this. An unshaven man in reflective council overalls stopped by for a chat (a lot of people talk to Robert), but Robert wasn't feeling very chatty. A well-dressed woman made a fuss of Lady and put a pound in Robert's upturned *Big Issue* baseball cap. Robert looked grateful. He admitted, under pressure, that financially he was 'a bit tight'. We had an agreement that we'd split my fee for this profile, so I stumped up an advance and bought him a packet of fags. He said he'd ring when he'd got himself straight.

Exactly what had happened to Robert still remains unclear. But it seems there had been a bit of a ruck with someone else staying at Lincoln's Inn, and that was why Robert had broken camp and gone back to sleeping in doorways. He had drowned his sorrows with a vengeance

and was now embroiled in a facedown with the clear light
of day.

Such breakdowns have happened before, with one
nasty upset triggering an avalanche of self-destruction.
Last summer, Robert spent a lot of time begging on the
glitzy pavements of Sloane Square. He entered into a
timeshare arrangement with another guy and his dog,
whereby they would take turns to sit outside holding out
their hands. While one blew all his money inside the pub,
the other would try to accumulate enough change to do
the same. Then, the pair would swap: different beggar,
same dog.

Sloane Square was an experience. Passers-by who were
obviously loaded were the least likely to give. One or two
would offer cheery heckles like: 'Why don't you get a job?'
Robert, though, had his repartee to hand: 'I'm a self-
employed beggar.' As ever, it was the less well-heeled who
put their hands in their pockets.

Robert remembers shabby pensioners pressing notes
into his hands: 'I used to tell them, "Keep it, you need it
more than me," but they wouldn't have that. In the end I'd
take it just to keep them happy.'

One night, after closing time, a man who'd had a skinful
produced a wad from his pocket. It contained, says Robert,
£175. 'He said, "Oh, it's only money." His wife probably
killed him the next day.'

Trouble came when a couple of drunks started winding
Robert up, trying to move in on his space. There was a
bust-up in the middle of the square. Robert was armed
with a chain, though if he used it he didn't say so.
Whatever, with the confrontation concluded and Robert
on his way, a police car and a van homed in on him.
Robert came quietly: 'I wasn't going to run anyway.' He
spent the night in a cell. The following morning he was
charged with committing grievous bodily harm.

For more than a fortnight he was kept at the young
men's remand centre in Feltham ('it was a free bed,

though,' he points out), then was bailed and arrested again on the same night. He was duly charged with affray and bailed again.

Nine days later he was arrested for a third time, this time the charges were threatening behaviour, drunk and disorderly, carrying an offensive weapon, and verbal abuse.

The upshot of this behavioural nose-dive was a suspended £200 fine, a suspended six months' sentence, a £50 fine and a week in jail. Robert didn't tell his mother until later. She wasn't very pleased.

What is, on the face of it, surprising about Robert is his deep conservatism. He has old-fashioned tastes in music, favouring Elvis, Freddie and the Dreamers, The Drifters, even Dean Martin – 'proper songs where you can hear the words'. His hero is salt-of-the-earth-bound Phil Collins, whom he has seen in the movie *Buster*. The backdrop to one of the film's scenes includes a block of run-down flats where Robert used to crash: 'My squat's famous!'

Many of Robert's attitudes are still those of the ultra-traditional, metropolitan working class among whom he grew up. For example, when we were first introduced, I'd come from the House of Commons and was wearing a jacket and tie. The second time we met, intending to head for the pub, I had reverted to T-shirt and jeans.

'Why aren't you wearing the suit?' he inquired.

There was no need for it, I explained.

'Oh, you should wear your suit,' he responded, quite perturbed.

Initially, Robert seemed surprised that I knew my way around the underground network, and I wondered if he'd assumed that a reporter from a posh newspaper would only travel by private car. Similarly, for a man of such rugged experience, he seemed unnerved by alien surroundings. He revealed that he'd once travelled by coach up to Newcastle to visit a girl he knew, but came back the same day. He'd spent two hours in the unfamiliar city and couldn't get away quickly enough: 'it was boring . . . I don't like Geordies,' he said and wouldn't be shifted in his view. The same stoutness of conviction informs his attitude to handouts – 'I won't go running to charity' – and to crime. 'I could steal, easy,' he says, 'but that's not me.' The one time he did indulge in thieving, his booty was one of those Help A London Child teddy bears with a bandage across its eye.

He took it, he explained, to give to his little girl on her birthday. He doesn't see her very often, he explained. And at least the bear was doing the job for which it was designed.

The feeling Robert communicates most strongly when he talks about himself, and when he's wound down with a pint or two, is a desolate and affecting sense of loss. He says sadly, for example, that if he could have his time again, he would take his schooling more seriously. A spell at adult-literacy classes helped and he even carries a diary these days. But for a long time his reading and writing skills largely centred on the pre-eminent brand names of his former trade: 'Michelin', 'Fiesta', 'Sierra' and so on. You sense you are in the company of a man with a hole in his soul which he is anxiously seeking to fill. At the moment, the vacancy looks most likely to be filled by God.

The last time I saw Robert, I found him outside the Body Shop talking to an ex-pat New Zealander called Steve. Steve had brought Robert a pair of sturdy secondhand boots which went well with Robert's new rig, a set of ex-US Army fatigues which, taken with his hard chin and cropped haircut, made him look like a GI who'd lost his platoon. Steve told me he'd spent more than a few nights sleeping on the Strand when he was new to Britain, and believed 'the Lord sent me there, to show me how these people lived'. Steve went on his way and Robert produced from his rucksack a new, shiny blue copy of the Bible. He turned the pages, poring over them, looking for a passage from Luke he particularly wanted to show. This evaded him. But we decided to set off round the corner to the Westminster Chapel, the source of this particular copy of the good book.

Robert had remarked previously that he had become a Christian, 'born again'. He attended services each Sunday morning and evening and joined friends and congregation in a back room for lunch. As we approached, the minister, a Dr R.T. Kendall from Kentucky, stepped forward with a good-news expression.

He had a word of warning for Robert, following a talk he had attended at the chapel a few nights before. The subject of the talk was the 'evil of drugs' and when the speaker – a celebrated anti-drugs campaigner – had asked if anybody present had messed with these sinful substances, Robert was the only one who had. 'God is watching you,' Dr Kendall said to Robert, putting an arm around his shoulder: 'That's all I'll say on the matter.'

Inside the church, which was impressive and smartly maintained, one of Dr Kendall's assistants elaborated his theology. Colin, a young Scotsman, had found Jesus while working as a rough-neck on the North Sea oil rigs. He explained that his was an evangelical church whose creed insisted on the absolute truth of the Bible and that Jesus was the literal son of God. We were all sinners, he explained, but if we put our faith in Jesus, we could achieve a state of forgiveness and be fit to enter heaven.

As we headed for the pub, I asked Robert how he assessed the strength of his own faith. He pondered this question gravely and replied that what the church had offered him so far was a sense of belonging to something, an institution where he could, for a time, be released from the unending stress of the kind of life he leads. 'It's given me more confidence in myself,' he reflected, striding down the pavement with Lady straining ahead, 'more confidence in myself. And you've got to have confidence in yourself when you live out on the streets. Otherwise, the pressure is too much.'

I wrote Robert a cheque for the balance of our 50/50 split. I thought he could add it to his Halifax account. He said he'd give it to his mum. In fact, he reckoned, supping up, he might go off and see her that very afternoon. I left him to his pint and his future, and set off through the throng of Saturday shoppers, down the steps of Victoria tube station and the start of the journey that would take me back to my warm and welcoming home.

March 28, 1992: Posy Simmonds

June 20, 1992: Erlend Clouston

Thin blue line

The dusty white Astra spluttered and shuddered up Steep Turnpike. In the driver's seat PC Alan Williams vainly hammered the accelerator to the floorboards. 'That's flat out,' he sighed. 'Ten to one if we had to chase anything, we'd lose it.'

If anything, PC Williams's odds were generous. The Astra's speedo was registering just under 20 mph.

'It grinds you down,' admitted PC Williams, 21 years with a force whose straitened circumstances are now acquiring music-hall status thanks to Geoffrey Dear, HM Inspector of Constabulary, whose series of reports are likely to lead to the Derbyshire force being the first to be refused a certificate of efficiency.

'I took a prisoner up to North Yorkshire and they said they'd expected to see me in a Lada,' moaned traffic-warden Jeffrey Vardy in the Matlock police-station yard. Beside him the wind whistled forlornly through the coat hanger that served as an aerial for the divisional Sherpa van.

All the bobbies in the canteen told the same story: loved the job, respected the chief and the 'top corridor', but they were stupidly understaffed and the equipment was crap. The cars were crap, the radios were crap, even the shirts were crap.

'Look at this,' snorted PC Williams, tugging out a tiny shirt tail. 'Cheap and nasty.' PC Paul Smith, lately transferred from Hampshire, to his ex-colleagues' general stupefaction, agreed. 'The buttons fall off and the collars go funny when you wash them.'

'Feel that, feel the quality of that rubbish!' said a disconsolate PC, rubbing a legful of lumpy black serge. Little relief is in prospect. One of the few approving paragraphs in Mr Dear's interim report, issued last September, discloses that £5,200 has been transferred from the uniform budget to the informants fund.

Perhaps the men were lucky to have a uniform at all. 'It was years before we had blue lights on the panda cars,' reminisced PC Bill Newbold. 'There's still no two-tones, except for the response Cavaliers.' Until recently Matlock policemen hot-pursuing big-city car thieves in force Metros had to turn a key in the boot if they wanted to switch on the official roof lamp. If they did not turn it off again in five minutes, the battery went flat.

Joint police support-unit exercises with other forces remain a humiliating experience for Derbyshire officers.

'You see these guys from Manchester and Leicester in their Robo-cop gear, and then we appear with shin pads and hockey players' arm protectors,' said one. 'Everything we do, we get this label on us, and it's unfair on the lads.'

Derbyshire's mounted policemen borrow their horses from outside the area. The underwater search unit has long gone. PC Williams's desk was held together by sticky tape.

Blame for their humiliating predicament is apportioned equally between the Government (feeble capital grant) and 'those prats up there' (Derbyshire county council, HQ in Matlock).

'We are pawns,' muttered PC Newbold.

'If only the public knew,' added PC Ivan Charlesworth.

'The officers of the force know that they are sliding fast,' rumbled paragraph 2:18 of Mr Dear's report. No one in the canteen quarrelled with that. 'We're not sliding – we've slid,' said PC Williams. 'We must be at the bottom. It's only our professional attitude to the public that keeps things going.'

At times that must seem an impossible task. Because of a past freeze on recruitment, the Matlock division is 12 men short; because of this, policing between 2am and 6am is often reduced to two or three officers and a manned patrol car. They have to protect a 60-by-20 mile strip of prosperous villages and market towns, surrounded by havens of fast-travelling criminality such as Manchester, Sheffield, Stoke and Derby.

'Sometimes we're really only a recording service,' said PC Charlesworth ruefully. Last year Matlock officers duly recorded 3,540 crimes, and cleared up 964 – 27.2 per cent. The national detection rate is 37.1 per cent. Mr Dear greatly offended county councillors, who suspect a political vendetta, by warning that their policemen were conceding 'more and more ground to the hooligans in the street'.

In his office on the top corridor divisional superintendent Mike Jackson put a brave face on things: 'We do a first-class job, in the circumstances,' he said. 'There are cock-ups occasionally, but by and large we are doing OK.'

Thanks to Mr Dear stirring things up, they had been given four new Astras and a fax machine. Mileage and overtime limits had been relaxed and recruits were promised. Mr Dear had spent several hours at the station during his visit to Derbyshire. He had been 'very supportive' and had talked to a cross-section of the lads.

In the canteen the inspector's chutzpah was much admired. 'He came up here to do a hatchet job,' said PC Williams, who has never quite recovered from the experience of sitting, unsuspectingly, in his area police office when council workmen arrived to brick it up.

June 13, 1992: Martin Wainwright

A twitch in time

A small grey bird with a curiously long tail lost its way this week, en route from Saharan Africa to the south of France, and disrupted a lot of very different British lives.

Nine-to-fivers, shift men, schoolboys – they came, to Spurn Point on the Humber; they saw, in spite of the murk that rare birds seem to favour; and they twitched.

Mark Chase, aged 29 and working shifts in an East Yorkshire chalk quarry, abandoned the leisurely plans he'd drawn up for his Wednesday and Thursday off. Chris Dobson, retired personnel officer in Lincolnshire social services, persuaded his wife to take him for a rapid 50-mile drive.

There was even a minimal effect on national security. A Ministry of Defence contractor, discreetly anonymous but accompanied by a cheery friend called Derek from Greenford, dropped his current project for the day, packed sandwiches and left London at 5.30am on the M1. They were among some 200 twitchers, avid collectors of rare-bird sightings, drawn by a rapid phone and CB radio grapevine to greet the exhausted Marmora's warbler on its landfall at the Humber mouth.

Thousands of pounds' worth of expensive optics was deployed on the little peninsula, spiky tripods balancing in the fog-bound buckthorn. Car-parking receipts shot up by a windfall £300. The wife of Spurn lifeboat's coxswain, Anne Bevan, missed ramming into the back of a twitchers' van by about an inch.

'It suddenly stopped in the middle of the road up Spurn,' said a colleague at the Crown and Anchor, Britain's most easterly pub, where Bevan works part-time. 'The four twitchers in the van thought they'd seen the bird, so they just jammed on the brakes and spilled out there and then. There was some swearing.'

Such sudden, dramatic dashes are one side of the fast-growing and compulsive habit of twitching (named, according to the most widely-accepted theory, after a birder called Howard Medhurst who used to tremble and twitch after motor-bike epics to spot rarities in the 1970s). Barry Spence, warden for the Yorkshire Wildlife Trust, which runs Spurn as a nature reserve, watches with wry detachment when a sighting cry goes up.

'They come from everywhere,' he said. 'They'll be spread out along Spurn [a good two miles] and they suddenly concentrate. It's quite a sight itself.'

The principal means is the twitcher-fed Birdline (0891 700222), updated almost every two hours and astonishingly detailed ('The rose-coloured starling is in the cherry tree by Bradfield post office in Windmill Road'). The dynamic is largely the collector's motivation of tracking down rarities and drawing up lists, with the rules and ritual that make such hobbies elaborate.

Twitchers must identify the bird for themselves, not rely on others' say-so; they sub-divide their prey – carefully disqualifying seabirds spotted outside territorial waters from the most popular, British list. Early June is a key time for the twitcher, when rarities find their way to Britain.

'The rarities are often, well, small and fairly boring-looking,' said Peter Jolly, a day late for the Marmora's warbler because he had to fulfil a promise to take his wife to an antiques fair. But their wonderfully eccentric names – ancient murrelet, Siberian-nesting great knot, long-toed stint – make up for the browns, greys and duns of plumage and look as good as Châteaux Latour or d'Yquem on a wine expert's list.

The Marmora's hunters at Spurn this week were not the superleague twitchers, men (and women) spoken of with some awe within birding, accompanied by a self-deprecating 'it's a bit mad, really'. The current Grail, a British list topping 500 birds, is almost within the grasp of Ron Johns, a gas-company manager from Staines, who started twitching in time to get the 1967 American brown thrasher, which has not been back since.

He is tailed by Chris Heard, a teacher from Maidenhead, Berkshire, at the frontline of twitching, where competition spurs the collecting instinct on. But the Spurn birders noticeably avoided the less pleasant side-effects of rivalry;

Richard Bolton, 16 and puffed after pedalling down from Withernsea, Humberside, and a GCSE exam, was obviously anxious to share his sighting of a specimen of the inaptly named common rosefinch deep in scrub on a long dune.

'There,' he said, notching up his 236th bird and guiding another group of twitchers, looking exactly like the royal ratpack as they trained their telescopes and £500 Zeiss bins on bushes less than five yards away. In spite of their furious scrambles when the cry goes up, the birders are strikingly patient. The finch's plaintive piping could be heard for more than an hour within less than 30 square yards of the buckthorn, before Richard finally spotted it.

No one suggested a miniature grouse-beat to flush it out. And the twitchers, as retired mining engineering lecturer Geoff Carr put it, are also generally knowledge-able and thoughtful about their quarry.

'I spend a lot of my time doing surveys on my own patch, Pugney's countryside park at Wakefield,' he said. 'A lot of twitchers will tell you they get as much interest out of watching robin or blackbird behaviour, as they do on these dashes.'

Their data provides a base for monitors of corn bunt-ings, whose unexplained decline is currently worrying Chris Dobson. The birds' usual acceptance of bird-watchers, even of hundreds of lenses pointing at them from close range, is put down by some to their 'goldfish memory' – by the time they realise they are being watched, they have forgotten what they have realised.

'Twitching tends to widen your natural history interests too,' says Dobson, aged 45, and retired early because of arthritis (a condition helped by the exercise, fresh air and countryside peace of his birding outings). 'If you're in a wood, say, and dull weather's keeping the bird numbers down, you naturally take an interest in the wild flowers.'

He records butterflies as well as birds in his patch of

Lincolnshire. Sheila Gear, also lugging £1,000-worth of optics round Spurn, has diversified from fish. 'I used to run Tingley Tropicals, just outside Leeds,' she said. 'When I took up twitching, it helped knowing how to deal with the Latin names, which we had with the fish as well.'

Women make up about 10 per cent of twitchers (and rising), and Gear was probably the best travelled twitcher on Spurn this week. Birding visits to Thailand, Siberia, Costa Rica and India have helped her to a world list of 2,080 birds.

She helps undermine the misconception that twitching is one of those strange, men-only occupations, like clubs and freemasonry. The Marmora's warbler was detected by another woman watcher – Gillian Grainger from Leeds, who heard its call while staying at Sandy Beaches caravan site this week, recognised that it was unfamiliar and managed to get it identified before catching the bus home.

Twitching as whacky, eccentric and typically Brit is another tenacious but misguided theory. On one of the hobby's furthest shores, the spotting and listing of birds shown on wine labels, the doyen is Peter Stangel, an American. He reported recently from Washington, DC, his delight at discovering passenger pigeons on a 1984 Californian Zinfandel and a Lady Amherst's pheasant on a bottle of Pinot Grigio from Italy.

September 10, 1991: David Ward

The play's not the thing

One week into a new school year. A time to record the first impressions of those on the first rung of the education ladder. A visit to Barwell county infants' school near Hinckley in the one-time Leicestershire hosiery belt.

A basic question to five-year-old Georgina in a pretty

dress: what do you do at school? 'You have to eat your dinner and then go home.' Pause. 'Your mummy or daddy comes to fetch you. Or your grandma.'

This wasn't quite what *Education Guardian* had in mind. Could you elaborate a bit, Georgina? 'You have to go to school because it's a school day. School is for playing.'

Cries of outrage from education's hard-liners: 'You see? No learning, just playing.' Hang on a minute. Listen while Georgina tells you what to do at a table in the middle of her bright classroom in a school built 80 years ago by Wesleyans with a taste for fancy brickwork.

She gestures towards the Plasticine and issues commands with the authority of a headmistress. 'Press down very hard. Now lift it up – and there's your thumb. Now look at it with the magnifying glass.' Done that. Now what? 'Press your finger in the ink pad and then press it on the paper. There's your fingerprint. You can put your name on the paper. Can you write your name? You can take the paper home if you want.'

This may be fun but it also has just a hint of National Curriculum science. *Education Guardian* takes a break from class to wash its inky finger at a low level wash basin. Georgina explains that you can discover which is the hot-water tap by (a) sticking your hand under it when the water is running and (b) by examining the colour dots on top of the tap. Some understanding of semiotics here. Another attainment target bites the dust.

A pause during the drying of hands to recall an introductory phrase from head teacher Jane Sanchez: 'This is the demanding end of the service. These sprogs need attention all the time.' You can say that again, Mrs Sanchez.

Back in the class, young Emma was trying it on at the writing table. School, she said, was boring-snoring. 'You write it for me,' she commanded. Not a hope, said the visitor. She sighed and got to work with her pencil.

Emma was hot. The sun was streaming through big

Wesleyan windows and the creative writers were wilting. Teacher Madeline Johnson considered a remedy: 'My job-share partner and I set the room out during the summer. Now we will have to do some rearranging.'

That was not all they did in the summer. They planned the work for the new term (based on autumn and the harvest) and codified it in topic and subject webs recorded in the kind of quality writing towards which Emma will eventually aspire. Attainment targets were plotted in red. 'None of this makes life any more difficult,' Mrs Johnson said. 'We have been doing this sort of thing for years. It's just that now we call it the National Curriculum.'

The first weeks of term are for watching, observing, assessing, creating order out of the infant's instinctive desire for anarchy. 'If you are a hot dinner, could you go and line up for Mrs Armstrong,' said Mrs Johnson, who *does* sound like Joyce Grenfell, but then you'd be hard pushed to find an infants' teacher who doesn't.

Mrs Johnson has 25 children in her class: the youngest just five, the oldest just six. 'These first few weeks are so important because you have got to get to know your children. You have to be flexible – they are developing all the time.'

Progress will be meticulously recorded. Daniel, clever lad, already knows what a rectangle is. But Mrs Johnson has also decided that she will need to speak to the whole class about their attitude to work and tidying up. There was a small flood in the water corner and a sticky sham-bles under the table where paper-plate faces were under construction. Perhaps that was why she chose to read them Mr Messy at story time.

When the children read for themselves, they start on familiar old Roger Red Hat but won't necessarily stick with him for ever. 'We use phonics, look-and-say, and real books,' said Jane Sanchez. 'You may need all three with one particular child at various stages in his development.

We are not raving trendies here. We are very middle of the road and cautious.'

It was getting still hotter. Mrs Johnson did her hands-in-the-air routine to get the attention of the class and led them to the playground for a break, skipping at the head of a sweltering crocodile. Then they played farmers in the den (the unreconstructed version, where the farmer still wants a wife rather than a partner) and *Education Guardian* prayed that it would not end up as the endlessly-patted bone.

After the break, Martyn, in luminous lime-green T-shirt with Ibiza on it, headed for the computer to ice a series of cakes on the screen. But after some exploration of the keyboard, he managed to escape, crash and abort simultaneously. The machine surrendered and cried: 'Error! Error!'.

The four class groups made their last shift in their integrated day, taking their places for writing, shape-drawing, sticking or play in the home corner. Here Kirsty and Amy celebrated a pretend birthday party at MacDonald's. 'Hurry up,' said Amy, 'we've got to go to the pub.'

Three-fifteen and *Education Guardian* was on its knees; especially since its micro tape recorder had been sussed out at the writing table. 'What's that for?' 'To take notes.' 'Why?' 'Because it saves me work.' 'Why does it save you work?'

Some of us can have enough of inquiring minds. Not so Mrs Johnson: 'During this year, I want these children to develop as individuals, socially, emotionally and intellectually. I also want them to have mastered the basics of reading and numeracy.'

Well, Georgina, what more do you want?

April 10, 1992: Melanie Phillips

Taking the Mickey

It could be the beginning of a sell-out. It might be an economic disaster. The world is watching to see if all the boasts and the promises live up to expectations. This is Mickey Mouse's weekend, the culmination of months of secretive planning, plastic fantasies and media hype.

On Sunday morning Euro Disney opens its doors to the public. Advance reaction, in print at least, has been appalled fascination. The size of it! The sinister discipline! The cultural colonisation of it! And in France of all places! The Euro Disneyland theme park, Europe's largest leisure complex, occupies some 5,000 acres of farmland near Paris, one-fifth of the size of the capital. The country that gave us Balzac, Asterix and Gerard Départieu now boasts features such as the Big Thunder Mountain Railroad and Dumbo the Flying Elephant.

Euro Disney, like military intelligence or Bavarian nouvelle cuisine, simply sounds implausible, a contradiction in terms. After all, everyone knows that the French are deeply suspicious of and even hostile towards any sign of creeping American cultural imperialism. French trade unionists have been outraged by the Disney dress ethic (no jeans, male deodorants encouraged *and* a permanent smile). Eyebrows have been raised at the spurning of the French culinary arts on site in favour of American fast food. Gastronomic imperialism indeed. For a fantasy within a fantasy, the facts associated with the enterprise are heroically solid.

Some 700 contractors and 1,000 suppliers have laboured to build 30 attractions, one lake, two rivers, six hotels, a camp site, a golf course and an entertainment centre. Around 14,000 staff, cunningly called cast members, representing 75 nationalities and speaking 40 languages, have been assembled to welcome 11 million visitors in the first year. They hope. A three-day stay, including flights and accommodation for a family of four from London, could easily sting them for £1,500. Once you're into that kind of money, why not go the whole hog and sample the real thing in Florida – where you can be sure of the weather?

One is indebted to Walt Disney Attractions, London, for a further 100 Euro Disney facts. Did you know, for example, that every year enough steaks will be sold on the theme park to make a stack, one on top of the other, three times as high as the Eiffel tower (fact 24)? Or that the Swiss Family Robinson Treehouse in Adventureland has 900 branches, 17,000 leaves and innumerable flowers all fixed by hand (fact 38)? Or that the Euro Disney resort hotels will have 62,400 coathangers (fact 65)?

Don't take the mickey: Disney is taking over. The buzz word among Disney executives is synergy: a word more commonly found on the unworldly lips of eco-crusaders but used here to describe the ruthless commercial philosophy that preaches that every individual Disney money-spinner, from toiletries to theme parks, promotes the company as a whole. At Disney shops in Britain you can buy T-shirts, hats, videos, toys, prints, records, sweets, pyjamas, underwear. Your life can be a total Disney experience.

And it's now a legitimate subject for academic inquiry, too. At New York university Marshall Blonsky, professor of semiotics, has apparently devoted thousands of words to a treatise on how Disney designers came to use the colour purple, an exercise in which he invoked Jacques Derrida, Wassily Kandinsky, Paul Virilio, Umberto Eco, Jacques Attali and Frederic Jameson. Soon, no doubt, you'll be able to take a B.Sc. in Disney Studies at one of the more forward-thinking polyversities, or at the very least (in these anything-goes days) a doctorate.

Britain, of course, is making its own Disneylands, its

London Dungeons and Dickens Experiences. Leisure is increasingly becoming divorced from culture whose images it plunders; it's even becoming divorced from weather, since holiday-makers can now sun themselves in the artificial equilibrium of the glass bubbles of Center-parcs; it is turning into a Virtual Reality. Materialism is all and Disney is still its slickest exponent. That's why it's sneered at. It sucks us in despite ourselves. Walt Disney was an animator of genius. His creativity endures because it touched upon reality and released the imagination in a way in which the industry that now exploits those creations utterly stifles. Who could remain dry-eyed during *Bambi*? Who was not entranced by *Fantasia*?

Now try a few more facts. Did you know that Euro Disney is the third largest construction project in Europe after the Channel Tunnel and Expo '92 in Seville (fact 55)? Or that two rhododendrums (*sic*) over 150 years old have been planted at the Davy Crockett Campground and the Disneyland hotel (fact 52)? Or that all the horses' manes and tails on the carousel in Fantasyland are painted in 23 carat gold leaf (fact 20)?

But what does any of this matter? It is, after all, only a theme park. Do the reservations about Euro Disney amount to no more than cultural arrogance, a belief that British fantasies are superior in every way to tawdry American commercial creations? After all, just think of Dracula, Svengali, Raffles, Peter Pan, Sherlock Holmes, Jekyll and Hyde – an imaginary popular culture with depth and resonance *and* global appeal. Imagine a British fiction theme park. You'd wait for an age for rides on the Roald Dahl Roller Coaster which would finally arrive bunched up in two and threes; Violet Elizabeth Bott would be into handbrake turns and Bilbo Baggins would be living in a cardboard box in a doorway. Maybe we're suspicious of the un-British efficiency of Disney, the way in which people are marshalled and packaged and directed, the quasi-authoritarian control of its staff. Maybe we fear being taken over by a homogenous pseudo-culture based on artifice, cheap sentimentality and commercial exploitation. But it *is* only a fun-fair. Why the fuss?

The thing about Euro Disney that really sticks in the craw is not that it is a glorified fun-fair but that people are going to travel to France solely and specifically to visit it. They won't be going to visit Paris, or the chateaux of the Loire, or the caves of the Dordogne, or to sit over a Ricard in a Normandy market square.

They will be paying a great deal of money to visit a corner not of France, nor even of America, but of a celluloid continent, a corruption of a fantasy which pretends to blur the distinction between fiction and reality and only succeeds in constructing a tacky sham that, unlike the original, leaves nothing to the imagination. Disneyworld's make-believe castles sit particularly ill in a country which has the real thing in such splendid abundance. Its government bribed Disney to set up shop there, seduced by the prospect of thousands of jobs. Materialism is all. In the process, the French government may have sold its country's culture short. Politics and Mickey Mouse: horses for courses.

February 6, 1992: Richard Gott

Culture Cellophane-wrapped

This is your new literary editor speaking . . . an unfamiliar and unsettling mode in which to be addressed, like listening to the voice of the guard on the Inter-City train that glides through the English countryside, reflecting the multicultural nature of our society.

Literary editors are traditionally seen and not much heard, and this particular one has spent more time in the past 25 years wandering around the swamps and plateaux of South America than in the gentle meadows of English middle class fiction (though he knows enough not to describe the Latin American novel dismissively as magic realism).

The books pages are the most unreformed area of British newspapers. While often perceived as precious ornaments, they sometimes have the feel and look of recovered artefacts – endowed with an archaic patina as part of the heritage industry. Once, they seemed to embody the fulfilment of an earlier, nobler tradition. When I was at school in the 1950s, it was gently suggested that we should write our weekly essays in the manner of Raymond Mortimer and Philip Toynbee, then the resident weekly reviewers at the *Sunday Times* and the *Observer*. Their urbane, intelligent, and discursive style, typical of the leisured middle class 'with no private means to speak of' but enough to live on, was itself inherited from the pre-war era of weekly reviews, and can be traced in direct line at least as far back as Matthew Arnold.

Over the past three decades – until the late 1980s – this civilised tradition was zealously maintained by two books editors, the late Terence Kilmartin at the *Observer*, and W.L. Webb at the *Guardian* (happily now ensconced at Nuffield). Any cultural history of Britain in the second half of the 20th century will record the significance of their long service in the twin temples of the liberal centre-left. Yet in the harsher 1990s, dominated by style, post-modernism, and a fear of the imminent collapse of reason itself, there has been a notable decline. The books pages of national newspapers sometimes appear as beleaguered islands in a sea of rock music and cinema, constantly under threat of erosion.

Writers and their publishers have not done much to help themselves. Far too many people in our bedraggled culture aspire to be writers. In spite of the invention of cinema and television, novels continue to pour out every week in an unending flow; some by genuine writers, others by people who ought to know better.

I first thought that the over-production of bad novels was simply a matter of those famous schools of creative writing, mistakenly introduced into universities in this country from the United States a couple of decades ago. They transplanted the illusion that everyone had the capacity to write the Great American Novel. Soon, there was a plethora of second-rate novelists entering an already over-stuffed market.

Then, in more charitable mood, I had second thoughts. This uncontrolled enthusiasm for writing fiction ought perhaps to be considered, not as the self-advertisement of a few inflated egos, but rather as an indictment of our late-20th-century English society. The reality is so unattractive, the politics so banal, the general level of culture so poor, that people desperately seek something different in the only other world available, the world of the imagination.

English culture – the culture of Norman Tebbit's cricket-playing England – has never been in such an appalling state. The English novel is in a poor and feeble condition. English contemporary art is largely without content. The English film has almost disappeared. Indigenous theatre is moribund. Live English modern music may be in good shape but lacks an audience. Our cultural critics have been forced to gaze westward – to the United States – to find anything to get their teeth into. We should not be surprised. We live in desperately conservative, not to say reactionary, times. It would be strange if this were not to be reflected in the culture.

And the English, still steeped in their imperial memories, have little sense of nationalism with which to redeem themselves. In Scotland, the newspapers review Scottish books; in Ireland, they review Irish books. In England, most books reviewed are American – American writers, American subjects, American publishers.

The publishers must bear a heavy responsibility for much of the current malaise. In among the imported American books, there is not much room for native flowers. It is the publishers, too, who have invented the Complan style of literary production, a method of serving up literature in soupy, digestible portions called the Book of this, the Companion to that, the Guide to the other, as though afraid we can take nothing stronger. The worst offender is the magazine *Granta* which delivers regular doses of culture in thin slices, Cellophane-wrapped, as though it were processed cheese.

So now I have got that off my chest, and alienated all my potential friends – authors, publishers, reviewers – I can tell you what we're planning to do. Our chief aim is to reintroduce old-fashioned criticism into the books pages. We shall tell you which books are good and which ones are bad, and why. We shall keep an eye on important paperbacks that you can afford, but we shall not be afraid to inform you of the ideas that are floating around within the pages of books that you may never be able to buy. And we shall seek to deliver all this with a polemical punch that will make you yearn for these pages from Thursday to Thursday. Lofty ambitions.

So that's it for now. Carry on reading and, as the Americans would say, enjoy.

February 27, 1992: Richard Gott

Sex with everything

The Literary Companion to Sex, by Fiona Pitt-Kethley (Sinclair-Stevenson, £18)

Living as we do in a conservative and decadent epoch, in which much art and literature serves to reinforce the stifling vacuity of the status quo, it is not altogether surprising that western culture should have become obsessed by sex. Gibbon was here before.

Few writers or publishers now seem able to resist the temptation to produce books that cater to the hunger they perceive. The subject once reserved for the topmost shelves at the newsagents has moved further and further down into eye range.

Typical of this trend is the arrival of a sexual vade-mecum by Fiona Pitt-Kethley, a book that should never have been suggested, commissioned, or published. There is, in fact, little sex in literature. The greatest writers have been sparing in their descriptions, and those readers who prefer a book as a companion to sex might better spend the money on a psychiatrist. But Ms Pitt-Kethley has made the subject her stock-in-trade and no one should begrudge her the necessity of earning a crust.

Her anthology does serve one useful contemporary purpose. In the current debate about the ubiquity and superfluity of sex in the English-language novel, it provides useful ammunition. It reminds us that the athletic, gymnastic view of sex that seems to characterise much late-20th-century fiction was never a significant part of earlier literature.

Our bawdy ancestors, with their strong sense of value, never got much beyond a little mild titillation – the depiction of the peasant Mary Combe, for example, of whom witnesses complained that she 'indecently would force an honest man to occupy her, spreading of her legs abroad and showing her commodity'.

Daniel Defoe, by the standards of today, was fairly decorous, earning his reputation as the founder of the 'then he had his way with her' school of fiction writing, but keeping graphic description to a minimum. 'He held her fast, and the wench being naked in bed with him, 'twas too late to look back, so she lay still and let him do what he would with her.' Defoe, happily, leaves the rest to the imagination of the reader.

Nowadays, such decorum has been thrown out of the literary bedroom. No coat is left buttoned, no trouser zipped, no physiological detail omitted. Many contemporary novels resemble a biology textbook. The novelist D.J. Taylor argued forcefully and regretfully that 'most commercial novels are built upon a ground plan of colossal orgasms'. His basic complaint, that there is far too much sex in the contemporary novel, seems eminently reasonable.

But how much is too much, and where does all this wantonness come from? As usual, it looks as though the Americans are to blame. Before D.H. Lawrence, there was little overt description of sex in English writing – and his contributions, once so controversial, now seem extremely discreet. The little that was written down was kept from a wider public by the censor.

But across the Atlantic in the United States – a completely different society from Britain and one which has elevated teenage values into an art form – a tradition has grown up of absolute explicitness with regard to sex. Intimate details of personal relationships are aired regularly on coast-to-coast television – from sexual harassment to rape, nothing is left to the imagination.

With this graphic reality impinging so regularly and insistently on fiction, American novelists have drawn their own conclusions. Rather like American film-makers, they now behave for the most part like retarded adolescents, keen to shock. What were once delicate references to private pleasures or emotions have been turned into pages of explicit sex, decked out in all the splendour of contemporary fine writing.

British (and some European) novelists, thinking (at best) that this is the key to unravelling the mysteries of their own societies, have followed suit. Indeed, it may well now be difficult to get a novel published in the current cultural climate without the inclusion of a suitably explicit description of the major characters caught up in a significant grope.

Puritanism today comes mostly from the right, and libertarians have understandably spent much of the past three decades in defending the gains that were made in the 1960s. They now get little help from writers and publishers, whose unbridled licence to publish is discrediting their cause. They ought now to advocate a self-denying ordinance, or at least a prolonged period of abstinence.

The puritan strain in British society, developed in the 17th century and earlier, once had a left-wing and radical element. In contemplating the current implant of high voltage sex into the novel, it is high time this tradition was revived.

July 4, 1991: Catherine Bennett

The prime of Miss Jean Plaidy

'Through my befugged sensations came the appalling realisation of what had happened. He had planned it and I had been the victim of . . . *rape*. I, Kate Collison, had been raped by the man I most detested . . . this arrogant Baron who thought he had only to beckon to a woman to make her come running. He had followed the customs of his marauding ancestors who had lived by rape and pillage. And I . . . *I* had been his victim.'

Not even the most passively receptive heroine actually likes to be raped. And Kate Collison has reason to protest, being a financially independent miniaturist, the toast of Paris. And yet, after four or five chapters, nature has taken its course: Kate has begun to be fond of the nobby brute who drugged and deflowered her, causing multiple contusions. By page 382 – a rape child, a war, two murders and a suicide later – it looks like wedding bells. Kate Collison, heroine of *The Demon Lover*, is all set to become the Baroness de Centeville: 'He looked at me, long and steadily, and I wondered how I could ever have thought of leaving him.'

Mrs Eleanor Hibbert, who, as Victoria Holt, devised these lively scenes, lives in graceful solitude, not far from the Albert Hall. Now in her mid eighties, she is at work on another suspenseful Gothic romance, her 31st Victoria Holt, after which, she will write her 87th historical novel as Jean Plaidy, and her 19th historical romance as Philippa Carr. All three novels will have been completed within a year. Under her assorted names – she has tried at least seven – Mrs Hibbert has written about 200 books, she is vague about the exact figure. Without doubt, she could have managed more, but she does not recommend over-production. 'If you do too many you find that one book is encroaching on another.'

So, every year, three new novels roll smoothly off Mrs Hibbert's effusive typewriter, at which, as her fans know, she works seven days a week, for five hours a day, starting at 7.30am. Predictable as proverbial bad luck, prolific Mrs Hibbert produces her three manuscripts, each faultlessly typed, impeccably matched to its market. For Plaidy readers, she writes a chunk of fictionalised history, usually told by a woman of royal extraction. The women watch their kings and princes go off to war and come back again: 'Mary was disturbed when Henry told her that he was going to attack the Barbary pirates.' They get married, they say 'mayhap', and suffer, with genteel understatement, the ageless trials of womankind: 'There *must* be an end to this incessant childbearing.' Sometimes they wish they could just be an ordinary person: 'Who would be born royal?' Then, as historical figures must, they die.

Victoria Holt readers prefer something racier, spookier, and less predictable than history. For them, Mrs Hibbert reliably supplies a remote, horse-drawn and frock-coated, pre-National Trust sort of past, when servants grinned with witless loyalty, and whopping houses were still closed to the public.

In *The Captive*, innocent, plucky Rosetta, a representative Holt heroine, is shipwrecked, washed up on a desert island with two potential suitors, kidnapped by pirates, thrown into a seraglio, freed from the seraglio, employed as a governess, then half-strangled by a murderous sergeant-major. She lives on to clear the reputation of one good man, heir to a noble fortune, then unexpectedly ends up with another: good-looking, affluent, Lucas Lorimer.

Hibbert's juvenile *nom de plume*, Philippa Carr, works

up Plaidyish historical interest with Holtesque plot and melodrama, then throws in a complicated family tree, to satisfy the readers of romantic sagas. Innocent Annora, heroine of Carr's *Midsummer's Eve*, is born an heiress, witnesses a witchburning, learns about fallen Victorian women, visits Australia, learns about the transportation of convicts, loses both parents, inherits a fortune and a castle, discovers she is illegitimate, and loses her fortune and castle, narrowly escapes being shot, discovers she is legitimate and regains her legacy, and marries tall, land-owning Rolf Hanson.

So consummately has Eleanor Hibbert mastered each type, that all three names, Plaidy, Holt and Carr, annually appear on the list of the top 100 library authors, which means that each has been borrowed at least 300,000 times in a year. Victoria Holt, Hibbert's most successful author, is in the top 10. Her agent in the States, Julie Fallowfield, estimates Holt's sales, in 20 different languages, at around 75 million. The less popular Plaidy still has 77 books in print. This has been achieved without help from the more exalted literary editors, who almost never have Plaidy reviewed, and resolutely ignore Holt and Carr. It was done, slowly and persistently, by Mrs Hibbert alone.

Benign, but somewhat austere, Mrs Hibbert offers only the blandest explanation for her furious output. She always read a lot. She always wanted to write. She loves writing. 'I think it's dedication more than anything,' she said. 'You see I'm more interested in this than anything else. I was determined to be a writer . . . I want to do this. So many people – I never understand them – so many writers don't want to write. I think the reason they don't do it regularly is, they're not in trim, as it were.'

Unlike the majority of her heroines, Mrs Hibbert was not born in a castle or a manor. She was born in Kennington, in south London, into a family she describes as 'very humble, really'. Her father 'didn't have a profession, he just did jobs'. But he was on the bookish side. Hibbert read books from the age of four, she thinks, and without restriction. 'I do feel that books were my thing, right from the word go.' But no one, neither her parents, nor her teachers, ever suggested she made a living out of them. At 16 she left school and went to work for a jeweller in Hatton Garden, where she typed, and occasionally weighed gems, or counted their carats. 'It was quite interesting,' she says. 'I liked it very much.' In her early twenties, she married a wholesale leather merchant, 20 years her senior, like herself an avid borrower from Harrods lending library. Mr Hibbert gave Mrs Hibbert the financial freedom to write.

The young Mrs Hibbert wrote 'a lot' of novels. They were all returned to sender. What were they like? Mrs Hibbert laughed. 'Oh, you know what you are when you're young. You're putting the world right, aren't you? And nobody wants to read them.'

Mrs Hibbert did not repine. She began writing stories for the *Daily Mail* and *Evening News*, which both ran short fiction every day, the kind of stories with 'a twist in the tale'. Then the former literary editor of the *Daily Mail* became an agent. 'He said, "You're barking up the wrong tree. You must write something which is salcable, and the best thing, and the easiest way, is to write a romantic novel." '

Mrs Hibbert had never read a romantic novel. Now, she diligently read 20, then wrote one, which was immediately accepted by Herbert Jenkins, then Mills and Boon, and published under her maiden name, Eleanor Burford. 'I could see how they were done, and what they were aiming at, and they were quite easy to do,' she said. 'And they turned out to be quite profitable, because we used to sell the serial rights to magazines, for quite a lot.' She thinks she might have written 40. 'It might be 30. It's difficult to know . . . I can't remember a word of them.'

The Burfords fitted, perfectly, the description which then decorated Mills and Boon wrappers. 'I always look

for the Mills and Boon when I want A PLEASANT BOOK!
No more doubts! No more disappointments! A Mills and
Boon novel will give you hours of happy reading.'

Married in Haste, a late Burford, published in 1956, is
flawlessly pleasant. Lorna, a sweet girl, marries her childhood sweetheart. She meets a rogue, who loves her. Her
husband begins to seem roguish. Confusion. Did she
marry the wrong man? No, she did not. It was all a mistake.
Her husband was not really a rogue. Lorna is a little wiser.
'So, Lorna passed into true happiness . . . '

By this time, Mrs Hibbert had discovered a feeling for
history. She wrote a long novel about transportation to
Australia, which many publishers' readers found too long,
until it went to Robert Hale. 'He wrote to my agent and
said, "Will you tell this author that, for anyone who can
write as she can, there are glittering prizes in the literary
world." ' The book was promulgated under the name of
Jean Plaidy, Plaidy being a Cornish town. 'That was going
to be an entirely different kind of book, and I really didn't
want it connected with these romantic novels,' Mrs Hibbert explained. 'You know how difficult it is in this literary
world. Labels get attached to you . . . The name of the
author tells the public what a book is like, doesn't it?'

In the libraries, Plaidy was much borrowed. Mrs Hibbert realised that was the way ahead. 'I could see by this
time, because I was studying this business very well, that
whatever I wrote was not going to be noticed. So the only
way to do it, because people in libraries had liked it so
much, was to go on building up through them. And to do
that it's no use writing a book and then waiting another
four years before you write another. Even three, or two, is
too long. You've got to keep giving them books, so they
don't forget your name. That's very important.'

Mrs Hibbert put her back into it, stepping up production to two Plaidys a year. Even that was not enough. 'I'd
realised that with a historical novel I really wasn't going to
get as far as I wanted, because it is rather an esoteric

public . . . And I made up my mind that I was going to write a book that was going to be a bestseller, and I started with some of these names . . . '

She tried Ellalice Tate. 'Now, what did she do?' Mrs Hibbert enquired. 'Some of those books were the long type of book with a great deal of action in them, and they were books which, I thought, because I'd been studying the bestseller, were what people really wanted to read.' And what is that?

'They want to read a good story, first and foremost,' said Mrs Hibbert. 'People now think it's dreadful to tell a story, which is absolutely crazy. People want a story, they will always want a story . . . And it's got to be an interesting story. It's no use trying to show off how clever you are with lots of quotations and references to the classics. No, not at all. You've got to get on with your story, and not hang about with it.'

She experimented with other pseudonyms. Elbur Ford, the (female) author of four novelised reconstructions of Victorian crimes. 'Elbur Ford was just a funny little flash in the pan,' said Mrs Hibbert. Then there was Kathleen Kellow. 'What books did she do?' asked Mrs Hibbert, forgetfully. One was *Danse Macabre,* a contemporary tale of masculine frustration and murder, with some nicely observed details of lower-middle-class pretension. 'I suppose that was experimenting again,' said Mrs Hibbert. 'That was before I realised that I had to do something different, something big. A big, plotty thing.' Plotty!

The names were not working. An American agent, Patricia Myrer, 'a wonderful woman', came to London to tell Hibbert she was, once again, industriously barking up the wrong tree. 'They are all saying this is Jean Plaidy,' Myrer told Hibbert. 'She doesn't think this is good enough to publish under Jean Plaidy and the thing's doomed from the start.' Myrer had an idea. She wanted Hibbert to revive the Gothic novel. So Mrs Hibbert did. She wrote *Mistress of Mellyn*. 'This was the sort of book that I loved to write, because I had read so much of Brontë's, over and over again, and Wilkie Collins, and all that sort of thing. So I knew it was my thing, really.' More important, it was the public's thing. It took you out of yourself. 'Once you begin to read it,' exulted one reader, 'it is like a drug for which, without in the least meaning to, you form an addiction.'

Cleverly, Hibbert and Myrer kept the true identity of Holt a secret for six books. 'That was another good selling idea,' said Mrs Hibbert, enthusiastically, 'to have a mystery writer.' By the time Hibbert was unmasked, Holt was a consistent bestseller. Why? 'I think one reason,' Mrs Hibbert offers, 'is it is about the past, and people really want to escape from the present, which may seem rather drab to them.' She is not keen on the present – 'on the whole the young people don't always behave very nicely, do they?' – but has hopes that it may, in time, come to resemble the past again.

So historical romances help people switch off? 'Oh, yes,' says Mrs Hibbert. 'And there's no reason why they shouldn't.' Switching off has not always been so heartily endorsed. From Jane Austen, exploring the idiocy of the Gothic in *Northanger Abbey*, to Queenie Leavis, excoriating the bestsellers of the 1930s, many have denounced the maleficent effects of fantastic literature.

Catherine Morland, Austen's fictional gobbler of romantic fiction, concludes that her shaming, Gothic delusions about life at the Abbey, 'might be traced to the influence of that sort of reading which she had there indulged'.

Q.D. Leavis, in torridly apocalyptic terms, decided that low-brow popular fiction was, to its readers, a 'means of easing a desolating sense of isolation and compensates for the poverty of their emotional lives . . . ' But not beneficially. It encouraged 'self-dramatisation', it interfered with the readers' 'spontaneities'; to the uncritical, it was 'fatally persuasive', even 'pernicious'.

It seems an unnecessarily harsh judgment on Mrs

Hibbert, whose novels are marked by her own sympathetic good nature. Even her murderers often kill from misguided kindness. And she does seem to be on the side of women. 'I think women certainly haven't been very well treated, and I do find that women are so much better than men at so many things. I think men are wonderful at getting to the moon, and that sort of thing, and carrying the bags, and making arrangements.' But they don't, she says, *understand*, as women do. They like novels about gadgets and guns; they aren't primarily interested in *people*.

But not all women would approve of Mrs Hibbert's people. Some feminist critics would read her stories – her baron's marriage to his rapee, for example – as a mystified representation of the patriarchal, bourgeois individualist myth, which teaches that since any adequately beautiful goosegirl might marry a king, it's only right that the world should be divided into kings and goosegirls.

They may be right. But Hibbert is not the instigator of this regrettable state of affairs. A popular romancer like Mrs Hibbert cannot operate at the leading edge of ideas. She does not have any ideas, as such. She writes she says, 'instinctively', and somehow her subconscious communicates with her readers' subconscious without a fully realised, fully conscious intermediary stage. 'I think I have the common touch,' she says, modestly. 'I think I feel as they feel. My emotions are like theirs.' Kate Parkin, her editor at Collins, believes that Mrs Hibbert could never have been a sophisticated, *literary* writer. 'Because she doesn't have an ounce of cynicism. She genuinely doesn't. There's nothing calculated about her writing.' Far from writing *down* to her readers, Mrs Hibbert labours to write *up*. That's one reason why she's a bestseller.

In Kensington library, which lends historical biographies to Mrs Hibbert, one of her own female borrowers said she had read all 30 Holts, and would 'jump on' any new ones. 'They're interesting, very readable. But I couldn't possibly remember all the names.' Could she remember the plots? 'Oh, no.' In the Romance section, other subscribers were rummaging, not looking at the words, but checking for the secret marks they leave at the back of a book, the only way of remembering whether or not they have read it.

Such forgetfulness is intrinsic, not accidental. Mrs Hibbert, who has a sharp memory for historical facts, cannot clearly recollect her own romantic fiction, and nor can her readers. If they could, her books would not be this kind of novel, or this kind of success. The effect of popular romances is cumulative. They're a habit, they flow into one another. As Kate Parkin says, 'Once the name is established, and they are marketed properly, provided the writer is consistent, there is no reason for sales to fall off.'

And Mrs Hibbert never wavers. Since her husband died, 20 years ago, she has continued to write and write, for reasons that could only be understood by herself, or other non-stop romantic writers such as Catherine Cookson or Barbara Cartland. 'It's truly a compulsion,' says Diane Pearson, romantic novelist, and president of the Romantic Novelists Association. 'There are quite a lot who just write because they must write.'

Mrs Hibbert cannot bear to talk about money, but clearly she has no need for more. While her backlists gather royalties, she lives modestly, in an unostentatious, pink and green flat decorated with home-made tapestries, copies of her own books, and numerous jade statuettes collected on the world cruises she has taken annually since her husband died. 'I don't want a rest,' Mrs Hibbert insisted. 'I take my typewriter with me . . . '

Her one known extravagance, the purchase of the King's Lodging, an historic house in Sandwich visited by several Plaidy-featured monarchs, she now regards as a 'terrible mistake'. Mrs Hibbert had the place lavishly restored, and filled with gothic chairs, and chests and fourposters, but once installed in a home worthy of her fantasies, she felt uneasy. 'It was a bit weird,' she said. 'Everybody said it was haunted. I felt there was something strange about it.' One day she looked at her view of London, 'and I thought, no, *this* is where I belong.'

Big, old houses can be uncomfortable, and, for all its dramatics, Mrs Hibbert's fiction is about safety and predictability. 'It's comfort reading,' says Antonia Byatt, 'I think a lot of people read for comfort. They read the way I still read fairy stories, when I'm really low . . . I know exactly what is going to happen, and I enjoy the calm of going through a plot with difficulties, coming out the right way.' When low, Byatt has even enjoyed Victoria Holt. 'She has just enough imagination to make a world for you, and not enough imagination or literary skill to make it difficult or problematic for you.' Mrs Hibbert, who, for all her 200 novels, turns out to be a woman of few words, gives a simple account of her powers. 'It's like God, isn't it? God is the creator, and you're in his image, you are creating. And you have created this world, which is your world. And that is a wonderful thing.' After all, 75 million believers can't be wrong. Can they?

January 8, 1992: leader

Cover stories

And so, farewell, the long-playing record: born 1948, expired by degrees from the late 1980s onwards squeezed out of your vinyl existence by the smooth, remorseless advance of the compact disc. Now even W.H. Smith are no longer to stock you. In a sense, you had it coming. You could not be played in cars. You had to be turned in mid-symphony, even the sort of symphony where the composer stipulates that the *allegretto* must follow the *largo* without a break. Quite early in life your music was often augmented by snaps, crackles and pops – even when you were carefully cosseted with arrays of odd brushes and cleansing fluids and even strange little guns which did something or other with ions. If left too long on the turntable, you were likely to warp, doing things to the music of Beethoven which the master never intended. Compared to the compact disc, you were cheap, but you might not last so long. And you never provided that useful service, a number on the screen to remind those whose attention has wandered that the Shostakovich prelude and fugue now in progress is actually number 16.

But what we will certainly miss, what may well be irreplaceable, is a form of recording technology which wore its art on its sleeve. In its great days, the LP cover was part of the pleasure of the purchase: even sometimes, on later reflection, the best thing about it. The Beatles, with the help of Peter Blake, created not just the music but a whole thronged kaleidoscopic entourage for their *Sergeant Pepper*. Thelonious Monk clung nonchalantly to the back of a San Francisco street car, the city paraded behind him. The Rolling Stones' *Sticky Fingers* came complete with a working zip, attributed to Mick Jagger; the first Velvet Underground album with a peelable banana, designed by Warhol. More austerely, one could prop a portrait of Rubinstein, or Arrau, or Kempff, alongside the gramophone while he was playing. Do that with a compact disc, and you get little more than a dot. And who, people used to wonder, was the dark-haired woman nursing a cat who appeared behind Bob Dylan on the cover of *Bringing It All Back Home*? We may never know. But in CD's Lilliput format, would we even bother to ask?

February 3, 1992: Roy Hattersley

Tropical tangles

I missed my first chance to hear the programme for which the whole nation has waited since 1942. But, as the combination of person and programme promised to be the biggest festival of kitsch for 50 years, I made a point of listening to *Desert Island Discs* last Friday morning. I was not disappointed.

Honesty requires me to explain that, although I am an enthusiast for the programme, the programme has treated me like a liquidated member of the Supreme Soviet after one of Stalin's purges. I was not invited to the anniversary party at which – according to the publicity – all previous participants discussed alternative luxury objects and held literary discussions at which all talk of Shakespeare and the Bible was prohibited. The reason why I was ignored was more painful than the snub itself. I have been written out of the history books.

They actually asked me to be castaway last summer. And when I thanked them for the honour of inviting me a second time, they denied absolutely that I had been on the show before. I suspect that, down in the bowels of Broadcasting House, a wall is decorated with composite photographs of *Desert Island Disc* laureates – and that some of the faces have been obliterated. The non-persons are (or were) the dissidents of the revisionist Michael Parkinson regime.

It is only fair to say that, as well as having a strange relationship with *Desert Island Discs*, I am not terribly close to John Major. My affection for him had not been increased by a problem which he had caused me on the day before I heard the choice of records which Conservative Central Office had made on his behalf. During Question Time in the House of Commons, I had to quote from one of the Prime Minister's previous answers. That is always a daunting task. Last Thursday my difficulty was grammatical.

Ad-libbing about VAT in June, Mr Major refused to give a 'categoric assurance' that it would not be increased. He added for emphasis that no government could ever make such a promise: 'none have and none will'. Considering how to reproduce those five words spoilt my lunch at the American Embassy. Fearful that the error would be attributed to me, I considered following the habit of my fellow Sheffielder, Mr Stainless Stephen, and speak the punctuation.

Brevity is all at Question Time and I doubted if the Speaker would allow 'as the Prime Minister said. Ping. Ping. None have and none will. Pong. Pong.' I could have added 'sic'. But it might have been misunderstood.

In short, I listened to last Friday's *Desert Island Discs* through a haze of complicated prejudice and what I write about it is probably conditioned by the bias. So I was probably wrong to suspect that when the Prime Minister twice spoke – with dismissive envy – of 'double firsts', a small effigy of Douglas Hurd was metaphorically rotating on the turntable. In consequence, it is better for me to concentrate on the questions rather than the answers.

Even dealing with what ought to have been the least contentious parts of the programme requires me to admit that I do not admire Sue Lawley's peek-a-boo interviewing technique. Whatever you may say about Sir Robin Day's mannerisms, his questions do sound like demands for information rather than invitations to be chased round the studio. But even Miss Lawley's style (which I am sure does not reflect her admirable character) is no excuse for treating a serious subject with such frivolity. And the Prime Minister is, whether *Private Eye* admits it or not, a serious subject.

On *Desert Island Discs*, Mr Major announced that no

one need sleep rough in London. He went on to claim that
the crisis of mortgage repossessions had largely been
solved. Both assertions were left to hang unchallenged in
the tropical air. Perhaps the producers thought that argument was inappropriate because the programme is not
political. Clearly, Mr Major did not share that opinion.

At first I was prepared to believe that he really liked the
Elgar and I can easily imagine him listening to Diana Ross.
Nor did it surprise me when he chose Don Bradman
being bowled for a duck at the end of his last Test innings.
But he did not mention that the England team gave three
cheers before Bradman took guard and John Arlott subsequently said that you cannot bat with tears in your eyes.
Funny, I thought. Funny. Perhaps such sentimentality is
out of fashion. Then he ended the programme with 'The
Best is Yet to Come' and I understood it all. The image
makers had been at work.

Perhaps the programme could not avoid being
hijacked. But even at the human interest level – the
standards that we expect from chateau-bottled gossip like
In the Psychiatrist's Chair – all the best opportunities were
left buried in the sand or sunk amongst the coral reefs.

The Prime Minister said that the desert island fantasy
was most appealing at quarter past three on Tuesday and
Thursday afternoons. I can think of few other interviewers
who, having been given that opening, would not have
gone on to ask if he was really saying that he did not enjoy
Prime Minister's questions and what it was that he found
so unattractive about the occasion. Perhaps he was merely
counterfeiting humility. Or it may be that he hates
wrestling with the grammar.

I am still worried about the way I quoted his answer last
Friday. ' . . . no government at any stage give [sic] categoric
assurances.' There is nothing that you can do with that
sentence except start again. Better the tropical moon, the
sleepy lagoon and Sue Lawley.

February 6, 1992: Letter

Just deserts

I am pleased that Roy Hattersley admits to listening to John Major's *Desert Island Discs* 'through a haze of complicated prejudice'. Nevertheless, I cannot allow that to excuse several unfair jibes at the programme and at my style of interviewing. Let me answer a few.

It is true Mr Hattersley was invited to be a castaway last summer. His publishers sent us his latest book, presumably in the hope of inspiring such an invitation. When it was discovered he had been a guest in the past few years, the invitation was withdrawn. No one denied he'd ever existed, but writers (and some politicians) don't like to destroy a good story for a ha'p'orth of fact.

Sadly, many former castaways were not invited to the party celebrating the fiftieth anniversary of the programme. Some 1500 are alive and no doubt capable of consuming large quantities of food and drink. The choice of about 200 of them was always going to be a somewhat arbitrary one. Sorry, Mr H if your number didn't come up. John Smith's and Neil Kinnock's did.

So we come to the more substantial charge that I treated a 'serious subject' (the Prime Minister) with 'frivolity'. To compare my style of interviewing unfavourably with that of Sir Robin Day is, in the context of *Desert Island Discs*, to misunderstand the nature of the programme. 'Demands for information' would sit uncomfortably in a conversation designed to elicit personal reminiscences and observations.

Neither is *Desert Island Discs* a platform for prolonged political debate. It is not the place and there is not the time. It is a forum for listening to the castaway's position on the subjects which most test him or her. Hence, John Major was asked about unemployment, homelessness and

Mrs Thatcher. Neil Kinnock was asked about his recalci-
trant left wing, the problems of being called a windbag
and his chances of coming to power. It is up to the listener
to decide whether the explanation is convincing or not.

Finally, Mr Hattersley suggests I missed an opening by
not pressing Mr Major on his stated desire to be on a
desert island at 3.15pm on Tuesdays and Thursdays.
Unlike Mr Hattersley on this occasion, I think I recognise a
joke when I hear one.
Sue Lawley
London SW15.

Notes & Queries

March 23, 1992

**QUESTION: What happens to the voting slips used
in British elections after they have been counted?**

Under the Representation of the People Act 1983 the
Returning Officer, usually a senior official of the local
council, has to ensure that all ballot papers, counterfoils
and the polling clerks' marked copies of the electoral
register are safely deposited with the Clerk of the Crown
in Chancery (a senior officer of the Lord Chancellor's
Department). This is so that if any corrupt or illegal
election practices are reported the appropriate documents are available for inspection.

All such documents are supposed to be officially sealed
so that there is no chance of interference by any party and,
according to the 1983 Act, the seal can only be broken by
the order of the High Court or Parliament itself. In
practice ballot papers are simply bundled up into paper
sacks and transported to a warehouse in Hayes, Middle-

sex, for the statutory period of one year and one day. Following the 1987 general election, I reported on the disposal of the 7,000 sacks of this 'low-grade confidential waste' for a national newspaper. The papers were transported by truck from the Hayes warehouse to be incinerated in the North London Waste Authority plant at Enfield.

During that process we witnessed dozens of sacks splitting and many hundreds of spent ballot papers spilling for all to see. This adds weight to the conspiracy theory that security around the election documents is very lax, and that the vote-tracing procedure has been used to identify people voting for fringe candidates.

Votes can be traced by matching the numbered ballot paper to its similarly numbered counterfoil; the numbered counterfoil also bears the voter's registration number from the electoral register which is hand-written by the polling clerk when the ballot paper is issued.

As all the ballot papers for each candidate – including fringe candidates such as Sinn Fein, communists, fascists, nationalists, etc – are bundled together, anyone having access to those documents can speedily trace the name and address of every voter for such candidates if they wish.

In 1981 Gordon Winter – a former agent of BOSS, the South African Secret Service – writing in his book, *Inside Boss*, claimed that the South African government knew the identity of everyone who voted for the Communist Party of Great Britain – thanks to British intelligence using this simple vote-tracing procedure. In any event, the notion that we have a secret vote is very misleading.

One positive outcome of the last general election, however, was that the incineration of 91 tons of ballot papers contributed to the 21 megawatts per hour output of the North London Waste Authority plant, which supplies electricity to Tottenham. – *David Northmore (author, The Freedom of Information Handbook), London W1.*

I do not know what happens to the voting slips for the Conservative candidates, after they have been counted, but in the mid 1960s those for communists were tallied against their counterfoils in the ballot books (just like chequebooks) and those who had had the temerity to vote for a communist were identified from the electoral roll. Their names were forwarded to Special Branch and to MI5, almost certainly as a matter of routine.

The source of this information was a good one. He was a postgraduate student doing his doctoral research on local government in a Midlands steel town where he was attached to the town clerk's department. One day he opened a cupboard, looking for some documents, and found instead a large number of ballot slips, all of which were marked in favour of a communist candidate in the local elections. The town clerk returned and found the student with the slips and told him (knowing the student's safely right-wing views) that it was one of his regular chores to forward the names of communist voters to the Special Branch.

As the town had a strong communist tradition it was a recurrent task for the town clerk and the slips had been put to one side until he had time to deal with them. The then student (my informant) saw nothing wrong with this procedure – which made his account the more believable.
– *Michael Wilson, Thame, Oxon.*

March 30, 1992
Two further questions are prompted by the letters about serial numbers on ballot papers. First: if I delete or cut off the serial number do I invalidate my vote? Second: have serial numbers ever been used for their official purpose – the investigation of electoral fraud? – *Janet Johnson, Rugby, Warwicks.*

What Michael Wilson describes was not the practice everywhere in the country. In the 1950s and 1960s I was the town clerk of two Lancashire authorities where we not only had Communist candidates but also Communist members on the councils for short periods.

While the ballot papers cast for the Communist candidates were dealt with in the same way as those for other parties, it is true that police acting on behalf of the Special Branch did take an interest in these candidates. They always came to the town hall and took the names of the proposer, seconder and assentors of the Communist candidates. However this information, unlike the ballot paper, is not secret and was published in an election notice. – *J.W. Blomeley, Streatley-on-Thames, Berks.*

April 13, 1992
Janet Johnson asks if serial numbers on ballot papers have ever been used for their official purpose: the investigation of electoral fraud. There was a case in the late 1970s in a council election in Richmond-upon-Thames. A German couple living in Gerard Road, Barnes, turned up to vote. They were not entitled to as they were not British citizens, but the poll clerk confused them with another family with a very similar name only two doors away, and they registered their vote.

When the correct Mrs Such & Such turned up to vote, she was told her name was marked as having already voted, and was allowed only a 'tendered' vote which meant she could mark a ballot paper which was not put in the ballot box but kept separate. In the same street a girl was unwisely persuaded by a political agent to vote although her name was marked with a 'Y' on the voting register as she had not quite reached voting age.

The result of the election in our ward was extremely close, but after recounts the Conservative candidate was declared the winner with a majority of only one or two votes. At this, the genuine voter with a German name demanded that her case be looked into. It was established that her vote was valid and her German neighbours' not. The under-age girl's vote was also ruled invalid.

By means of the serial numbers of the ballot papers copied on to the voting register, the invalid papers were traced and it was discovered that all three were for the Conservative candidate. The 'tendered' vote was for the Liberal. Thus the result was to reverse the outcome of the election in our ward. – *Margaret Sharp, Barnes, London SW13.*

March 23, 1992

QUESTION: Given that my feet enjoy a bath as much as the rest of me, why are they the only bits that smell of mature Stilton?

Your feet are infected with a close relative of the fungus that gives Stilton its blue veins. Washing is of no use because your footwear provides a humid, anaerobic environment which the fungus spores find irresistible. This 'bugs' Benidorm' is achieved by wearing nylon stretch socks and shoes made from impermeable synthetic materials, along with never baring your feet outside the bedroom or the bathroom.

The solution is twofold. First, for immediate relief use a fungicidal foot-powder available from any chemist. Second, for a permanent solution, wear natural fibre socks and leather shoes (which let out the sweat and let in the air) along with going barefoot or be-sandalled whenever possible.

Alternatively, go into cheesemaking. – *Val Dobson, Bamber Bridge, Preston, Lancs.*

April 13, 1992
I can't provide an explanation but I can offer a cheap, effective and long-lasting cure. Buy some boracic acid powder from a chemist, sprinkle a small amount on clean

feet, socks, shoes, etc. for a few days. Wear leather insoles in trainers, wellingtons, etc. at all times. This worked for me. – *Dick Bergman, Guildford, Surrey.*

April 20, 1992

Among the bacteria resident on the human skin is a species named *Brevibacterium epidermis*. A related species, *Brevibacterium linens*, is actually used as a culture in, surprise, surprise, cheesemaking. Both species of bacteria break down long chain fatty acids found both in milk and on skin secretions to produce the malodorous gases methane thiol and hydrogen sulphide – hence the characteristic smell.

The skin of the sole of the foot contains a very high number of sweat glands which, in combination with the higher skin temperatures of a shod foot, creates a tropical pedal micro-climate which encourages proliferation of the bacteria.

In addition to the sound advice offered by D. Bergman, I recommend natural fibre socks or stockings, (synthetics tend to aggravate the condition), changing these during the day if the feet perspire excessively, and ensuring that shoes are alternated so that the moisture accumulating inside them has at least 24 hours to evaporate. – *Michael A. Nicol (podiatry lecturer), London W5.*

March 30, 1992
QUESTION: Is it true that tapeworms were used as an aid to slimming in the 1920s? Did it work and, if so, how can I contract this parasite?

Arthur Jackson, in his book *More Tales of a Country Practice* (Souvenir Press), describes how segments of a northern Scandinavian tapeworm, *diphyllobothrium latum*, were found in the faeces of an emaciated elderly patient.

Some time before the war, she had taken 'Dr Simpson's

famous simple slimming pills'. Two pills containing the flesh of a worm-infested freshwater fish were swallowed to start the slimming process and two more, presumably containing a vermicide, should have been taken when the desired weight was attained. The patient, happy to be thin, never took the antidote.

The author does not name the species of fish concerned, nor does he mention whether it must be eaten raw. Perhaps a ticket to Finland would be of further help to the enquirer. – *Ruth Mundy, Cornwall County Library, Redruth*.

Around 1930 a tablet was advertised as 'slimming without dieting'. It was said in letters to the press that tablets left untaken erupted and maggots crawled out. – *L. Clarke, Northampton*.

There are various human tapeworms but the only one which could safely be used is the beef tapeworm. This might be contracted in France or other European countries from eating very rare beef or steak tartare but infection could more easily be picked up in Ethiopia, where it is particularly common.

However, there are many reasons why this should not be attempted. There is no evidence that it does aid slimming and the tapeworm has rather unpleasant habits best not outlined in a newspaper read over the breakfast table. – *(Dr) R. Muller, St Albans, Herts*.

August 15, 1991: Judy Rumbold

No, Nicholas

It was in 1978, after the break-up of Nicholas Fairbairn's first marriage, that he decided to give up fidelity in order to spend more time with his libido. 'I'm not crazy about the concept of monogamy,' he says. 'The reason it's successful to the extent it is, is because most people are comparatively unlibidinal. It may be that MPs have a high libido, but that's not because they are MPs. No, it's the other way around. They become MPs because their libidos are high. Power is the ultimate aphrodisiac.'

The difference between Fairbairn, MP for Perth and Kinross, and the rest of his purportedly sex-crazed colleagues at Westminster is that he wears his dick on his sleeve. In 1973's *Who's Who* he states his recreations as 'making love, ends meet and people laugh' and the most public of his sexual indiscretions was when, in 1981, spurned parliamentary secretary and sometime mistress Pamela Milne took an overdose and reportedly survived after hanging herself with a pair of sturdy 15-deniers from a lamp-post outside Fairbairn's London flat.

The question that has exercised Fairbairn's mind through all his roguish philanderings is: why do women so often say no when they mean yes? Before he became Solicitor General for Scotland, he defended countless rape suspects, during which time he accused judges of 'leaning over backwards to protect women', found 90 per cent of his accused clients to be victims of a 'game gone wrong', and said rape involved 'an activity that is normal'.

Fairbairn still reckons he knows a thing or two about the psychosexual jiggery-pokery involved in taking no for an answer. 'What,' he asks, sloshing champagne all over the table, 'do you imagine my secretary thinks I'm doing with you?' Not just being interviewed, that's for sure. No, we're playing games, says Fairbairn. Elaborate *sexual* games.

While the 58-year-old scarecrow from hell – all tartan, mad hair and assorted watch-fobbery – struggles to focus through a miasma of bubbly and raised hopes, he endeavours to make his point about the sexual fireworks that, in his experience, inevitably visit such chance meetings as ours. He starts going on about men 'wielding the sabres of paradise' and women's 'wounds'. As far as he is concerned, asking newspaperly questions and Asking For It are suddenly not such remote concepts. 'For goodness sake!' he booms. 'You don't dress in order to be sexually undesirable; you dress in a way that makes a man want to *undress* you! It's all a libidinal game. A woman may say no when she means yes.'

Still, the man who is fond of such maxims as 'A sexy mistress is better than a boring wife' says it is unfair to label him a womaniser. 'What is wrong with the adoration of women? You can't be a womaniser unless women are menisers. It's fantasy that men take advantage and women get no advantage.'

Fairbairn can't understand why all men aren't as openly adoring of women as he is. He has even tried a touch of self-styled Outing. 'I remember being on a parliamentary trip once and saying, "Right then, fellas, tell me about your sex lives. Do you enjoy it? Does your wife enjoy it? Are you faithful, are you unfaithful?" '

He wasn't surprised they clammed up on him. 'I think the reason they resent the fact that I'm perfectly happy to say I love women and have loved many women is because it creates in them a feeling of inadequacy.'

No such sexual enshrivelment for Fairbairn, who says he 'worships and adores' women, not least Mrs Thatcher, with whom he claims to enjoy a 'special chemistry'. Not all women inspire the same sort of rapport. For a start, he finds ugliness in women 'an inappropriate characteristic'. Edwina Currie's character is singled out for special criticism. 'I said to her, do not forget that you yourself were an egg once. Some of us regret its fertilisation.'

He has strong ideas about how women should dress and besides creating his own eccentric wardrobe to match the baronial excesses of his 16th-century castle in Fife, he also designs clothes for his second wife, Suzanne McInnes. The better to demonstrate this prowess for sartorial wizardry, he whips from his pocket a grotesquely encrusted old handkerchief and drapes it around the champagne bottle in Dioresque folds. 'You can create the most wondersome *creation* if you have taste.'

Generally, he despairs of current trends in women's clothing ('It never ceases to amaze me that women can't judge their own legs! God in heaven, it's beyond belief'), especially those worn by women MPs. 'I can't say I've ever got visually, artistically or sexually excited by any of them. On the whole, they dress like frumps. What has happened to pride of dress? It's an expression of belief in yourself!'

The pinnacle of pride, thinks Fairbairn, is a woman's awareness of her own delicious *differentness*. If this happens to incorporate acres of cleavage, high heels and a bit of leg, all the better.

Feminism he dismisses as 'idiotic. It's a cover for lesbian homosexuality, in fact. It's a sort of phallic resentment concept.' And it is all the more futile, he says, because male and female characteristics are, for better or worse, preordained in the womb. 'The male has the most appalling experience. By the time the nine months are up, that bitch of a landlady, so far as he's concerned, has brought all the walls in. Without so much as a bloody warning, he's just pushed out of the porthole. And then has the indignity of having to go back to her and say, "Hey, bitch, can I have some milk? I love you and you kicked me out."

'If you take the female child, who has the same experience, she says, "Well, she would kick me out, wouldn't she? She's my rival, she's a bitch, so I'll go and take some milk off her and bloody well make her suffer." So the initial traumata of relationships are totally distinctive. Now, if women were born of men, and men were born of men, women would be the aggressive ones because they would be rejected by the love object. And men would have the characteristics of women. Of that I am certain.'

In case you were in any doubt, Fairbairn is all man, a fact that was first brought to his notice at the age of eight by his school matron. 'I think she showed a special preference for me. Other boys would mess up my hair but she never sent me off to brush it like she did everyone else. It gave me that first feeling of sexual arousal.'

Fairbairn's parents, on the other hand, were neglectful hair monitors. His father was a psychoanalyst, his mother an aristocrat. 'By the time I was born,' he says, 'they were totally estranged. My mother turned to the bottle, my father became emolliated in his theories. But in those days you didn't divorce, you merely tolerated an assiduation of horror, aggression, resentment and separation.'

Still, it didn't put him off marrying at the age of 28. 'It was the thing you did,' he says. 'Like the life cycle of the eel worm, it was preordained.' But he has since rebelled, dismissing matrimony as a 'questionable concept. Life is no longer preordained. If you have 10 wives, 10 mistresses and 10 lovers, it is less predictable.'

And possibly a touch complicated. How does he keep it up, so to speak? Moreover, where does his wife stand in the lusty Fairbairn 30? Will they stay together, does he think?

Now, for some appalling reason, Fairbairn extracts a romantic subtext from this last question and takes it as a come-on. He lunges across the table and tries to engage me in a whiskery snog. Even as I prepare to stash the Fairbairn tapes in my bag, he's still banging on about sex games and the fabulous unpredictability of a life that just seems to dump an endless succession of yielding women at his feet.

'You don't choose who's in your life,' he slurs. 'How they come about isn't something you can either arrange, deflect or complain of. I mean, I didn't know I was going to meet you, for instance. Life is about chance. A wonderful game of chance . . . Shall we go to bed?'

He was right, after all. No doesn't always mean no. Sometimes it means, simply, go to hell.

Nice to be back

March 19, 1992: Andrew Rawnsley

Reading between the lies

Who said that the choice at this general election was between Tweedlejohn and Tweedleneil? Probably Tweedlepaddy.

Yesterday the Conservatives and Labour both sought to make manifest their differences by unveiling their manifestos. Reading between the lies, the ideological battle was stark.

It will not surprise you to learn that only one of the manifestos talks about 'going back to socialism'. That's the Conservative one. And at only one of the manifesto launches was there any mention of 'the legacy of Thatcherism'. That was the Labour one.

The first choice facing the sophisticated voter is which manifesto colour scheme will best go with your toilet suite. If it is a Royal Navy blue cover flying a Union flag, you're a Labour supporter. You're a Tory voter if you prefer your manifesto bearing a mugshot of John Major stonewashed into faded denim.

An extremely important decision for the musical elector is what sort of tune you like your policies to be set to. Those who want a manifesto you can dance to, though not terribly well, will vote for Andrew Lloyd Webber's class-less synthesised remix of Purcell, and John Major's class-less synthesised remix of Toryism.

If you prefer a manifesto you can hum to, though not terribly well, Labour has your ear. Its recomposed policies were unveiled to a new tune by Michael Kamen. The party was unwise enough to reveal that he also composed the theme to *Robin Hood: Prince of Thieves*, the film which inspired Neil Kinnock's tax policies.

Poetry-lovers will not warm to Labour. The first page is given over to a poem written by Adrian Henri, a member of the Liverpool School of Worse Verse. Socialism does not appear in the poem either, because it cannot be made to rhyme with power.

The opening page of the Tory manifesto is a composi-tion by a lesser known artist, a John Major, member of the Huntingdon School of Blank Prose. 'All my own work,' he grinned yesterday morning, like a seven-year-old present-ing his first effort at creative writing to a teacher.

The word you need an electron microscope to find in the Tory manifesto is 'recession'.

It does not scan with re-election.

To help further inform your choice, here's a word game for the family to play at home. Which party's commitment to free enterprise and the free market leads it to say 'the only way for Britain to build a strong economy is to make the goods and services which people at home and abroad want to buy'? Wrong. It's Labour.

Which party's commitment to care and compassion leads it to say: 'We believe we have a responsibility to one another. We will care for those in need to establish a society that is generous'? Wrong. The Conservatives.

Which party pledges 'to enhance the quality of life for the British people'? Right. Both of them.

Which party presents itself as the friend of field sports

by making it clear 'that there will be no new limitations on the country sports of angling or shooting'? That's the shootin', fishin', vote huntin' Labour Party.

Which party projects concern for our furry friends? 'We are firmly opposed to international trade in rare and protected species such as rhinoceroses, cheetahs, leopards and bears.' That's the carin', sharin', animal-lovin' Conservative Party. Which party's environmental policy pledges to make our rivers so clean that it can promise to 'introduce crocodiles to the Thames'? No, neither. That's the Monster Raving Loony Party.

The gap between the parties is particularly wide when it comes to charters for the citizen, as the Tories call us, or the consumer, as Labour calls us. The Conservatives 'want each police force to produce a charter telling local people how quickly the police will aim to respond to emergency calls' – the Burglar's Charter.

Labour will crack down on overcharging by British Telecom and particularly 'regulate telephone services which demean women' – the Heavy Breather's Charter. Both parties saved some policy surprises. The Conservatives' remarkable pledge 'we will not legalise any banned drugs' is a dangerous gamble with the Heroin Vote, while Labour's surprise promise 'to fight crime' risks losing the support of floating murderers.

Of course, what many voters will be looking for is the party with the Big Idea for the nineties. Labour's Big Idea is to get elected, the most naked example of a policy stolen from its opponents. The Conservatives' Big Idea was harder to locate. But it finally turned up on page 43: 'We will introduce a Hedgerow Incentive Scheme.'

It's a Big Choice.

March 20, 1992: Andrew Rawnsley

Thunderpaddy One

It is 0700 hours at Liberal Democrat headquarters. Officer-commanding constitutional reformers, Captain Paddy Ashdown, is on parade. He likes to call reveille before dawn has fully broken, and journalists have fully woken.

In preparation for the day's forced march through target seats, the captain is putting his media auxiliaries through some brisk phrase-bashing.

'The Conservative Party doesn't care, the Labour Party doesn't dare.' Left, right, left, right. 'Only the Liberal Democrats have a tough, powerful, realistic action programme.'

Today's action programme will begin with an airborne assault on the West Country.

In the week since the election broke out, he and his Dan-Air jet will have ricocheted from Yeovil to London to Edinburgh to Cardiff to Essex to Leicester to Liverpool to Preston to Plymouth to Birmingham to Yeovil. By polling day he will have travelled a complete circumnavigation of the globe without leaving Britain.

For the first time in recent history, the third party has only one leader. Where there was the Gang of Four and the Two Davids, now there is only the One Paddy – one and a half if you count Des Wilson and the parliamentary auxiliaries.

The advantage over the old double-headed leadership arrangement is that in this campaign the leader can only contradict himself. The disadvantage is that his face has to almost completely front the campaign, a burden the face wears with a smile.

Such is the pace, as Thunderpaddy One dips over the north Devon coast, it is a surprise that he decides to wait until the plane has landed before throwing himself out of the door.

Touching down at RAF Chivenor, he points to a hedge at the edge of the base which had once been his home during a Royal Marines exercise. 'I spent 24 hours in that hedge.'

Though he has always emphasised he wants to fight this election on policies, he conducts his campaign by constant reference to personalities. His own. The day's unemployment figures will be underscored by memories of how he lost his job in the first Conservative recession. Former UB40 may not have the same glamorous ring as former commando. But when he shouts to a market place crowd – 'I am angry' – it sounds more than just Paddy throwing a paddy for the cameras.

The first target is a factory which makes optical equipment. In the photo-opportunity election taken to its logical extension, the camera lenses crowd round to film the leader examining camera lenses. The company chairmen proudly show off their latest product, a 'hi-tech image manipulator and enlarger'. Mr Ashdown examines it with professional interest and inquires about the price. Could his cash-strapped party afford another £10,000?

Deciding no, he gives the media their next ration of opinions. 'Only Liberal Democrats offer tough, realistic, and powerful measures. The Conservative Party . . . '

Meeting up with local Liberal Democrat ground forces in Barnstaple, the captain storms the High Street, now ricocheting from toddler to shopper to pensioner to toddler. The nightmare of the Ashdown campaign must be that somebody will accost him about You-Know-What. And that nightmare comes true in the formidable shape of a middle-aged woman, who engages him in direct voter-to-politician combat.

She has heard all he has said about putting past mistakes behind him, his commitment to a 'stable partnership' and a 'long-term relationship', but who would he jump into coalition with? The uncaring Tories or undaring Labour?

Mr Ashdown tries to explain that he dealt with all that weeks ago, and it is a personal matter only of continuing interest to prurient journalists.

Pressing deeper behind enemy lines, the next attack is a yomp through Tory-occupied areas of north Cornwall where Liberal resistance has been historically high. Addressing supporters in Launceston, he fixes that famous visionary gaze on the horizon, or at least at the Gateway supermarket, and detects 'a new mood in our country'.

After the mood of the country, it is time to find another of campaigning politicians' favourite things, country food. The Ashdown forces raid the local bakery. A traditional Cornish pasty is served up for the traditional Cornish pasty-opportunity.

'Eat it!' demand the photographers. Mr Ashdown laughs that this is a sound-bite too far. It is an exuberant campaign and, compared with those of his rivals, much more relaxed. Unlike John Major or Neil Kinnock, for one of whom this battle will very likely be fatal, he will survive to fight another election.

March 24, 1992: Andrew Rawnsley

Ducking the people

As part of the Conservatives' increased offensive on the voters, Norman Lamont was sent to Birmingham for a Meet The People Tour. During seven hours in Britain's second city, the Chancellor of the Exchequer met a grand total of three of the people, two by mistake, four if you count the man who shouted from the pavement a rhyme for merchant banker. His longest public walkabout was 10 feet down a garden path from the safety of a car to the sanctuary of a local Conservative Association.

It is not that Mr Lamont, who can be a gregarious and witty man in secret, is against people. It is even said that some of the Chancellor's best friends are people. He seemed game to go out and tell the voters to their faces that economic recovery 'is imminent'. It is just that people have strong feelings about Mr Lamont, particularly Conservative colleagues defending fragile majorities.

The local Tory MPs obviously felt that they had been quite courageous enough letting him into the city, without endangering his personal safety or their majorities by letting him loose among the voters.

For his press conference, they had provided a chilly backroom in the Conservative club. 'What are the people like here?' I asked Roger King, MP for Northfield. 'C2s,' replied Mr King with the brutal sociological insight that comes from wobbling on a majority vulnerable to a 2.9 per cent swing.

The C2s are that fabled tribe whom the psephologists tell us will decide the election, whose votes are more precious than gold dust. No wonder Mr King was keeping the Chancellor safely locked away. He did promise he would introduce him to a man who did believe in the economic recovery.

As we drove off on this quest, the rain which had poured down all morning turned to snow. Snow, in the middle of Birmingham, at the end of March. You suppose it does happen occasionally, but there was something inevitable about it happening to Mr Lamont. We reached a car showroom where the Chancellor was to hand over the keys to the buyer of a new £16,000 Rover.

We waited for the man to turn up, while the staff tactfully tried to cover up notices begging customers to 'ask about our redundancy protection scheme'.

We waited some more. The man who believed in the economic recovery was as late turning up as the economy.

One of the staff finally announced: 'He's phoned to say he's not coming.'

Eventually somebody else was found prepared to buy a car from the Chancellor after getting assurances that it wasn't second-hand. The man said he usually voted Tory, but was worried about the economy. 'Quick,' said Mr Lamont to Mr King, 'give him the keys.'

'What! Are you giving me this car?' said the voter, staggered at the desperate bribes the Tories appeared to be offering now. Mr King had to explain that they were not. The man was crestfallen.

Mr King, alarmed that some passing C2s might by now be at the point of recognising those famous arching eyebrows, bundled the Chancellor away. Just to put the voters really off the scent, he also switched vehicles, persuading another local Tory MP to take the Chancellor in his blue Bentley. Despite these precautions, coming out of a local-radio studio brought the moment all the MPs had been fearing. One of their voters put a name to that famous pekinese face. He asked for the Chancellor's autograph. We seemed to have located the founder-member of the Norman Lamont Fan Club.

The autograph-hunter would be voting Tory? The man laughed uproariously.

Mr Lamont was hurried back into the car before he did any more damage, on the promise that he really would find somebody who believed in the economic recovery in the neighbouring constituency of Selly Oak. The local MP, Anthony Beaumont-Dark, introduced him to a novelty-cake entrepreneur. Among the novelty sponges on sale was one bearing the message 'Best Wishes on Your Retirement' and a 'Playboy' cake wearing a black icing basque and fish-net stockings.

'Naughty but nice,' chuckled Mr Beaumont-Dark. Suddenly realising they were attracting the attention of some loitering voters, he propelled the Chancellor out of his constituency in the direction of a private lunch with businessmen.

At the door he was welcomed by a handful of people yelling 'Norman Lamont! A Price Worth Paying!' and placards yelling 'Capitalism Sucks!' Just Norman's luck to run into the entire membership of Birmingham's Revolutionary Communist Party.

The Chancellor rushed inside to complete his whirlwind Avoid The People Tour.

April 8, 1992: Hugo Young

Goodfella versus the godfather

If this had been a presidential election, there seems no doubt who would have won. Most voters think Paddy Ashdown fought the best campaign and most floating voters, according to Mori, think he would make the best prime minister.

The election is not presidential. It has not been fought primarily on the leadership question. All the same, we have learnt a lot about the leaders in this time. Either Major or Kinnock will be prime minister on Friday (say Sunday, to be safe). Either will make a great difference to the government, perhaps more than to the election. If we judged on these men alone and what we've seen in the past month, we would be driven towards a puzzling verdict.

John Major proved a poor campaigner. He went sharply down in public estimation. This is not a negligible weakness. If you can't set the country ablaze, arguably you should not be seeking the highest office in this day and age. Not everyone can be a great rhetorician. But Major's campaigning strategy often looked like that of the neophyte he is. He had neither experience nor the panache to make up for it.

But he has been, within the limits history imposed on him, a good prime minister. As a leader of government, he inspires confidence if not a trace of excitement.

He is intelligent and eminently straight. He understands the most arid of issues, has an orderly approach to everything that crosses his desk. He did a tremendous job at the Maastricht Summit, with the Foreign Office machine behind him. Few if any of the participants at that occasion would deny Major and Douglas Hurd did better than anyone in maximising the hand they had to play.

The campaign has taught us that these bureaucratic qualities remain through rain or shine, and are allied to a fierce partisanship. It is to Major's credit, not his disgrace, that mendacious excess, the stock-in-trade of the most hymned performers on the stump, is beyond him. He is a reasonable, collegiate politician, unseduced by ego trips. He would never let the country down.

On the other hand, what about vision? If he has one, it is a cloudy, pallid thing. He is caught between the millstones of the Thatcher and post-Thatcher worlds, and doesn't know what posture to assume. He's had four months since Maastricht to work out the lineaments and four weeks to drive home what he believes in. But this has evidently not been long enough. His discovery of the constitution's overarching importance less than a week before the vote says it all about the fixity of his vision.

Neil Kinnock's campaign revealed new qualities as well as old ones. It was disciplined and smoothly organised as well as energetic. He disclosed a surprising capacity to stay cool. He secured a powerful lock on the agenda and seldom had his arm twisted off it.

One remembered that he had done it all before. For a professional politician such long years in Opposition, tirelessly derided by the other side, provide a hardening apprenticeship. At this level of the game, the men whose lives have preserved them from the indignity of Opposition suddenly looked like the ones who didn't know what they were doing. Kinnock will never be a senior wrangler in the technicalities of public finance. He would be a terrible Chancellor of the Exchequer, and perhaps none too acute as Foreign Secretary. Whether he has an aptitude for the grinding slog of the prime ministerial in-tray is a question on which his previous life offers little guidance. He is reputed to be idle. We may soon see.

But emerging, as the recent weeks have passed, from the shadows of predicted defeat into the ripening sunlight that greets a potential prime minister, he has made clearer why this post may be appropriate to the time and place in which he fills it.

First, he is the party boss supreme. At his press conference appearances, increasingly frequent as the polls firmed up in his favour, he emerged more clearly as the acknowledged leader of a team no longer in any important way superior to himself. He regards them with a benign countenance. For the first time, they owe him far more than he owes them. As the leader of a cabinet, he would want to retain the power Margaret Thatcher gathered round herself. But his lack of zeal for policy detail improves the chances that he would supply what the leader must: a sense of perspective and priority.

Second, he would preside over an unexpectedly convincing team. The campaign paraded a body of Labour politicians who, although few have held any office, are better groomed for power than their most obvious historic analogues, the Wilson government of 1964. That contained more practised public men. But it was strangely unprepared for government, as the diaries and memoirs copiously make clear. It did not have a strategy, and its preparations were strangely uncollective. Harold Wilson's own account suggests much of it was worked out on something not much less substantial than the back of his own envelope. A Kinnock government might face a not dissimilar economic crisis, with devaluation in the wings. But it has an intensely collective approach – another product of so many years in Siberia.

Third, Kinnock would be playing to the strengths of his own style. He may not be at home with the finer points of currency reform. But the likely stuff of politics will be what the years have made him good at: haggling, dealing, parleying the votes. Whether it's the politics of proportional representation or of party unity, the Godfather will be in his element.

What Kinnock likewise lacks is a vision, or at any rate one that corresponds to achievable reality. He deploys the passion and the glitz, but the votes he will get are far more negative than positive.

Essentially, power for power's sake: that is the overwhelming, though not the exclusive, drive behind each man. Understandable and not unworthy, just uninspiring in the world beyond politics. But neither man is a crook or a demagogue. They are capable politicians who want to succeed. And the election, in any case and strangely, is not about who they really are.

April 9, 1992: Matthew Engel

Labour's bricks

Tomorrow the world, or so he presumes. The Daimler past the palace gates; the commission from Her Majesty; the brief, graceful speech on the steps of No. 10, which he might just have rehearsed once or twice during the past 8½ years.

Then the call from President Bush ('Honestly, we're all mighty pleased in Washington, er Nick. Say again, what's

the name of your Foreign Secretary?'), the first sight of the
Treasury and MI5 documents ('Perhaps you ought to
know, Prime Minister . . . '), and the honeymoon period
with the Conservative press, which could easily last as
long as 20 minutes.

And yesterday it was the brickworks. Truly. Neil Kinnock's sole engagement between the morning press conference in London and the evening rallies in South Wales
was a visit to Marshall's Clay Products in Accrington to 'see
how acid-resistant and other specialist bricks are made'.

Now for a politician who, famously, has negligible
experience of non-political life, this is all thoroughly
useful. You never know when Chancellor Kohl might slip
him a tricky one on the Common Acid-resistant Brick
Policy. But it does smack of panic-stricken last-minute
revision to be swotting up on the brick industry now.

But the Labour Party has become obsessed with brickworks. 'It's my third,' groaned one reporter. This is presumably because of the subliminal image of re-building.
Tricky blighters, though, bricks. They get thrown, they get
(as Mr Kinnock noted) dropped, they get built without
straw. And this brickworks is next to the municipal rubbish tip and overlooks the football ground used by poor,
extinct, Accrington Stanley.

The Kinnock campaign is beyond such details. It is not
just prime ministerial any more, it is positively
presidential.

He has even adopted Ronald Reagan's habit of curtail-
ing contact with the travelling press to bantering questions, shouted above the din of aircraft noise. It happened
that the plane making the noise in Accrington was flying a
banner marked 'Get Stuffed, Boyo'. It merely added to the
air of triumphalism: the equivalent of frustrated left-
wingers chanting rude slogans at demos in the 1980s.

At other times it seems like a royal progress. Mr Kinnock walked across the tarmac at Blackpool airport, arms
behind his back, like Prince Philip; the staff greeted him as

though this was a rare honour. In fact he had been there the previous night on his way back from Blackburn to London. Accrington is next to Blackburn.

The nub of Labour's case is that they can make more efficient use of scarce resources than the Conservatives.

They can certainly run a more ordered campaign. The press are chivvied on and off buses and behind barriers as though it were a fourth-form outing. The new bossiness lies before us: You Know It Makes Sense.

The leader is a distant figure, occasionally glimpsed listening intently while an executive explains about thermal conductivity and abrasion resistance. It happened that the brick being turned out yesterday was called Robin Hood Red Smooth. Somewhere in the factory an alarm bell was ringing, faintly but insistently.

The Red Smooths had been out in force at the last press conference too. Ten prospective ministers were paraded in crisply pressed suits to the compulsory martial music. One imagined that a Walworth Road official had inspected behind their ears before they were allowed into the hall.

There they all were: John Smith, as ever a tribute to Tie Rack; Gordon Brown, arms folded and jaw jutting; Jack Straw, staring statesman-like into the distance; Ann Taylor and Harriet Harman, looking as if they were fresh from a Swiss finishing school.

Would anyone ever have persuaded Labour cabinet ministers of old – George Brown, Ray Gunter, Arthur Bottomley and all those grey men called Fred – to act like this? Would the party have done better if they had?

The Labour Party will try and play anything for symbolism now. As the leader's plane approached Cardiff – where he was heading for the two election-eve rallies – they played the campaign theme again on the plane's muzak system. At that moment the clouds cleared away and the sun broke through on to the fields of Glamorgan below. 'Isn't that appropriate?' said an aide.

Then we hit an air pocket and the plane lurched. And

somewhere in the back of my head the alarm bell from Accrington was still ringing. Tomorrow morning it will be easier to work out what on earth it signified.

April 9, 1992: Andrew Rawnsley

Punch drunk on optimism

How would you have spent what the opinion polls were all saying would be your last day enjoying the perks and privileges of being Prime Minister?

Throwing a party at Chequers, perhaps, and making sure to leave lots of mess for the Kinnocks to clear up? Taking the VC-10 out for one last spin, possibly, and leaving a nasty dent in the paintwork? Or packing up what souvenirs of your brief stay you could legally lift from No. 10 before going back to your constituency to prepare for Opposition?

John Major is too nice a man or too unimaginative a man to do any of that. Or maybe he just knows something nobody else does. He spent his last day on the campaign trail, as he has spent the last 30 days – insisting he was not a loser.

'We are going to have a clear majority when the result is announced,' he declared at his morning press conference and repeated it like a mantra all day.

His top dogs of war – Boxer Patten, Ratter Baker, Alsatian Howard, Pekinese Lamont, Afghan Hurd, Terrier Clarke and Golden Retriever Heseltine – had been brought on to take turns having one final sound-bite at the voters.

As the seven spelled out the disaster that would be a

Tory defeat, for the first time in this election they began to sound like conviction politicians. The flat tone of their voices, and the glazed look in their eyes, spoke of men convinced they were going down to a disastrous defeat. Mr Heseltine even refused an offer to bet £1,000 – the sort of money he can afford to leave as a taxi tip – against a Tory defeat. Even though, for him, victory or defeat is an each-way bet.

Only Mr Major was still smiling on through, as if he would bet the entire Public Sector Borrowing Requirement on it.

He dismissed the opinion poll projections, preferring to put his faith in the weather forecast. 'It's going to be sunny tomorrow, a sunny day in every way,' he said, forgetting that the margin of error among weather-men is notoriously higher than that among pollsters.

Setting off on the last leg of his campaign tour, a dash around some London marginals, a visit to Lewisham reunited him with the inventor of his famous soapbox. Derek Stone, a builder aged 53, said he had recruited Mr Major to the Tory Party more than 30 years ago when he was just another failed conductor. If he becomes just another failed Prime Minister, the Tories now know who to blame.

Admitting to being the first to have had the idea of finding a wooden platform to match Mr Major's oratorical style, Mr Stone went on: 'We used to trundle up to wind them up.'

Mr Major had trundled up to wind up two of his most vulnerable ministers. The local bookies' bet is that John Maples and Colin Moynihan will both swing.

'I'm confident of winning. I'm remarkably confident,' Mr Major comforted them. They would get off on the final appeal. 'It's going to be all right.'

On to Dulwich, where just 180 votes stand between the defending Conservative, Gerald Bowden, and the dole queue.

Mr Major stood on the doorstep of the Tory head-quarters and shouted through a megaphone, although the only hecklers were trying to be friendly.

'Well done, John! After four years of Labour, they'll want us back!' shouted one man, wearing a hat saying: JM 4 PM.

JM was still insisting he was not about to become the forgotten PM. 'We're going to win this election. Absolutely stone-cold certain of it, I am.'

Today he will find out whether he would have been better off getting absolutely slewed on the Chequers wine cellar.

April 11, 1992: Posy Simmonds

© Posy Simmonds 1992

April 11, 1992: Andrew Rawnsley

Happy Eater

For once he didn't say it, but everybody else was using John Major's most celebrated catchphrase as the country woke up, pinched itself, and found it really had voted for five more years of Citizens' Charters. It was really quite remarkable.

Mild-mannered Clark Kent had turned out to be Superman after all. Or, at least, Considerably Satisfactory Man. Able to leap a soapbox in a single bound, John Major emerged on the doorstep of No. 10 as unamazed to find himself still there as everybody else was fazed.

His work done, he had already put his underpants back inside his trousers, and returned to the familiar disguise of the bespectacled accountant. You would have to be in on his secret to know that, in the teeth of all the economic indicators and all the expert forecasts, he had won the first consecutive fourth Tory term since the Napoleonic Wars.

'I have only one thing to say,' he told applauding Downing Street staff as he emerged after a quick kip. 'It's nice to be back' – for all the world as if he and Norma had just come back from a fortnight's coach holiday, rather than pulling off the biggest electoral upset in 20 years.

Bottles of champagne from the grateful flowed to the door of No. 10 all morning, but the word from inside was that he had chosen egg, sausage, bacon and fried bread.

By lunchtime he was ready to come out and say how he planned to continue his work making the whole of Britain a land fit for Happy Eaters.

Mr Major walked down Downing Street to shake hands with those who had come to congratulate him. All the well-wishers insisted that, when everybody else in the country had written him off as a nice guy who was going to come last, they alone had never doubted for a moment that he would win.

Among them, I think I spotted several members of the Cabinet, most of Conservative Central Office, all the opinion pollsters, and several distinguished political correspondents and eminent pundits.

Mr Major may have spent much of his campaign getting pelted with eggs, but they had all ended up on other people's faces.

'You must be shattered,' said one supporter in the crowd. No, that condition belongs to the Labour Party. Neil Kinnock spent his day at home in Ealing, hosting a barbecue for friends, and preparing to fall on his own kebab. His speech at the count in Islwyn, promising to serve the nation 'in any capacity', could not fail to touch even his bitterest opponents.

But Mr Major, although he has some new posts to fill, was not saying yesterday whether he would be putting Mr Kinnock's name forward for the presidency of the Millennium Fund or the chairmanship of the Hedgerow Incentive Scheme.

Mr Kinnock's colleagues filled the airwaves all day, saying that they would let the Labour leader go from his present job with dignity and in his own time. And could he make it Monday at the latest?

April 11, 1992: Hugo Young

Holding on to nurse

Britain is, above all, a conservative country. That is the verdict of the people. At present there is reason to suspect that it is inextinguishably conservative. The shape of John Major's victory makes a strong case against the possibility of radical change of any kind. In the circumstances that is an astonishing judgment, but the more impressive for it. From 1950 to 2000, 35 years will have been Tory years. From 1800 to 2000, no party will have held office unbroken for so long as the Conservative government that began in 1979. This record compels politicians of all interests to ask what, if anything, the people want of them.

Mr Major perfectly personifies conservative sentiment. He is unexciting, but also unalarming. He fought a campaign that was true to his character, presented himself to us as he is. The country, desperate to express its conservatism, sank gratefully into the arms of his reassuring integrity.

His victory is potent. It leaves him in a position of unresented authority such as few leaders enjoy. He can make a cabinet free of debts to anyone, and now is the time to be cruel. But he gains the special advantage of having won when everything was loaded against him. He is the quiet miracle-worker who never really knew he had it in him: ignore all talk about the high command being stone-cold certain of winning. The Conservative triumph breaks all the laws of electoral politics, under a leader whose part in this was, if not incidental, in no way dominant or demagogic. It leaves him without a rival or an enemy, banishing every taint of the illegitimacy that hung over his 16 months as the candidate of nothing more convincing than the 1922 Committee.

The fourth term vindicates the conservatism which began with that inaugurating moment in November 1990. Mrs Thatcher was among the first to give her opinion on Thursday night. Victory, she said, locked her record into place. But its more emphatic message was to confirm that her deposing was one of the most brilliant acts of self-renewal any party has ever executed. It disposed of an old leader, which satisfied the public appetite for change. Just as important, it ended an era of harsh and relentless radicalism which the people put up with only because no effective voice could speak against it. The radicalism left a deep mark, which included a deep desire for it to yield to a period of quiet consolidation.

Perversely, conservatism found a new source of succour in the Conservative-led recession. The clues were there to see, if we had only seen them straight. Why could Labour never convert the endless recession into a steady 10-point opinion-poll lead? It was the mystery of the last six months. The answer delivered on Thursday is that, in some kinds of crisis, the people hold on to nurse for fear of something worse. The old conservatism rules. Fear of Labour's tax demands obliterated resentment of the recession, in enough of those people whose businesses, jobs and houses were put in jeopardy by both prospects. The instinct to punish collapsed before the instinct to preserve.

But the conservatism goes deeper, and is more positive. Besides trusting the Tories with the economy, more people than anyone expected trust them with the health service as well. One thing for sure is that the NHS reforms and the radical shifts in the administration of schools will be fixed immovably in place well before another election. A whole swathe of social reform, for better or for worse, will have taken root in the 1990s: one more Conservative installation that Labour must grope to adjust to. This too argues for a conservative country sensing that yet another upheaval in basic services is a priority to be avoided.

Some instincts in the Tory Party will lust to challenge this scenario. Although Major has only a modest majority, the way he got it might tempt some colleagues towards as many hubristic adventures as Mrs Thatcher launched into from her much larger power-base. After all, if Conservatism can receive this vote of confidence when every current economic indicator suggests it has presided over a disaster, the more tigerish ministers must ask what's to stop them moving faster towards a privatised society on American lines: the withering of the NHS, more aggressive inequality, and the other nostrums of the far right. But

Major has set himself against this. No more tax cuts for the rich, he said as the campaign ended. And definitely no privatisation of health care. A conservative man, with moderate instincts, is left to handle the economic imponderables that made every party's election promises academic.

The tigers, however, are in one way right. The Labour Party has ceased to be a credible alternative government. The 1992 election strongly suggests that Labour as we now know it is incapable of securing any mandate and is, in short, terminally exhausted.

Thursday was its blackest night in the last 30 years, and arguably in its history. For Labour sincerely expected to win. And for not winning it has no alibis.

One alibi will be sought in the identity of the leader. The months, indeed years, of Neil Kinnock's tenure have been marked by powerful spasms of feeling against him. He was always going to be a loser, it was said, because he was palpably unfit to be prime minister. No doubt the tabloid mobs will today be torn between derision for his latest shattering failure and gratitude that he wasn't replaced long ago.

But Kinnock is not the problem. His ratings actually rose during the campaign. He proved more than able enough to handle most of the questions. He may attract a lot of venomous sneerers outside the Labour Party, but his colleagues' admiration for him grew. Nor are there any excuses to be found in incompetence elsewhere at the top. Even the Tory press was saying that the Labour front bench outshone some of the deadbeats across the chamber. The campaign itself, moreover, was flawlessly professional. The confusions and dissensions even of 1987, let alone 1983, were entirely absent. As for the objective circumstances, they could not have been more favourably arranged.

So it is hard to persuade oneself that a change in the cosmetics, including the change of leader which in due

April 11, 1992: Steve Bell

time will surely happen, can be relied on to carry Labour, with one more heave, through the iron gates of Downing Street.

The fault lies somewhere deeper. Although there remains a large anti-Conservative majority in the country, the configuration of left politics makes it impossible to mobilise. For this the Labour Party carries the largest responsibility: not because it has not tried to modernise, but because somehow it has failed, even now, to relate to modern times.

It remains a 'socialist' party. Although the word has vanished, significant traces of the idea remain. British socialism, unlike most of its continental counterparts, still aspires to an organised programme that is unashamedly and prominently egalitarian. Equality remains its creed to an extent that outfaces its new commitment, so sedulously worked on, to present itself as a party of capitalism as well. This may be partly the work of its infamous paymasters, the trade unions, that got it committed to a statutory minimum wage. But what is striking about the younger generation of leaders, the Blairs and the Browns, is that they retain this powerful strain of selfless idealism, epitomised by John Smith's tax plans, which is serious about a more equal society: more serious, apparently, than the British middle-class masses are ever prepared to be.

The longer Labour is out of office, moreover, the more its core collectivist philosophy seems to look like a challenge to middle-class life. Ownership, one of the great Thatcherite legacies, has played an immense part in creating a conservative nation. John Major's brand of Conservatism proposes its modifications of Thatcherism, with an enhanced understanding that the law of the jungle is not the kind of social policy the British want. Society has been reinstated as an entity that exists; a development which plays no small part in Major's quiet populism. But the Tories' fundamental message, of more reliable respect for individuals and their choices, is one that Labour, for all its acquiescence in privatisation and nuclear deterrence, finds it impossible to match.

The hope attached to a Labour victory was that it would have completed the party's modernisation and established it as credibly as the German SPD. Such an evolution, when the tide of disappointment has ebbed, must now be conducted anyway. One way Labour will not respond to defeat is by hardening leftwards. One way it must eventually respond is with the most serious consideration of links with the Liberal Democrats and their voters. Electoral reform will provide an interest in common. But that's academic until these parties together get some power. The examination of self must precede it: how can Labour speak to a conservative nation with radical inspiration?

They thought they had done that during the campaign. It was not a very radical campaign. It was bemoaned for not being inspiring enough. But the sad truth was that it was not conservative enough.

One truth emerged from it, however, which was entirely reassuring and a great surprise. It was that the very instruments of modern politics can no longer be relied on to perform the tasks assigned to them. Whatever one may think of the prospect of the next five years, the electoral process has been taken out of the hands of the gurus who were thought increasingly to control it.

Take campaigning itself. The 1992 result suggests that the rules of 'campaigning' as currently defined need to be rewritten. The best campaigns, as assessed everywhere including in this space, were run by the big losers. Paddy Ashdown did brilliantly, but scored worse. Kinnock was Kinnock. Since 'good' campaigning includes a high degree of manipulation, its failure should be a comfort to democrats. The Tories have their own manipulators, performing daily in the tabloid press (although coverage by the broadsheet Tories was admirably fair). But in Major they had unmanipulable raw material, who certainly did not win because of his mastery of factitious modern devices.

Perhaps more profoundly, the opinion poll business has proved to rest on fantasy. What is plain is that voters decline to specify their ultimate intentions, and make the whole predictive business sweetly unreliable. The polls were not only wrong at the end, but their lurchings in the middle, not one of which came anywhere near the final figure, were quite misleading as well. They simply did not find out what sort of nation this really is.

The question now is how far its conservatism reaches, and how long it can be made to last. For at some point the political system might be expected to implode under the strain of unceasing Conservative government.

There are points where the breakdown can easily be imagined. The Scottish result was a disaster for rational government, possibly for the Union. It was messy, with the Scottish National Party doing far worse than expected, and the Tories effectively applying a cynical squeeze on the Labour vote to gain unlikely ground. They've discovered some political astuteness, hung on to seats they should have lost, and in general gained not lost. Labour and the Nats will now get down to bloody fighting.

None the less, the equation of illegitimacy remains. Scotland will be run unremittingly from Westminster, having rejected the Conservative proposition. Every word spoken before the election about this breakdown of democracy holds good, and Mr Major's last-minute repentance, conceding that he ought 'to do something' for Scotland, holds no promise that it will be rectified. What Labour must fear is a surge for independence. That's what they were saying in the Labour strongholds when they contemplated the result that has come about. So should we all fear it. Perhaps the stoic conservatism of the Scots, tested for so long and not yet found wanting, has its limits.

Equally, with the unfairness of the voting system, and the weakness of the constitution, lodged in the public mind by this campaign more vividly than ever before, the arguments for change will not stop. A four-term government is an offence against the two-party system. It is the seedbed of intellectual if not moral corruption, of idleness, complacency and, on all other sides, despair. When the grievances of the dispossessed find no outlet in the political system, they reach for alternatives.

These are harbingers of trouble. They might confront a four-term government with eruptions it cannot control. But I do not expect it. The mandate for conservatism reaches far, wide, and to the fringes. The people accept the people's verdict, however incredulously. It is, after all, their own.

April 11, 1992: Michael Kinsley

You ain't seen nut'n yet

Channel Four News asked in alarmist tones two nights before the election: 'How much American razzmatazz has crept into British election campaigns?' Paddy Ashdown, at his last morning news conference, said smugly: 'I do think that Britain was in danger of slipping into American-style negative campaigning,' a descent he saw no irony in blaming on the other two parties. A journalist then attacked Ashdown: 'Aren't you, the Liberal Democrats, as responsible as anyone else for a presidential style of campaigning?'

Britain, relax. When it comes to cheesy politics, you've got a long way to go.

The complaint that British democracy is adopting deplorable American habits seems to have three elements. One is negative campaigning. Another is a supposed 'presidential' style. A third is campaign staginess and artifice: spin doctors, people meters and so on.

Let's be clear: there is nothing wrong with negative campaigning. Pointing out the faults of the other guy is perfectly legitimate. In fact, in an election where (as in America) there is a general consensus that it is a choice among evils, emphasising the opposition's defects is arguably more honest than emphasising one's own alleged strengths. What people mean, or ought to mean, when they complain of 'negative' campaigning is two other things: triviality and dishonesty.

As for triviality, the only issue during this campaign (and it wasn't a very large one) that left an outsider wondering, 'Why on earth are they wasting their time arguing about *that*?' was foxhunting. Compare the situation in America: there, President Bush last month won the crucial Michigan primary by running ads pointing out that his opponent, Pat Buchanan, drives a Mercedes. Buchanan's noisiest issue against Bush was that the government had funded a film about black gays. Embarrassingly, this turned out to have been under Bush's predecessor – and Buchanan's hero – Ronald Reagan.

Big issues in this week's New York Democratic primary were the fact that Governor Bill Clinton had played a round of golf at a racially restricted club, and that Governor Jerry Brown – dazzled by meeting Mother Theresa – had made an anti-abortion remark years ago, though he was pro-choice before and has been since.

This kind of 'gotcha' stuff is the result of what's called 'negative research'. That means looking for embarrassing things about some prominent person that are not already known. Almost by definition, such things are likely to be of limited significance. And don't think the trivia is limited to primaries. Based on the experience of 1988, the election in the autumn will not be any more elevated.

As for political dishonesty, it certainly flourishes on both sides of the Atlantic. The big lie of the British campaign, it seems, was Labour's preposterous insistence that Conservatives would privatise the Health Service. But at least that is a lie about something important.

What passes here for a 'dirty trick' is simply pathetic. In Chingford, where the *Guardian* sent me for three hours to take the pulse of the nation, the Tories were making an issue of an allegedly deceptive leaflet being distributed by Labour. The deception consisted of saying that Labour's proposed National Insurance tax increase would be phased in, whereas the Labour manifesto said it would be imposed immediately. The papers were reporting this seriously and Labour was actually regretful. This would not be regarded as a significant breach of campaign decorum in Chicago.

The 'presidential' question apparently reflects a concern that there was too much emphasis on party leaders; that they were overly packaged, glamorised, and isolated from the voters. What impressed me was just the opposite.

John Major's final campaign gaffe – admitting the possibility of a Labour government – came during a voter call-in television show the day before the election. It is inconceivable that the president of the United States would risk such unmediated contact with the electorate so close to the voting.

When you are one of several candidates for the opposing party's nomination, you are happy to do call-in shows. By the time you are the opposition front-runner or nominee, you might still be willing to be grilled on rare occasions by the more prominent TV interviewers. But when you are president, the only access to your mind comes at massive press conferences, where reporters are lucky for a single follow-up question, and at one or two over-rehearsed so-called 'debates' with your opponent.

The *Guardian*'s Hugo Young, writing about the British election in the American publication I work for, *The New Republic*, commented that Neil Kinnock cannot survive five minutes of close economic questioning. I wouldn't know if George Bush could survive five minutes of close economic questioning (although I have my guess). The point is that he never need submit to it.

The isolating grandeur of the president is partly due to the constitutional fact that he is head of state, like the Queen, as well as head of government, like the prime minister. The absurdly overblown secret service protection, which descends on opposing candidates as well, also contributes to the sense of imperial remove. But there is also much cynical calculation by presidential imageologists to aggrandise the incumbent.

The sight of John Major, at the Tory news conferences, sitting in a row with other ministers, politely waiting his turn to speak, suggests that prime ministerial imageology is not a fully developed art. Labour imageologists clearly put a lot of work into giving Neil Kinnock all the gravitas they could, but that was surely a matter of 'damage control'. Surely neither leading party built its strategy around its leader's personage. Reasonably enough.

On the other hand, other sorts of electoral artifice actually seem more developed here than in the United States. Three sequential morning news conferences every day of the campaign allows parties to create issues of the day and play the 'spin' game with almost comical efficiency. NHS patients may suffer in multi-year queues for medical doctors, but journalists here never have to wait long for a spin doctor.

Believe it or not, British campaigns seem to feature even more polls, more people meters, and similar bits of democratic (or anti-democratic, depending on your point of view) technology than American ones. And, aesthetically, America's fractious political parties could never be packaged like a product by ad men – with coordination of colour, graphics, slogans and even music – the way British parties are.

And just so that you don't think that these are the ravings of a hopeless Anglophile, let me add that to American ears there is still something patronising about the way many

British politicians talk. Tories are the worse offenders, of course. But even among Labour campaigning there is the faint flavour of 'what *we*, your leaders, are going to do for *you*, the ordinary folks' that any American political consultant would be sure to get rid of.

But back to Anglophile ravings. Although Britain's campaigns are clearly becoming more like America's with each election, I suspect they will always be more serious and more honest. That is not because British voters are less susceptible to bullshit, or because British politicians and their 'handlers' are less adept at razzmatazz. It is because of your different constitutional arrangement.

It is startling for an American to realise that, when a British politician says that something or other will happen if he is elected, it may actually happen. And it may happen within a week! The stately pace of American campaigns; the gap between election and inauguration; the separation of powers between the executive and legislative branches of government; the seemingly permanent tradition of a Republican president and a Democratic Congress; the lack of cohesion within the parties themselves – all these elements conspire to weaken the connection between what is debated in elections and what happens in government.

If a British prime minister is elected on a manifesto promising that the government will do X, Y, or Z, he or she has no excuse for not doing X, Y, or Z, and nowhere to hide from the consequences if X, Y, or Z turns out badly. An American presidential candidate has an infinity of excuses and, so, can be far more creative in what he says to get elected. Political party manifestos (called 'platforms') are unread wish lists of legislative proposals. The campaigns themselves increasingly turn more on atmospherics than on specific government action.

What, if anything, has President Bush done about prison furloughs – a central concern of his 1988 campaign? No one has even bothered to ask.

Voters, too, have it undeservedly easy in the American system. It allows them the luxury of believing unbelievable promises and then complaining of betrayal when the promises are not fulfilled. Or of voting on the basis of irrelevant issues, then blaming the politicians as the country goes to hell.

Sound tempting?

April 13, 1992: Ian Aitken

The City strikes again

Improbable as it may seem, I managed to raise a glass of fizz early on Friday morning. This wasn't because I had misread the Basildon result, and still less because I welcomed its baleful message. It was because I had, just for once, established a modest but welcome personal milestone.

After voting in the same constituency in every election since 1950, I finally put my cross beside the name of a winning candidate. I voted for Barbara Roche, the admirable new Labour MP for Hornsey and Wood Green – a constituency that has been Tory since the beginning of time.

There was also a second, more shamefaced, reason for raising my glass. Mr Major's victory means that I will not have to pay the cash price of my vote. There is no denying that, thanks to Essex Man and his allies, I can now bask in my own righteousness without facing a higher tax bill. It may not be very nice, but it helps to ease the pain.

Happily, I also have an uplifting reason for not being entirely depressed. I've said before that every election leaves me with a memorable image, and Polling Day 1992 provided one which, even in defeat, helps to counter the growing cynicism about politics and the democratic process.

It happened while I was doing a stint as a Labour teller at my local polling station, matched by a splendid colonel's widow for the Tories, though no one from the Lib Dems. Suddenly a battered car wheezed into the school yard and lurched to a halt. Inside was a dreadfully disabled young man, who proceeded to lever himself painfully out of his seat.

It took a very long time, and longer still to reach the building. But a thoughtful polling-station clerk offered (no doubt illegally) to bring a ballot paper out to him. Having voted, this intrepid crusader for democracy returned just as painfully and slowly to his car.

The colonel's lady and I were both profoundly moved by this young man's determination to do his civic duty. It seemed even more amazing when he cheerfully informed us, as he let in the clutch, that he had voted Lib Dem in what he accepted was a two-horse, Tory v Labour race. Somehow, it didn't seem a wasted vote after all.

Now Mr Major has produced his post-Thatcher cabinet. And a pretty rum lot they are if one is looking for some consistent message. Lashings of un-Thatcherite intervention in industry from Hezzie, perhaps? But what about Peter Lilley at Social Security, Michael Howard at Environment, and Mrs Bottomley acting the Lady Almoner at Health?

And then there is Poll Tax Portillo, whose No Turning Back convictions still show through the thin coat of camouflage paint he applied 18 months ago. He will be in charge of public spending – two very dirty words in his Thatcherite vocabulary – while Norman the do-nothing Chancellor remains in control of the Treasury. Perhaps Mrs Thatcher could have cuffed such a crew into obedience, but Mr Major does not seem to have sufficient sense of direction to keep them all travelling the same way.

Meanwhile, I offer no excuse for averting my gaze from the tear-stained wreck that is the Labour Party. Rummaging through the transcripts and videos of the campaign to find an instant scapegoat is distasteful, and plumping for drastic remedies like a new alliance with the Ashdownites is clearly premature. There will, alas, be plenty of time for that kind of thing in the long, Tory years that lie ahead.

But politicians are remarkable people, and do not remain cast down for long. Like Milton's Satan, they soon rise up and resume their defiance, and there is nothing quite like a leadership contest to make a politician's heart beat faster. If there is a resignation statement from Mr Kinnock today it will bring the corpses back to life more certainly than a draught of virgin's blood.

But before the inquest begins in earnest, and the inevitable accusations are levelled at those responsible for organising what was still seen as Labour's best-ever campaign only a few days ago, MPs might do well to consider the possibility that Thursday's defeat really had very little to do with the campaign, or with the quality of leadership, or even with the policies on offer. There are good grounds for thinking that Labour's defeat was engineered, partly by accident and partly by design, by what we used to call the Gnomes of Zurich and now have to describe as the City of London yuppies.

Consider the circumstances of the week before last. It looked as if the Tory onslaught on Labour's alternative budget had failed, and that John Smith was succeeding in persuading voters that he was at least as safe a pair of economic hands as Mr Lamont. Then came those weird polls alleging Labour had made the breakthrough and was six or even seven points ahead.

Never mind the panic this generated in Central Office. The important panic took place in the City. Over the next few days the pound slipped, share prices plunged, businessmen queued to express their alarm at every available broadcasting outlet. The process checked briefly, then resumed a few days later when the polls continued to register the message that, even if there wouldn't be a majority Labour government, a minority one was the most probable outcome.

Even devoted anti-Thatcherite economic writers like William Keegan of the *Observer* wrote stories last Sunday predicting a crisis rise in interest rates in the event of such a result. Messrs Smith and Brown faced endless questioning about what they would do if the pound was threatened.

The result, in my view, fits the idea that the polls were right throughout the campaign, but that their very correctness precipitated Labour's eventual defeat. Former Labour supporters who had deserted in 1983 and 1987, but were considering voting Labour this time, may not have been convinced by the wild warnings of the Tory posters. But they were halted in their tracks by what seemed to be objective evidence that there would be a collapse of business confidence if Mr Kinnock crossed the threshold of Downing Street.

Though it rules out the search for personal scapegoats, this explanation is really even bleaker news for Labour than any identifiable failure by the party. For it means that changes in personalities or policies will do next to nothing to put things right in time for the next election. Almost the only thing that could help would be incompetence by the new Major Government on such a scale that it would convince the financial world that a John Smith government would actually serve the City better.

None of this would be valid if it were not for the fact that the financial institutions now have more power than at any time since the war to bring down governments – a power they owe to Sir Geoffrey Howe, the chancellor who ended controls over the export of capital in the early 1980s. Could this, one wonders, be the first election ever to be won by a dead sheep?

Exit Gorby, stage right

August 23, 1991: Jonathan Steele's exclusive report on the release of President Gorbachev from house arrest in the Crimea after the hardliners' attempted coup

Defiance at the dacha

It was Bŏris Yeltsin who gave the first announcement that the Soviet *putsch* was on its last legs. There is a report that the Gang of Eight are on their way to Vnukovo, he told the Russian parliament early on Tuesday afternoon.

The deputies looked delighted, and journalists headed for the door.

The road to Vnukovo was strewn with evidence that the coup was indeed over. A policeman was preventing traffic turning on to it from the outer ring road, but we drove past him flashing our press passes.

We passed a huge column of tanks moving away from the city, spewing earth all over the asphalt, as they moved out from the fields where they had spent two nights. The Kantimirovskaya Division was lumbering home to Narofominsk. But where was the Gang of Eight?

Outside the black grille gates of Vnukovo's VIP airfield an officer was setting up a communications post, a tall aerial sprouting up like a speeded-up film of a plant growing. It was nothing to do with the coup leaders' escape, he said. 'We are co-ordinating our departure from Moscow.'

Alexei Fomin, a police lieutenant, drove up and told us a plane with some of the coup plotters had left Vnukovo at 2.30pm. By then it was 3.20. There are four Zil machines hidden in the airport compound, he tipped us off. We peered through the fir trees but could see nothing. They could have been round the side or on the apron behind the building.

A man in a dark-blue Aeroflot uniform came slowly towards us from the airport building.

'There's nothing here.'

Clearly he had been sent by someone to put us off.

'No one has flown off from here. The building's under repairs. The buffet isn't working. The water's been cut off.' (Three weeks ago President Bush came through the building which is the normal arrival point for all foreign visitors.)

'Why are there four Zils here then?' we asked. The Aeroflot captain looked startled and shifty.

'Is this an interrogation?' he countered.

'Just a question,' we parried. 'Do you have an answer?'

He denied any knowledge of Zils and turned away. 'Can we have your name, please?' He had no answer to that either.

Frustrated by the closed gates of Vnukovo Two, we drove round to Vnukovo One, the usual civilian section, a mile away. A police car tried to block the road as a convoy of three cars roared into the access road. We took the car on to the soft shoulder and joined the end of the motorcade which drove straight on to the apron.

A crowd of airport workers was waiting near the

gangway of a TU-134. The Russian prime minister, Ivan Silayev, stepped out to cheers and good-luck wishes. He was on his mission to the Crimea to try to fetch Mr Gorbachev back.

He sped up the gangway and disappeared inside. About 30 officers of the Interior Ministry troops were blocking access to the steps, but I walked round and climbed on to the mudguards of the gangway. I managed to catch the attention of Valentin Sergeyev, an official of the Russian parliament's press service, who was standing on the gangway. I reminded him of Mr Silayev's suggestion in parliament that morning that the delegation should include a small group of foreign and Soviet journalists as well as a medical team, and some Russian deputies. Mr Sergeyev pondered and then said 'Get on. Quick.' Two other reporters, from *Agence France Presse* and *La Vanguardia* followed me on.

Once on board, it emerged that the Silayev mission was not as easy as it seemed. There was no guarantee that the coup plotters who were thought to be heading for the Crimea had yet given up.

The Russian vice-president Alexandr Rutskoi had reached Vnukovo before Mr Silayev and told reporters: 'The group of criminals has flown off secretly. They have deceived everyone. There is a danger that they may do something to Gorbachev.'

Colonel Rutskoi, an Afghan war hero, who shot to political prominence only four months ago, explained his chilling warning. 'They have three options. They may flee the country. They will bring Gorbachev here. Or they may try to conduct medical experiments on him to change him into a different man. Our job is to prevent it.'

The 30 police officers boarded the plane, ready to do battle if necessary.

Colonel Rutskoi spoke in highly emotional terms of Marshal Yazov, the Defence Minister: 'When I saw those columns of tanks, I have only one thought. Yazov is a traitor and scum.'

Later that evening down in the Crimea at the airport which the President uses we found two air hostesses who confirmed that a plane had indeed left from Vnukovo's VIP field at 2.30pm. They had been on the same plane, they said. Its passengers included two of the security chiefs who took part in the coup, Marshal Dmitry Yazov and Vladimir Kryuchkov, the head of the KGB.

Intriguingly, with them also was Anatoly Lukyanov, the chairman of the Soviet parliament, who had taken an ambiguous position throughout the coup attempt. He conspicuously failed to condemn it, although according to his spokesman, Arkady Maslennikov, Mr Lukyanov did not know about it in advance.

'They all sat together, and were smiling some of the time. Their mood seemed good,' the air hostess said. 'They ate well,' she added.

Shortly before Mr Silayev landed at the Crimean airfield of Belbek, the mood had changed. The coup plotters who flew there two hours earlier with Mr Lukyanov had reached Mr Gorbachev's holiday dacha. It was clear they had come, if not to surrender, then to apologise for what they had done.

The popular reaction in the streets, the foreign reaction from the West, the firmness of Boris Yeltsin, and above all their awareness of their field commanders' views must have finally made them see the light.

With the coup now all but over, Mr Silayev and Vice-President Rutskoi were greeted by local officials in a relaxed mood. Shortly before landing they were able to tell the team of crack Interior Ministry officers on board the TU-134 that they need not get off the plane.

The 45-minute high-speed drive to the presidential villa at Cape Sarich was relaxed. Had it not been for the speed of the convoy and nervousness over the mood in which we would find Mr Gorbachev, we might have been able to enjoy the spectacular scenery of the Crimean peninsula.

Rolling hills and olive trees flashed past the window of the Volga in which we were driving. The air was a balmy 75 degrees. After Sevastopol we turned into wilder country, with large outcrops of white rock breaking through the trees. The sun was setting as we drove.

We passed one checkpoint on the road where a barrier like a railway level crossing stopped traffic. Our convoy was waved through. There was a proper check 50 yards from the house, as guards peered into the cars and sized us all up. Then the road plunged down towards the presidential dacha.

A blue lorry was drawn up diagonally in front of the black gates, preventing any other vehicle getting past. In spite of checkpoints on the approach road which drops down from a spectacular coastal cliff road, the lorry was being kept as a security precaution.

Mr Silayev and his delegation, which also consisted of two of Mr Gorbachev's liberal advisers, Yevgeni Primakov and Vadim Bakatin, walked the last few yards and were allowed through the main gates.

The five Russian and three foreign reporters, as well as two doctors brought down by Mr Silayev, were taken back on a separate road to a side entrance, guarded by a double set of security gates. A soldier in camouflage uniform opened the second gate.

We were brought to a three-storey hotel for security personnel. Off-duty soldiers were playing billiards. After about 50 minutes we were escorted on foot up a winding road to the presidential villa. It overlooks peach trees and an olive grove, leading down to a sandy beach. The cicadas were clicking furiously in the gathering twilight.

Mr Gorbachev's daughter, Irina, wearing a blue denim miniskirt, stood in the ornate wood-panelled hall of the villa when we walked in. There was no sign of Mr Gorbachev's wife Raisa, or of Irina's husband and their small daughter. The whole family had been on holiday since shortly after President Bush left Moscow after the July summit.

A security guard who preferred not to give his name said the family had carried on their normal holiday activities of walking and swimming while they were imprisoned on the compound. 'Mr Gorbachev likes to use the beach rather than the swimming-pool, but they went out of the house less than usual during these three days,' he said.

It was a tanned and tired-looking President, his body visibly trembling with excitement, his face expressing relief at being free, who received us less than an hour after our arrival.

'Complete rubbish, the crudest pretext,' he answered unhesitatingly when asked if there was any validity in the coup leaders' assertion that he had fallen ill last weekend and could not run the country.

Mr Gorbachev said no physical intimidation had been used against him, but indicated he had been under pressure to make a deal with the coup leaders. Had he done so, he said, he would have had to kill himself.

'There's one thing I want to say,' he told us. 'I made no deals. I maintained a firm position, demanding the immediate summoning of a session of the Congress [of People's Deputies] or the Supreme Soviet. Only they can decide the issue.'

'Otherwise,' he had told them, trying to find the most delicate way of expressing the point, 'after any other step I would have to finish myself off. There could be no other way out.'

Mr Gorbachev was standing in a small sitting-room, wearing a grey sweater over an open-necked shirt. Beside him stood the vice-president, Aleksandr Rutskoi, and the prime minister, Ivan Silayev.

The president made it clear that for a man as active as himself the worst thing was to have all his telephone and other communications cut off, as well of course as radio and television. 'I was cut off from any communication. The sea was closed by ships. There were troops all round. It was complete and total isolation.'

His usual corps of bodyguards remained with the prisoner president at his luxury compound on a picturesque promontory overlooking the Black Sea. They were captives as much as he, but he said that together 'we held a front line'.

'Even in these conditions I acted, and got my demands out through the people here on my side, constantly, regularly during the day, and managed to do everything. My guards were given orders to open fire and defend us against anyone who tried to break in. That's how we lived in complete isolation for almost four days and nights.'

Two doctors from Moscow's Medical Institute Number Two, apparently a special government hospital, travelled to the Crimea on Mr Silayev's plane. They would not give their names, but said they were heart specialists. They came into the room with us, but were not asked to conduct any medical examination of the president. Afterwards, one of them said: 'There was obviously no need. He looked amazingly well.'

A reporter asked if he was still under arrest. 'Not now,' Mr Gorbachev said, laughing. 'But I was.' The president was cautious about declaring the coup to be over, and declined to say whether the plotters would be punished. 'I think this gamble has collapsed,' he said. 'It needs to be investigated by the competent organs.'

One of his bodyguards who flew home to Moscow with us in a TU-134 of the presidential fleet said communications at the villa were cut at 3.45pm on Sunday afternoon. About two hours later Vice-President Gennady Yanayev arrived with Oleg Baklanov, the first deputy chairman of the State Defence Committee.

Mr Baklanov is a conservative who used to be a secretary of the Communist Party central committee in charge of links with the military-industrial complex. He has often been mentioned as the *éminence grise* of the civilian hardliners in the apparatus.

The two men flew back to Moscow later that evening and shortly after dawn on Monday the official news agency Tass published Mr Yanayev's decree saying that he had assumed the duties of the president. It was the first public sign that the coup was under way.

What became Mr Gorbachev's prison is a large compound which sprawls round a bay on the southern tip of the Crimea, about halfway between Sevastopol and Yalta. Foreign reporters have never visited it before. Under *glasnost*, the Soviet press has carried critical comments about the multi-million rouble construction project which Mr Gorbachev launched as general secretary of the Communist Party. In response to complaints in the press and parliament Mr Gorbachev transferred ownership of it to the Office of the Presidency last year.

Mr Gorbachev told us that the main reason the coup had not succeeded was that Soviet society had changed. It was a triumph for *perestroika*. He particularly cited the support for democracy from the republics.

'As you see, the consensus of the winter, the difficult consensus, when we felt danger and the need for consensus, is getting stronger. All republics came to the defence. The coup didn't succeed. That's the main thing. We haven't worked in vain these six years. Our society is already different, and the army in its great majority did not go against the people, and it will not.'

His bodyguards were still not completely sure it was all over. At the Belbek air force base from which he took off just after midnight on Wednesday night, his staff played an elaborate fiction.

The presidential plane, an Il-62 airliner, marked Sovietsky Soyuz (Soviet Union) stood on the main apron. Half a mile away in an unlit part of the airfield, close to the camouflaged hangars of a squadron of Mig-29s, the smaller TU-134 which had brought Aleksandr Rutskoi from Moscow had its engines running. As we were brought by minibus towards the plane, and then hastily driven back towards the main apron, we saw several Zil limousines race between the two planes, apparently to mask which one Mr Gorbachev was on.

A senior officer of the Soviet interior ministry who was bounced off the TU-134 to make room for the extra passengers told us he saw the president with Mr Silayev and the KGB chief, General Kryuchkov, in the TU-134. We were briefly allowed on to Sovietsky Soyuz and saw Anatoly Lukyanov, the speaker of the Soviet parliament, sitting with Vladimir Ivashko, the Communist Party deputy general secretary.

General Kryuchkov returned to Moscow in the same plane as the president, and was arrested on landing early yesterday morning, Mr Gorbachev's security officials said yesterday. Marshal Yazov, who was on a separate plane, was also arrested on landing.

September 23, 1991: Jonathan Steele

Saying goodbye to Lenin

I went to the mausoleum last week to say goodbye to Lenin. These days the queue has never been so short. It took barely 10 minutes to get into the vault compared with the hour or two you always used to need when the line ended out in the Alexander Gardens and people shuffled solemnly into Red Square waiting for The Moment.

Now you pick up the queue 30 yards from the entrance and before you have time to compose yourself you are going down the steps. Instead of having the guards form you into twos so that the walk past the lighted bier is disciplined and constantly moving, people stroll by and take their time. At least they still insist on silence, and cameras are forbidden.

My first visit 30 years ago was altogether different. Stalin still lay alongside Lenin, his bristling moustache and all-too-lifelike appearance giving a sinister aura to the glass case in which both men were trapped. A second visit years later was more satisfying. The villain had been taken away, the saint remained. The veneration of the crowd, the anticipation, the dimly lit room, the first view as you turned the corner – there was a sense of dignity, a feeling you were joining some special Soviet communion.

It is all over now, and when I talked to people in the queue as we re-emerged into Red Square last week, it was clear that everyone had the same thought. We were seeing Lenin for the last time. The majority wanted him to be buried in the ground, as he and his widow had insisted, but there was still a contradictory sense of loss. A young woman popping bubblegum with two friends said she first saw Lenin as a primary-school girl. 'They say the mausoleum may be closed, so this could be our last chance,' she said. Although she favoured putting Lenin in a grave, 'it's part of our culture, part of our history. However bad it was, you can't just wipe it out. Lenin's ideas were all right, but what we got wasn't the same thing.'

Faina and Abram Mortkovich from Novosibirsk said the first time they had tried to see Lenin some years ago the mausoleum was closed. 'We wanted to see him this time because we will probably never come to Moscow again,' they explained.

'Why not?' I asked.

'We're emigrating to Israel. We decided to visit the Kremlin and the mausoleum. This is our motherland. We're saying goodbye to our motherland.' They hoped Lenin's last wish to be buried in the ground beside his mother would be fulfilled.

There were dissenting voices but they were a minority. Lydia Dubkova, a woman in her fifties, was on her third visit to the mausoleum. 'It's a sacred place, and I'm upset they may remove Lenin. He's part of our history. So many generations have passed by here.' The firmest loyalist was an Armenian wearing his wartime medals. The October revolution was a legal revolution, and took place thanks to Lenin. It was thanks to Stalin that all the peoples of the Soviet Union joined together in the war 'like a single fist to stop the Germans'.

Two men from a village in Azerbaijan, neither of them Communist Party members, were all for Lenin staying in the mausoleum. So was a farmworker from Uzbekistan. But it was an elderly Russian couple from Kazakhstan whose answers I shall remember longest.

'It's my sixty-second birthday so I came to Red Square,' Rufina Usacheva said. 'To be here is to touch history.' She was against moving monuments 'because they are linked to people's roots. They are not just political statements.' Her husband Vladimir, a retired professor of journalism, used to be a party member, 'but it's finished and we no longer pay our subscriptions,' he beamed.

As for the October revolution, 'we only know about it from films. History is permanent evolution. I believe in dialectical development. Everything has elements of progress and regression,' he said. 'It's hard to ask our generation,' she chipped in. 'We're not objective. We were brought up on the revolution and patriotism.'

He would never join another party, he said. Every generation had finite resources. 'We've given up our energy, and anyway our experience stands in the way of getting political again,' he said. They wanted Lenin to be buried properly because he had never wanted to be displayed in a mausoleum. Why then had they come to view him? 'According to our custom,' she explained, 'we always keep the coffin open for a little time so that relatives and friends can say farewell.' Sixty-seven years, and now they are going to find the lid.

December 24, 1991: Alexander Kabakov

Gorbachev's children

As with many personal relationships, mine with Gorbachev changed from cold to adoration, from adoration to
resentment and back to love, sympathy and understanding . . . Don't imagine that I exaggerate: in our country,
where people are used to considering themselves in
personal touch with the ruling power, I believe there has
never before been a ruler to whom the intelligentsia has
been so strongly attached.

Nor am I alone. There are many people like me. So it
may be that my honest life story during those six years
would be a story of a large part of our society. It was spring
1985 when the new Master – after a succession of old men
('the era of pompous funerals') – produced a double-
faced impression. On the one hand, he was energetic and
presentable (though his birthmark immediately gave him
the rather rude nickname 'Marked', which had apocalyptic
undertones) and he could easily speak without following
his notes.

The only thing he had in common with his prede-
cessors was a strong southern accent, but as Kremlin
inhabitants never spoke standard Russian, we were well
used to this.

On the other hand, his first appeals were a direct sequel
to Andropov's campaign for discipline and order, totally
unacceptable to the traditionally anarchic Russian
intelligentsia.

During Andropov's war against corruption and dis-
order – welcomed by many common people looking
forward to 'a strong hand' – the intelligentsia was not
enthusiastic. Having once experienced Stalin's 'strong
hand', we didn't want even a hint of a dictatorial power.
That was why the first steps of the new general secretary of

the party, who announced *uskoreniye* (speeding-up) and
launched an uncompromising struggle against alcohol,
scared me.

For those who had been living under the old system,
the word 'order' was immediately associated with total-
itarianism. And the whole history of our country has
demonstrated that this fear was justified.

However, it became clear a year later that Gorbachev
was able to change his mind faster than any of his prede-
cessors (except Lenin), and that we, who grew up learning
to read the leadership's intentions between the lines of its
declarations, were not shrewd enough.

From around 1986, Gorbachev's speeches acquired a
strange, human undertone, reminding us of Khrushchev's
'thaw'. Life was changing. The first changes affected the
intelligentsia, which meant that we became Gorbachev's
true allies. Books which would have been unpublishable
during the past 20 years appeared on the shelves of
bookshops and libraries. They were mostly old novels by
authors inspired by Khrushchev's campaign against Stalin-
ism, but they were not published at the time.

So, after a 20-year-break, literary journals began to
publish novels by Rubakov and Dudintsev, theatres staged
Shatrov's plays, which portrayed Lenin in an unusual,
liberal way. We 'pricked up our ears': an old habit not to
trust any acts of Communist leadership.

I remember that at the time, I was inclined to believe
that Gorbachev would 'tighten the bolts of oppression' as
Khrushchev had done. I used to say that soon, after
everybody believed that the thaw had set in, new frosts
would come: another meeting with intelligentsia at a
government dacha, expulsion from the Union of Writers,
withdrawal of magazines from libraries, etc.

I was wrong. Instead, something absolutely new had
appeared: *glasnost*. Articles full of striking criticism of
Brezhnev and Stalin were published in newspapers and
political magazines. And the very nature of the criticism

was different from ever before. It was not 'personal flaws' that were being criticised, but the fundamental character of the system. It was at that time that my own life changed, too.

First of all, I was allowed to publish my stories and novels which had been piling up for many years in the drawer of my desk. I didn't have any hope of publishing them in Russia and had a real fear that the KGB would be interested in my literary activities. Instead one of the works has been screened by the studio, Mosfilm. Another, *The Man Who Wouldn't Return*, which became quite famous, was published by the magazine *Iskusstvo Kino*. That had particularly impressed me: in *The Man Who Wouldn't Return* I wasn't criticising the past, but describing the gloomy future of Gorbachev's reforms, the end of perestroika and the forthcoming civil war.

For the first time I was allowed to go abroad, to France, and for me, having been used to consider myself 'lower class' according to the main Soviet criteria, that was the crucial moment of my life.

Finally, after 17 years on an insignificant newspaper, *Gudok*, I was invited to work on the *Moscow News*, a popular weekly newspaper, which became the herald of the new policy, the mirror of *perestroika*.

For 17 years I had put up with the thought that, not being a member of the Communist Party, and, above all, being Jewish, I would never be allowed to work on any prominent publication. Now my life changed totally. From being an unknown journalist, hiding my literary ambitions, I have turned into a popular writer and publicist.

After years of poverty, I became quite wealthy by Soviet standards. I travelled to many European countries, enjoying some popularity. *The Man Who Wouldn't Return* has been published in France, Germany, Scandinavia, Spain, Italy . . .

I am convinced that a similar story could have been told by hundreds of Soviet intellectuals, who realised that our time had come. We are 'children of Gorbachev' – the first generation of intelligentsia after the so-called 'children of the sixties', who became aware of the thought that the leadership was prepared to co-operate.

The 'children of the sixties' during Khrushchev's era had been trying to improve socialism. We, at the end of the eighties, were prepared to help Gorbachev to change the system radically, and to abandon Utopia. It looked as if Gorbachev had the same goal.

Those who started in the sixties were invited by Gorbachev to take power – for at the beginning he too intended 'to improve socialism' and wanted to co-operate with the children of the '20th Party congress' and the 'Prague spring'. We, the next generation, didn't get real power, but instead were given the freedom to do more or less what we wanted to. We were able to approach the readers, spectators and audiences and express our thoughts and opinions. What else could one do to conquer the hearts of the intelligentsia? Not to mention fees and exciting journeys . . .

Today we are often blamed for having forgotten about the people's needs, having been 'bought' by *glasnost*. But I can't agree with this. Firstly, because I believe the intelligentsia is part of the people and not some group of individuals whose interests can be neglected. And, the improvement of our lives during Gorbachev's rule meant everyone's lives had improved. Secondly, I am convinced that 'a mouthful' of truth brings the same satisfaction to the common people as a slice of bread does. It has always been like this in Russia.

. . . And then many other things happened: human values were announced to be more important that those of the classes, the fall of the Berlin Wall, along with the series of 'velvet' revolutions in eastern Europe, rehabilitation of private ownership – all the steps towards freedom out of totalitarian slavery, which had been watched by the whole world.

We were happy. Never before could we have lived so happily, breathed so easily. The crushing of communism had been started, an event we couldn't even have dreamt of during Brezhnev's time: stagnation had made the idea of socialism eternal for us. The fall of the cruel system had become obvious and everything that interfered with that happiness we put to the backs of our minds. We could have been more realistic – myself in particular. I felt the danger as far back as 1988, when I was writing *The Man Who Wouldn't Return*; I felt it more strongly in 1990, when I was writing my new novel, *The Storyteller*, anticipating the events of August 1991.

However, using *glasnost* and the new freedom from censorship to criticise the mistakes and crimes of Gorbachev's leadership – events in Tbilisi, the Baltic states, the delay of the law, introducing land ownership – we were still in the power of illusions. We still had been thinking that Gorbachev's devotion to 'the socialist choice' and 'the ideals of October' were simply a camouflage to comfort party fundamentalists. Having trusted the ruling power, probably for the first time in the history of the Russian intelligentsia, we didn't want to destroy our belief.

The beginning of the end of our mutual love happened in January 1991 – after the events in Vilnius. We realised that Gorbachev was prepared to fight for his 'democratic socialism' not by democratic but by Soviet socialist means. Khrushchev's Budapest of 1956 had been reflected in Gorbachev's Vilnius of 1991 – and the second disappointment in the 'enlightened communist' turned out to be the last one.

Many of us immediately took Yeltsin's side. Others, including myself, have chosen a more natural position for an intellectual – doubting any leadership and keeping our distance. The lesson was too good. I think it will be remembered for a long time.

Today, listening to the last appeals of Mikhail Gorbachev, I say goodbye to the best years of my life. I think that many others feel the same. We were able to express ourselves during those years. We got what we didn't get when we were young: we believed in ourselves. As always with happiness, it was a mixture of euphoria and selfishness; as always with happiness, it didn't last long and has left a bitter taste.

Gorbachev is leaving politics for history in his usual way: with a mixture of elegance and fuss, the sharpest mind and striking narrow-mindedness, great charm and repulsive cynicism. But there is no doubt on one matter: he is leaving as a great man and will stay forever in people's memories as a demolisher of the most cruel social system that ever existed.

I believe he will find an honorary place in the future and, who knows, maybe as an international politician he will be as significant as he was in the national arena. In any case he already deserves a monument with the inscription: 'To the conqueror of communism, from the rescued'. Words I sincerely agree with.

December 27, 1991: Martin Woollacott

Fin de siècle

The twentieth century came to an end at 7pm Moscow time on December 25, 1991. The moment when Mikhail Sergeyevich Gorbachev, the last leader of the Soviet Union, ceded place to Boris Nicolayevich Yeltsin, the first ruler of the new Russia, seems a marker of far more importance than any on the horizon eight years from now.

It is as if the business of our century is over ahead of the calendar. The two enormous conflicts which have characterised it, that between capitalism and communism, and that between the old empires and the new powers –

struggles that have interacted through the decades – have ended. 'Bolshevism,' as Winston Churchill in 1918 imperiously demanded it should, has finally 'committed suicide'.

The other great fight, that between the Anglo-Saxon powers and the newcomer states of Germany and Japan, has terminated with it. The Soviet Union's eclipse has been the basis for Germany's emergence as the main European power: without it Germany's renaissance after the disaster of the second world war would have remained incomplete. As for Japan, America's industrial decline and the end of the cold war has created the space in which the post-1945 renewal could be rounded out into real power.

Of course, certain facts remain unchanged. The Russian empire is, from one point of view, the last old empire to disappear, going the way of the British and French empires, its allies in two world wars. Yet those maritime domains were essentially different from Moscow's land empire, which in some sense will continue.

The struggle between Boris Yeltsin and Mikhail Gorbachev was often perceived as an ideological contest – between a nationalist and an internationalist, between an ex-communist and a communist. This was overdone. Both men were ex-communists, but one was in a position to repudiate the party and the past more completely than the other. And both believed that Russia's historic influence over neighbouring peoples ought to be preserved, but Yeltsin could offer a more neutral and hence more acceptable version of union.

The struggle was something else as well – an epic, perhaps a tragic, contest between two men of utterly incompatible temperaments. For Gorbachev, Yeltsin was impetuous, wilful, a bully boy, the ultimate wrecker. For Yeltsin, Gorbachev was the 'lover of half measures and half steps', who wished to appear as a 'wise, omniscient hero' but who was in fact a devious manager and manipulator of men.

Yeltsin has now harried Gorbachev from office; yet those who criticise should remember Yeltsin's own humiliation in 1987, dragged from a hospital bed to be abused and cast into the political wilderness. In the hour of Yeltsin's revenge it is worth recalling what he wrote in his autobiography: 'Our huge country is balanced on a razor's edge and nobody knows what will happen to it tomorrow.' That is as true today under Boris as it was under Mikhail.

Yet, in saluting Mikhail Gorbachev, a man to whom we all have reason to be grateful, we have at the same time to accept that after the coup the division of power in Russia between two rival leaders and governments was unstable. That dualism was dangerous – one man had to win, and Gorbachev had to be the loser. Russia is a safer place, and the world with it, because that rivalry has ended.

December 27, 1991: Edward Pearce

False icon

The chorus of approval for the departing Gorbachev is absurd. Mrs Thatcher, sounding crazier than ever, her voice making those swooping, breathy stresses, the verbal equivalent of underlining in green ink, says we will want to tell him, as he travels the world, what a very, very great man he was. The give-away is that bit about travelling the world.

Mrs Thatcher assumes a parallel with her own phantom statesman's itinerary in pursuit of the money she hardly requires and the importance she needs like blood. Per-

haps Gorbachev will be like that: in failure he will need
solace and cash. For a little season the Americans will be
good for both. Their attention-span exceeds that of the
seven second goldfish and they owe him a debt. Time to
pay up for Gorby. But do we need the little-witted
applause at the greatness of this man? Mikhail Gorbachev
is not great. Decent, certainly, also well intentioned, he
has chiefly been the master of inadvertence. He did not
plan early departure, nor the abolition of the Communist
Party, nor the rise of the carnivorous Boris Yeltsin, nor the
loss of Eastern Europe. But they happened and the crash-
ing ineptitude of Mikhail Gorbachev made them happen.

It will be argued that the odds were enormous and that
he did his gallant best, customary excuses for a well-loved
incompetent. If there is a parallel it is probably Jacques
Necker, the Swiss banker, whose masterful mystique and
excellent intentions did not prevent liberal reform
government collapsing before the wheels of revolutionary France. Like Necker, Gorbachev was the acceptable
reformer of the old order admired abroad.

He was better placed than Necker, inheriting together
with its economic failure, all the instruments of the Soviet
state. It was open to him to concentrate on the economy,
starting at the bottom up, employing minimal rhetoric and
while forgoing all barbarism, in no way abandoning the
police mechanics of that state. The arguments against such
surrender are stated best in *King Lear*, but trendy politicians don't read such arcania.

Gorbachev didn't read economics either, and more
important, failed to hire those who had, then to trust
them, and stick to properly advised decisions. A vain,
shallow man with the instincts of royalty, he fled the dull
economy, preferring to be seen getting on and off aeroplanes. The official justification was that world statesmanship demanded that peace should be created first. To
which one can only reply: 'Sod world statesmanship.'
Peace was easy and bought by giving the Americans

everything. Gorbachev's greatness was of the inverse kind admired by those to whom are made relentless concessions on ever easier terms. To a degree, he seemed frequently to be negotiating his face on to the cover of *Time*. His attitude to the USA was abject and defeatist, 'naked in the council chamber' indeed; naked rather at the start of a game of poker.

It was open to Gorbachev to husband what resources he did have, that operatic American fear and the fact of Soviet nuclear weapons. 'Peace', a rhetorical word demanding inverted commas, could have come in its own good time. Enough economically necessary military savings could have been undertaken, taking every advantage of Soviet secrecy but not the public concessions which proclaimed private despair.

A leader who treats, who shows the courtesy and charm which rightly make friends, but whose concessions come dropping slow, a man exploiting a husbanded and well paraded strength will always out-perform one begging that advantage be not taken of his weakness. In his international dealings, Gorbachev threw himself on the world parish. He is praised for candour, and candid he was. But how long has candour been a virtue in politics other than as a sort of fragrance, a lavender water of public affairs?

Just as it was open to him to bargain hard abroad, so it was within the Soviet Union, which might then, following his wishes, have remained the Soviet Union. Calling a parliament to deal with redress was as foolish as it was for Louis XVI. Since all holders of power wish to maintain power, the supreme folly is to take the step likely to extinguish it. 'Democracy' is a word that Americans and cunning-obtuse English people like Mrs Thatcher really believe to be co-terminous with their state of affairs. It is a condition only remotely approached in either country: fifty per cent voluntary disfranchisement and the power of rich men and newspapers signifying something rather less ambitious. But neither true democracy, nor its simulation have utility for a man trying to amend the country of the aristocratic knout and the people's democratic purge.

Gorbachev offered *glasnost* and *perestroika*, openness and re-organisation. This in practice, given the infinitely foreseeable inability of anyone to put anything right, meant openness about the failure of reorganisation! The Soviets needed a delicate gentling of authority under a carapace of continuing authority. Only a fool, confident with absolutely no cause, would have thrown away the façade of order.

If Gorbachev had been, not great but ordinarily resourceful and sensible, he would have skipped world statesmanship – settling for civil, hopeful noises in a holding operation – and set all hands and brains to getting food into the cities. Similar advice was given to Nicholas II, an even sillier man, and ignored at some cost. Suppose the people, whose discontents were coming noisily through because they were greater discontents, had been assuaged non-miraculously with the loaves and fishes which a concentration of effort and trouble could have brought, with how much greater hopes could he then have treated with the West!

The reality was neglect of public need, the talking away of power bases, and international diplomacy undertaken as escapism. Gorbachev posed for pictures while citizens queued for bread and Soviet soldiers sold their uniforms to Gypsies at the Brandenburg gate. As a consequence of Gorbachev's greatness the Soviet state is broken into shards and its people at the mercy of opportunists, racialist-nationalists, spivs, trainee-Mark Thatchers and the 'economic reformers' introducing kerflip prices with kerflop employment.

Gorbachev has an actor's understanding; given a difficult hand, he made it impossible. Yet he has the qualities America loves. They, getting so much of their thought from films, adore appearance, hence the cult of John Kennedy, another handsome frothbottle. Gorbachev

seems wise, seems dignified, seems impressive. He exists
to seem, and could thus proceed forthwith to the US
Senate which his dignified features and handsome limitations would adorn. If that is an iconoclastic account of an
attractive, decent man, the icon is its own witness, shattered in glittering pieces.

February 27, 1992: Jonathan Steele

A Russian winter ahead

Russia's democrats will one day look back on Gorbachev's
era as a golden age. Just as the law-and-order crowd
remembers the Brezhnev period, even the Stalin one, as a
time of civic tranquillity and economic discipline, the
country's progressives could soon be regretting the passing of Mikhail Gorbachev. For all the chaos and political
turmoil, the next few years are likely to be worse. In
comparison the Gorbachev years will seem uncommonly
good.

Gorbachev's great achievement was not only to launch
the revolution which he called *perestroika*, but to keep it
in democratic channels. Without him *perestroika* would
have started anyway. It might have been delayed by five or
10 years, but it would have started. After all, Gorbachev
was not alone in understanding that the political system
was rotten.

Many people, particularly in the middle ranks of the
apparatus, shared his view that the economy could not
develop by adding more capital and labour in the old way.
They saw it needed fundamental reform. There were also
numerous analysts in the foreign ministry and the think-
tanks who saw that the arms race was crippling the system.

It was Gorbachev who managed to take these heretical
ideas and turn them into the dominant ideology of the

party. It was not the majority view, since even up to the party's dying day *perestroika* was not popular in the Central Committee. But Gorbachev made *perestroika* respectable. He ensured that the party had to pay it lip service, whatever people thought of it privately.

Gorbachev realised that the party was not a monolith, but an unacknowledged multi-party system playing by dictatorial rules. What he did was to bring the divisions into the open, put the social democratic tendency on top, and force its opponents to play a more or less democratic game. By August, public support for the changes that Gorbachev had brought about was too strong for the doomed plotters.

Historians will long debate whether *perestroika* was reform or revolution. The simplistic distinction between reform as peaceful and revolution as violent breaks down in Gorbachev's case. Rarely can so much change have taken place in any society with so little violence. A system of government that had run the country for years fell apart virtually without a shot being fired. Whether by explosion or implosion, few undemocratic social systems have collapsed so painlessly.

Perhaps the system was not as totalitarian as it is said to have been, even by Gorbachev. With success assured he had a vested interest in exaggerating the awfulness of the Brezhnev legacy. The Soviet Union had already changed. The neo-Stalinism of Brezhnev was not a Stalin terror, and there were opportunities in the last pre-*perestroika* years to argue in private, even to express veiled criticism at party meetings.

What Gorbachev did was to institute a series of gradual reforms over a time span that was long enough to allow the process, collectively, to become a kind of revolution. The sum of *perestroika*'s parts amounted to less than the whole. The whole was a new way of democratic behaviour whereby political conflict – for the first time in Russia – was resolved by non-violent means.

Some say this may have looked like revolution, but it was not. The first Russian revolution in October 1917, by contrast, was a genuine revolution. It involved a great shift of power. A ruling class was destroyed. Even if a few tsarist officers took up the Red Flag, even if some pre-1917 property owners re-emerged in the 1920s as NEP men, 1917 produced a stratification of society and a system of property relations which were different and new.

Neither *perestroika* nor the subsequent project of privatisation, Yeltsin-style, produced an equivalent upheaval. The old party and management élite remains in charge and is dividing up the state sector primarily for its own benefit.

Gorbachev's 'revolution' was one of style and thought. He tried to instil respect for the law. It was no accident that his most frequent catchphrase in domestic politics was about the need for a 'law-based state'. It is true that he asked the Soviet parliament for extra powers on numerous occasions, and got them. He created the executive presidency. But he never used the powers to declare a state of emergency and was suspicious of calls for a 'strong hand'.

He felt the need to preserve social stability. To blame him for ethnic violence is not fair. He can be criticised for under-estimating the strength of nationalism, but it is absurd to suggest that the short-sightedness he showed, along with many other Russians, exacerbated ethnic relations.

He also sensed that a rapid switch to a market economy and the application of 'shock therapy' would tear at the fabric of Russia's social cohesion. Better, he argued, to have a regulated market economy and a gradual transition than an avalanche of change.

Gorbachev enters retirement, as he entered office – a pragmatist, a democrat, and intelligently cautious. He is obviously unhappy to be forced from his job. The harsh and ungrateful way it was done was a clear source of disappointment, but as he watches developments from the sidelines he may be glad that he left when he did.

The next few years will be hard and threatening. The danger of a return to authoritarianism is real. The chances of economic revival before the end of the century are slim.

April 24, 1992: David Fairhall

The death zone

Anatoly Artemenko had two quite different reasons for offering to accompany me to the devastated Ukrainian power station. As a founder of the Children of Chernobyl relief organisation, with first-hand experience of how the Soviet authorities handled the 1986 disaster, he did not want a foreigner to have the wool pulled over his eyes by the nuclear 'mafia'. But Anatoly is also a native of Chernobyl. So this was a rare opportunity to return to his deserted family home inside the evacuated exclusion zone, and perhaps also to his mother's grave in the heavily contaminated pine woods just west of the station. He worried that the wild boars, irradiated but no longer hunted, were rooting round the abandoned cemetery.

On the drive from Kiev I learnt how the exclusion zone worked. Before reaching the main checkpoint we passed a sign warning against fishing and mushrooming. But at a certain arbitrary level of contamination the land was ruled to be uninhabitable. In other areas people were given the option to leave.

Within a radius of about 30km from the burnt-out No. 4 reactor everybody was evacuated, mainly to protect them from caesium, one of the nastier products of nuclear decay. Then there is an inner 10km zone also contaminated by plutonium.

More than 110,000 people were evacuated, and to some extent financially compensated. About 1,000 have since returned – old people who either do not care or do not understand. Among them was Anatoly's 84-year-old grand-mother, who pined for her orchard and her village, famous for its pottery. Last November the family finally tricked her into leaving again, by deliberately chopping too little firewood to see her through the winter.

Chernobyl looks like a village, but used to proclaim itself a town. Anatoly reckoned the local lemonade syrup was the finest in the region. 'The water here was good,' he said, smiling at his own irony. Down an overgrown side road, the chalk-blue door of his family's small house gaped open, the rooms littered with the looters' rubbish.

Where Chernobyl's excellent water came from I do not know. The important question now, everyone agrees, is where it will end up. In some places near the power station, the water table is obviously just a metre or two below the surface of the light, sandy soil. The average depth is four metres. Yet in the rush to clear the worst of the contamination, so as to keep the remaining three reactors in operation, abandoned holiday dachas and dead pine trees have simply been bulldozed into rough mounds. There are said to be hundreds of such dumps.

Water movement is being constantly monitored, I was assured by the head of the research and decontamination institute. Dams are being constructed to prevent radio-activity seeping into the Pripyat River, which feeds the Dnieper and hence the capital city of Kiev. But it looks a hopeless battle. The river is right next to the power station, visible behind the famous red and white chimney, and separated from its cooling reservoirs by a narrow dyke.

The first signs that the station's shift workers take the dangers of their radioactive environment at all seriously were the white coats and plastic galoshes issued to us on entering the main power-station building. Linking the entire reactor block is the 'golden corridor', lined with heavy yellowing plastic to keep the radioactivity at bay. It ends suddenly in a concrete wall behind which is the damaged No. 4 reactor, buried in its crude 'sarcophagus'. Nearby was another blocked entrance, covered by a memorial to the engineer whose body was lost in the burning wreckage. We did not stop long. Indeed I would have been out even more sharply if I had known the level of gamma radiation Anatoly was registering on his meter.

Trying to establish why people choose to work in this grim environment was like asking a private what he thinks of army life with his commanding officer standing two paces behind him. 'We're used to the radiation,' someone said, in an effort to reassure. Money is obviously a big factor. I gather Chernobyl workers get three times what they would receive for similar work in Kiev. But beyond that there is a extraordinary indifference, or perhaps just resignation, to the invisible danger all around them.

The sarcophagus is not just cracking, as previous visitors have noted. It was never sealed. Heroic construction workers did their best to minimise gaps between the rough panels they were able to put in place. In the ghost town of Pripyat, from which 50,000 people were evacuated after taking the first brunt of the radioactive cloud for 36 hours, I met a scientist quietly tending rows of mutating pine seedlings. He expects many foreign scientists will soon join him in this unique radiobiological laboratory.

The power-station manager Nicolai Sorokin told me he was also seeking international help in designing a second, properly sealed sarcophagus. He accepts the decision of the Ukrainian Parliament to cease generating electricity at Chernobyl next year, but evidently with reluctance. Technically, he said, the remaining reactors could continue until the end of the century. Alternative jobs would be hard to find.

When I suggested there might be a case for closing all

16 Chernobyl-type RBMK reactors, especially following the recent accident near St Petersburg, Sorokin was understandably circumspect. The St Petersburg failure was 'not unexpected', he said. While the RBMKs could not be updated to the latest safety standards, they were 'good enough for their time'.

The man in charge at Chernobyl on the night of the explosion six years ago, Anatoly Dyatlov, sees the same situation from a much gloomier perspective. His health was shattered by the appalling radiation he absorbed as he rushed to see what had happened to No. 4 reactor. He found the wall of the reactor building had simply disappeared. The exposed core was 'like a scene from Dante's *Inferno*', both beautiful and terrible.

As the senior engineer on site, Dyatlov took the blame – wrongly in his view – and spent four years in prison. Now he sits in his slippers, in the bleak apartment-block suburbs of Kiev, hoping at last to justify his conduct to experts of the International Atomic Energy Agency now busy rewriting their account of how it happened and preparing to investigate the RBMK design in detail.

His case is that the operators were not aware of the dangers they ran by letting the reactor drift into the unstable low power regime from which it exploded. To suggest otherwise, he says, is almost to imply that he and his staff were insane. So why did they blame him? Because to admit that the weakness lay in the reactor would have meant admitting that the Soviet nuclear industry was incompetent and that the safety inspectorate was not doing its job. They might have been forced to close all the other RBMK power stations.

Whatever happened six years ago, the crucial question for the future is whether the steam explosion which opened up the Chernobyl reactor like a can of beans could be caused by physical failure, without any operator error. Within months of the St Petersburg plant opening in 1975 there was an alarming incident – also an operational error apparently – Western experts believe could have been disastrous. Dyatlov told me of another, at Chernobyl in 1982, after which the chief engineer was fired. But last month's radioactive release from the Sosnovy Bor plant near St Petersburg was caused by a ruptured fuel channel. How close were we to another explosion?

All but two of the Soviet RBMKs, he explained, were designed to tolerate the simultaneous failure of two of their 1,600 pressurised fuel channels (the latest pair of reactors at Smolensk could take nine simultaneous failures). Officially, the probability of this happening was extremely low – 10 to the minus eight per reactor/year – but 'that calculation could be wrong'. And if more than two channels failed, he believed the consequences would be comparable to Chernobyl in 1986.

Dyatlov carefully stopped short of calling for all RBMKs to be shut down. But his warning was unequivocal: 'I can say that another explosion similar to Chernobyl is possible. I cannot calculate the probability, but it does exist.'

Other worldly matters

September 2, 1991: Martin Walker

Drinking with the President

The engine of the President's boat *Fidelity* suddenly roared into full power and I reached for a stanchion as we began to hammer the hull across the grey Maine seas.

'Never seen so many seals as this year,' George Bush told me. 'I've been here every summer of my life apart from that time in the war when I was in the Pacific, but this year the seals are really something.'

The President and I had been drinking beer from the bottle and nibbling amiably from his little cone hat of popcorn. We each wiped butter from our chins with paper napkins bearing the Great Seal of the United States. It was a marvellous summer's day, and back ashore the smell of the barbecue drifted across the Bush family lawn. Mrs Bush had just asked if we would like to use the swimming-pool . . .

Before you get the wrong impression, I am not an intimate of the First Family, but I joined about a hundred other journalists who happened to be in Kennebunkport last Friday for an impromptu barbecue at Walker's Point. The point is that any one of us could write an entire article in the vein of those first few paragraphs, and suggest without a word of a lie that one enjoyed a closeness to the Bushes which is in fact illusory, misleading, and more than a little worrying.

This barbecue event for the White House press and their children is held every year. It starts with a registration queue at the press centre where our names are checked against the security list of journalists who actually covered the summer White House, the endless golf games, the boat trips and the strenuous tennis. Had I not flown up in John Major's RAF VC-10, I would never have gone to the event.

Lift your eyes beyond the machine guns discreetly wrapped in carry-bags, and beyond the US Navy Seals diving out to check the Libyans have not been doing something ingenious with the lobster pots, and the view of the President's family home is stunning. Twenty-six rooms means a big house.

When John Major first laid his eyes on this place, they widened like saucers, not because of the sprawling ease of American power but just at his awe of the money. Eleven acres, 11 subsidiary cottages, a value of $4 million and annual property taxes of $25,000. The rich live well in America and the old rich like the Bushes live with an effortless assurance, a plain and simple style that put John Major at his ease, even as he looked like the poor boy from school come to spend the night at the rich kid's house.

And who could blame him? The sea glinted on both sides of the small peninsula where the house has stood, weathered shingles and good grey stone, for nearly 90 years. The walls of the little cottages are thick with photographs of the Bush children in their Texas school sports teams. This place is a home.

It is delightful to spend a day here, to chat with George Bush about the house, to gossip about mutual friends in Moscow with Brent Scowcroft, or to ask White House chief of staff John Sununu about the difference between Maine and New Hampshire. But when I watched a line of colleagues form to have their pictures taken with the President, and another line to take a snapshot of one's infant daughter with first dog Millie, a warning voice began to mutter that we are meant to cover these people, not fawn on them.

When John Major and George Bush said farewell at Walker's Point they said nothing of substance. But they made the TV news bulletins because they gave each other presents, a cricket bat for a baseball bat, and spoke of exchanging a 'curve ball' for a 'googly'. They were following a script drawn up back in December between their press officers to make us think a profound male-bonding experience had taken place, that an Anglo-American sporting jest proved that all was well with the special relationship.

In fact, a legend is being deliberately constructed before our eyes, and a photo opportunity is being mistaken for a real event. George Bush is a charming, hospitable and wealthy man, who genuinely likes to entertain and to be on particularly amiable terms with the White House press corps that has hounded so many other Presidencies to an early grave. He is also a dangerously seductive expert at the manipulation of the media. I am glad I have been on the speedboat where Bush and Major worked out how little aid to the Soviets they thought they could get away with; but I still need the right to say they look like cheapskates who could yet lose the strategic prize of the 20th century.

November 23, 1991: Simon Tisdall

Motor City's sidewalk army

Dusk on Detroit's East Side and the shadows are beginning to gather. As the sun dies, the Victorian brick frontages of the boarded, gutted buildings on Cass Street turn blood-red. The rutted sidewalks, darkening alleys, and overgrown demolition sites are deserted.

Suddenly a shot rings out, followed by another, and another, apparently random, too fast to count. Then silence.

Wherever the firing came from, nobody is hit, not on this block at least. The shadows pull up their collars. Another cold, hungry, fearful night on the streets has begun for the Cass Street foot-soldiers of Detroit's army of homeless.

Wrapped in all they own, they have gathered here, outside Cass United Methodist Church, because they are trying to fight back.

'Welcome to Englerville Tent City' says a sign, referring to Michigan state's Republican governor, John Engler. 'We pray for him, that he will become more humane,' said James Ford, a homeless man.

'In 11 years, I've never seen it this bad,' said the Rev. Edwin Rowe, pastor of Cass church. 'There were only 1,000 shelter beds for 30,000 people before October 1. That's when they cut off the general assistance programme for 90,000 people. Forty-five thousand of those people are in Wayne County, right here.'

Allowing the Cass homeless to pitch a tent on derelict church land is, he said, 'an act of solidarity with people who Engler has decided are expendable. If the church does not stand up now, it's finished.'

Tent City was intended to symbolise the plight of the Detroit homeless, according to Ruth Williams, a handicapped black woman from the Michigan Up and Out of Poverty Now Coalition. Five times in recent days the coalition has put up a tent, only for the police to come at night and pull it down.

'They say tents are hazardous, that it's unhygienic,' said Marian Kramer. 'But it's hazardous living on the streets.'

She pointed down the road to the silhouettes of two high rise apartment blocks known as the Jefferies Project and Herman Gardens. 'They're empty. They [the Detroit City government] want to demolish them. They say they're not habitable. The real reason they don't want folks inside is 'cos they want to build the area up for middle income people. They don't want us. This was an industrialised area. The people here worked all their lives. We're not against technology. We just don't want it used against us.'

'We're not dumb and shiftless and lazy,' Mr Ford said. 'These people want to work. But there ain't no work and they ain't got no place to live.'

That Detroit is the basket-case of the American Rust-belt is beyond dispute. It has lost almost half its population in the past 40 years. In the past decade, demolition permits have been issued for 47,059 city buildings. As Motor City stumbled, from one slump to the next, the auto industry went hi-tech and shed thousands of jobs; businesses, shops, and restaurants closed or moved away.

But what is now being described here as the homeless crisis was precipitated by Governor Engler's efforts to cut the state's budget deficit. As winter approaches, hundreds – if not thousands – of impoverished adults who received help under the now-abolished general assistance programme are facing eviction.

There will be 100,000 homeless in the Detroit area by Christmas, Ms Kramer said. 'And 43 per cent of all public housing buildings are empty.'

Teresa Blossom, spokeswoman for Detroit's Democrat

mayor, Coleman Young, said: 'We have made homelessness a priority. We have opened up "warming centres"
where they can get out of the inclement weather. We are
also acting to stop evictions. The mayor recognises that
people are being driven to desperate measures. We are
trying to renovate public housing, and provide more
shelters. They are venting their frustration [but] the tents
are not a safe course. It is a public-safety hazard.'

Amid the steaming sewers of the East Side there is
something monstrous about such measured statements.
'Bush needs to get down here and do something fast,' said
Ernestine Johnson. 'Coleman's throwing people out on to
the streets. It's total war between the people and the
government. We've drawn our line in the sand.'

'The warming centres are a joke,' James Ford said. 'They
let you stay a while and then they kick you out. Right now
my worst enemy is not street violence or the elements, it's
the government.'

Mr Ford, an air-force veteran, keeps going by doing a
part-time job raking leaves. Twice a week he sells his
blood for $10 at a hospital donor centre. He sleeps at the
Homeless Union shelter, if he can get a bed.

After a meeting this week with Jack Kemp, the Housing
and Urban Development secretary, Mr Young said that up
to $222.5 million in emergency funding could be made
available to Detroit.

Governor Engler, whose popularity ratings are plung-
ing, has offered a 'job pact' which would give minimum
wage part-time employment to some of those affected by
the welfare cuts.

But in the hellish netherworld of the East Side, outside
the tent on Cass Street, in the now complete darkness, a
ragged chorus of voices say they have heard such promises and plans before.

'The emergency is now. We're not going to allow them
to wage genocide on a community,' Ms Kramer said. 'We

must never let such inhuman behaviour stand,' said Mr Rowe.

Come the morning, the shadows may disperse but, said Mr Ford, the problem would still be there.

'You'll find them everywhere, in abandoned buildings, in viaducts, under bridges, in the morgue. They're gonna be dying soon.'

February 1, 1992: Martin Walker

Primary colours

The snow was thick on the ground, the temperature was twelve degrees below zero, and the possible next President of the United States was wearing thin training shoes and turning visibly blue as the smell of roasting pork merged with the acrid whiff of roasting reputation to drift across Jan Pascal's back yard.

'The things you do to get elected,' murmured the Governor of Arkansas, Bill Clinton, as he grinned and shivered and braced himself against the cold to apply his bare hands to the boar's carcass on the slowly turning spit above the smoking embers. It was a perfect metaphor for his own plight, as the three-million circulation supermarket tabloid *The Star* was trumpeting his extra-marital affairs with five women.

Over a warming cup of hot chocolate, I said to Mrs Hillary Clinton, wearing massive metal earrings that carried their own threat of frostbite, how pleasant it was to see her suddenly in the forefront of the campaign.

'I have been campaigning hard for weeks,' she replied, with a brittle grin. 'Only I have been talking about health care and children and education – and you in the media don't seem to have been too interested in that.' Game and set to the formidable Mrs Clinton, a Yale law school graduate with the looks, brains and sheer force that suggest her husband would be both otiose and foolhardy to fool around outside that marriage.

Beyond Mrs Clinton, the 6,000 ft White Mountains loomed dimly through a sky that was sullen with snow. The wind whipped across the half-frozen Lake Winnipesaukee, provoking a booming hum from the satellite dishes that bring TV to the homes that dot the lakeshore. This is a schizoid state, at once hi-tech and deeply rural. New Hampshire's biggest employer is the Digital Electronic Corporation and yet its biggest city has fewer than 100,000 people and over 200 of the state's drivers collided with straying moose on the roads last year.

Hardly any Blacks, no inner city nightmare, no state income taxes and the best school results in the country, New Hampshire is a most untypical place in which to hold the election that defines America's Presidential year. But the state's record of picking White House winners is remarkable. Since 1952, every American President has won his party's New Hampshire primary.

This moose-and-microchip culture also defines the losers. Back in 1952, President Harry Truman decided not to run again because he had been beaten in the primary by Estes Kefauver, just as Lyndon Johnson dropped out of the race in 1968, even though he won the primary by a 46–42 margin against the anti-Vietnam War candidate Eugene McCarthy.

And it all takes place on a neighbourhood scale. George Bush is President today because when he was trailing badly after losing the Iowa caucuses four years ago, the Governor of New Hampshire John Sununu got up early on the Saturday morning, four days before the election. Sununu drove to the home of the station manager of the MMUR TV station, woke him up and showed him a very large cheque. Bush's media team had worked through the night to make a new set of TV ads. Sununu persuaded the station to junk its weekend schedule, and run the Bush ads

that launched a devastating attack on his opponent Bob
Dole as 'Senator Straddle'. Lagging ten points in the polls
on the Friday, Bush beat Dole 38–28 on the Tuesday.

That was one reason why Bush rewarded Sununu with
the job of White House chief of staff. Another was Sununu's daughter's wedding, which he cannily decided to
hold in the northern part of the state, moose country,
where he feared Bush was weak.

The state legislature of New Hampshire is America's
largest, with 400 members, each paid a token $100 a year,
which means it is packed with 160 retired people and with
students and others who can use the money. Each
member is responsible to about 1,200 voters, which in
turn means he or she knows most of them.

'It's a great job for a retired person,' says Representative
Gary Gilmore, a carpenter. 'They feel a little important, get
out of the house, meet people a lot.'

Municipal affairs are run by town meetings, in which
every adult gets to speak and vote on the issues of local
government, which helps explain the visceral antipathy to
taxes, New Hampshire's insistence on the personal campaign by Presidential hopefuls, and its deep conservatism.
The state's motto, emblazoned on every car's licence
plate, is 'Live Free Or Die'.

In New Hampshire they bluntly refuse to repeal the
1848 law which makes abortion a criminal offence. Nor
will they repeal the 1791 statute which declares adultery a
crime punishable by 39 lashes, a year in jail, or standing
on the gallows for one hour with the noose around one's
neck. Not that they enforce this stuff, but they keep the
laws on the books on the principle that if it was good
enough for grandpa . . .

This unusual state plays a talismanic role in the American political process, a rite of Presidential passage that
must be undergone. It requires a human baptism of town
meeting, factory gate, local store and front parlour before

sending the survivors into the nationwide electronic campaign of press conference and soundbite.

'We get to watch the candidates' eyes as they answer our questions, and the rest of the country watches us watching,' says the local poet Donald Hall. He has another insight which explains the uniqueness of this state but also its comfort, its reassurance that somewhere in the televised blandness of the modern presidential election there is a real America making its choices in the old and intimate way. You have to begin, says Donald Hall, by looking at the names on the plaques beneath the statues and the memorials of the war against slavery, the war between the states.

'Only in small towns of the rural South and in northern towns of New England does the Civil War survive. In the present United States, this War recedes into olden times, like Homer, the Roaring Twenties, the Crusades. But outside Atlanta and Birmingham, and north of Boston, the Blue and the Grey still march, bugle call and amputated limb in the fierce cannonade of old memory. The past continues into the present because the plaques' family names remain on the land. Only in the rural South and the rural North do you find Americans who live where their great-grandfathers lived. Or who know the maiden names of their great-grandmothers.'

This curious empathy between the old North and the old South may help to explain why Bill Clinton, from the small southern state of Arkansas, campaigns so well up here. 'The political rhythms are familiar,' he confides. But as Clinton shivered beside the slowly roasting pig in the New Hampshire snows, this rural familiarity can be deceptive.

With its balmy climate, the American South is famous for its open-air barbecues, and an old-fashioned Arkansas hog roast probably sounded like a great way for Clinton to get to know the Democratic voters of the small New Hampshire town of Meredith. Or at least, it must have sounded good when first planned, before the Arctic cold front swept down across the Canadian border, followed hard by the tabloid chill of Miss Gennifer Flowers's claims of a 12-year affair with Governor Clinton, complete with titillating details of his prowess at oral sex.

After 12 hours of roasting, the pig was still so under-done that by the time Clinton and the guests and the cameras left, the cooks were still slicing chunks of almost raw meat from the carcass, trying to grill them into edibility over a hastily erected barbecue. Too late. As the early darkness fell, the Pascal family were stuffing three months' supply of roast pork into their freezer. They might have another disposal problem with the stacks of 'Clinton for President' campaign literature . . .

Back in Manchester, the state's biggest city, Ron Roy was setting out biscuits and a coffee urn in his sitting room and opening the double doors to his dining room.The neigh-bours were all invited to hear another candidate, Iowa Senator Tom Harkin. A local school teacher, Ron Roy sees the quadrennial primary as a crash course in civics. Four years ago, he walked Michael Dukakis round the nearby streets. This year, he brought in a kitchen chair for the candidate to stand on as Harkin addressed the crowded rooms, the Senator's head just brushing the low ceiling.

'I'm the only man in this race who's not a microwave Democrat,' Harkin began in his prairie drawl. 'Tell you what I mean. The other night I got home late after campaigning. Wife and daughters in bed, so I looked in the freezer, fix myself something to eat. Found some lasagna. Ah like lasagna. Took it out. Put it in the micro-wave. Zapped it, two minutes. You all done this.'

Every head in the room was nodding. Harkin has the delivery of a consummate actor. The entire audience was sympathising with this folksy image, murmuring approval. Possible President but he microwaves leftover lasagna just like us.

'When it was done, little bell went, and ah took it out, all steaming, smellin' real good.' Harkin smiled. He was telling this so well, we could almost taste it. 'Got mah fork, cut into it, and it was warm as toast on the outside. But the inside of that sucker was as cold as a Republican's heart – and that's what ah mean by a microwave Democrat.'

The room erupted, the biscuits were trampled underfoot, the coffee urn leaked unnoticed on to the carpet beneath the framed family heirloom of Mrs Roy's family tree. It went back to a German ancestor called Joachim born in Bavaria in 1630, which was by coincidence the year New Hampshire was named by the English settler, Captain John Mason. Joachim's family tree swayed uneasily as the neighbours jostled to put their names down as helpers for Harkin. Hard to believe that Harkin stood at a dismal five per cent in the polls.

Back in the city centre, Elm Street looked prosperous. Only a handful of empty shops. Then you see why. The old clothes store had been rented temporarily for the Clinton offices and the Jerry Brown campaign was on the next block and Harkin's HQ just down the street. From the first-floor offices of Senator Bob Kerrey came the sound of a party. His volunteers, busloads of students from his home state of Nebraska, were tossing buns and beer cans back and forth like a fraternity house party. Sleeping bags were stacked against the walls and a couple of pairs of skis.

Just around the corner in cheaper side street premises, the offices of the ex-Senator of Massachusetts Paul Tsongas face the rented room of the write-in campaign for the consumer crusader Ralph Nader. A man called Jerry, dressed up in a woollen cap, three pairs of trousers and several sweaters, had parked the supermarket trolley which contains his worldly goods just beside the Tsongas doorway.

'I was gonna go for Kerrey, 'cos he's a Vietnam vet like me. We gotta stick together. But now it's Tsongas or Nader for me,' Jerry explains. 'They're the only ones that welcome the homeless in to get warm. So I'm watching this campaign pretty close. It's a serious business and I got my vote to cast too.'

The northern state of New Hampshire plays a cruel and unusual trick upon the modern American political system. It forces all presidential candidates into a pre-television time warp of old-fashioned politics, meeting the voters, looking them in the eye and explaining why they want to get elected. The tarmac-to-tarmac campaign of airport press conferences is held in abeyance as the state's 511,000 registered voters assert their traditional right to hold America's only intimate by-election.

Only 150,360 of them are registered Democrats, being wooed by five Democrat hopefuls, and on the evidence of 1988, only 52 per cent of them are likely to vote in the primary. To persuade a plurality of those 75,000 likely voters, Bill Clinton has bought two hours and two minutes of TV time on WMUR, the state's only TV station.

It charges $1,000 for 30 seconds in prime time but only $10 between midnight and 5am. Much of Clinton's TV buy is prime time and Republican challenger Pat Buchanan has bought over three hours. The other two leading Democrats, Paul Tsongas and Bob Kerrey, have each bought over an hour.

Then there is the radio time, the hotel and apartment bills for the candidate and his campaign staff and the 300-strong press corps that accompanies President Bush on his three forays into the state, and it is obvious why the New Hampshire assembly passed a law to ensure that their state will always be 'First in the Nation' to hold its presidential primary. The campaign pumps over $40 million into the hard-pressed local economy.

This year, New Hampshire is doing even better from its primary. Beset by the challenge of Pat Buchanan, President Bush has launched a form of local Keynesianism to boost his chances. A new passport office, bringing 400 jobs, has been opened at the redundant Pease Air Force base. A new pilot project to help individual states fund their Medicare budgets is being launched in New Hampshire, bringing an immediate boost of $200 million to the state budget. The Small Business Administration has suddenly picked on New Hampshire as the perfect place to field-test their new job creation scheme.

'Let me give you good people a word of advice on what to do when the pollsters call,' says Bill Clinton at a town hall meeting in Bedford. 'I want you all to vote for me on February 18, but you needn't tell them that. Tell those guys you're for Pat Buchanan, because this state got $200 million when Buchanan hit 30 per cent. Once the polls give Buchanan 60 per cent, George Bush will pump money up here faster than you can blink.'

New Hampshire needs it. The last time George Bush came up to fight a presidential primary, New Hampshire had the lowest unemployment rate in the US at just over two per cent.

The jobless rate has tripled to 7.4 per cent, and so has the number of bankruptcies, and of people going on welfare. Last October, the Federal regulators forced five of the state's biggest banks to close.

In moose-'n'-microchip country, unemployment takes unusual forms. At the unemployment office in Concord this week, Paul White was wearing a business suit and Burberry raincoat and reading *Business Week*. Laid off in October from his job as general manager of a computerised graphic-arts company, he has a mortgage to pay, a daughter in college, another at school, and half his $179 a week in unemployment pay goes on the family medical insurance. Without his wife's salary, as an executive for a charity, the White family would be homeless by now.

'There is a whole stratum of middle-class managers being laid off – it's almost age discrimination. They get rid of us guys in our forties and fifties because they can pay the youngsters less,' he says. 'I'm a Republican, but I think I'll vote for Buchanan as a protest, to send Bush a message.'

Sitting just down the bench is George Comtois, made redundant from his job as director of an industrial museum in a disused textile mill. Concord has a population of 40,000 and new unemployment claims are coming in to this office at a rate of 1,200 a month. George Comtois jerks his thumb at the list of vacancies: 'Anyone can be out of work in this country – it's a classless society,' he grins. 'But right here, the middle class is getting it in the neck, and a lot of people reckon we have had more Republicanism than we can stand. Something fundamental is changing here in New Hampshire. People always voted very seriously in the primary, tried to pick the best man from the nation's point of view. New Hampshire always used to feel we had a responsibility to do right by the rest of the country. Not any more. Boy, we're gonna vote our pain. George Bush will pay for this.'

January 27, 1992: Playthell Benjamin

Beauties and the beast

I first saw Mike Tyson in the flesh at a party to announce his 1988 fight with Michael Spinks, the only light heavyweight champion to defeat a reigning heavyweight champion in history. On paper it looked like a dream match.

Both were undefeated. In one corner stood Spinks, Olympic gold medallist, undefeated and undisputed light heavyweight champion and International Boxing Federation (IBF) heavyweight champion – a title he took from the great Larry Holmes. In the other corner stood 'Iron' Mike Tyson, the reigning heavyweight champion. His title should have been shared with Spinks but, due to a conflict with the IBF over mandatory defences, Spinks's portion of the title was revoked. Hence in the minds of many boxing fans and pugilistic pundits Tyson's title was tainted.

Drawing: Peter Clarke

This fight then – colourfully called 'the Brawl for All' – was greeted with great expectation. Donald Trump, billionaire businessman and flamboyant playboy, threw a party worthy of the event at New York's Plaza Hotel and attracted a glittering crowd of beautiful people. Everyone was dressed to the nines. Everyone but Tyson.

While Spinks arrived punctually, perfumed, pomaded and tuxedoed, Tyson stumbled in late, unkempt and dressed like a ragamuffin. His clothes consisted of nondescript trousers, a wrinkled shirt hanging halfway out, scuffed shoes and no socks. The guests were aghast.

Compared to his wife, Robin Givens, Tyson looked like a derelict. Givens, a beautiful actress with an élite education promenaded about the room with the studied grace and elegance of a princess, charming the press corps in what seemed an attempt at damage control, hoping that her social graces would neutralise Tyson's boorishness. Her task was complicated by her husband's surly demeanour and total lack of the polite manners one expects from a public figure of his stature. They seemed an obvious mismatch, Beauty and the Beast – though some thought Samson and Delilah a more appropriate reference.

Spinks was the first to take the microphone. He spoke eloquently with the self-effacing humour that has endeared him to the American press. Tyson, on the other hand, was verbally pugnacious and exuded about as much emotional warmth as a Mafia hit man. For me, the most revealing clue as to Tyson's character came when, just as Spinks started to speak, someone shouted: 'Let's hear it from the true champ!' Tyson gave the Spinks partisan a murderous stare that made us all thankful that looks can't kill.

If the heckler had persisted, I feel sure Tyson would have bounded from the stage and smashed him. I have spent a good deal of time around pugilists but I have never felt that a fan or journalist was in danger of assault by a professional prize-fighter. Only around Tyson have I felt that way. Later on, I discovered my perceptions were widely shared by other guests. Further investigation would reveal that the views of the party crowd were par for the course in the boxing business; this guy was a loose cannon.

The opinion that Tyson has long been like a jet plane on automatic pilot heading nowhere fast is widely held in the fight game. Milt Swarsky, a lawyer who represents several top fighters, offered this Tyson observation: 'When I was handling the legal affairs for the Spinks camp, the questions that constantly came up among the promoters was "Will the fight happen before this guy self-destructs?". We had a $13 million purse riding on this fight. We knew he was going to self-destruct sooner or later. We just didn't want him to take us down with him.'

And Dan Duva, the streetwise manager-trainer of world heavyweight champ Evander Holyfield, once protested to the press upon receiving the news that a proposed Tyson-Holyfield fight had been postponed: 'Look, I know where my guy will be a year from now. But who knows where this other guy will be?'

Today Mike Tyson goes on trial for allegedly raping an 18-year-old contestant in the 1991 Miss Black America contest in Indianapolis, Indiana. He is charged with confinement, rape, digital penetration and oral sex. The last two counts are classified as 'criminal deviate conduct'. If convicted, he faces a maximum sentence of 63 years.

Tyson's problems with the opposite sex appear to have begun early in life. And so did his violent tendencies. José Torres, a writer and former light heavyweight champion of the world, who was for years a confidant of Tyson, recounts a conversation with him in his biography of Tyson, *Fear and Fire.* Angry about having broken a cherished toy gun when he was nine or 10, Tyson recalled: 'I was so pissed off that I took a doll and banged it against the floor and then pulled its head off.'

This display of violent temperament on the part of a child is frightening enough, but Tyson's description of his emotional response to it is worse. 'I felt an immense thrill when I ripped the head off the doll. It was like an orgasm.' This association of pain inflicted on females with erotic pleasure persisted into manhood, according to Torres, who quotes Tyson: 'I like to hurt women when I make love to them . . . I like to hear them scream with pain, to see them bleed . . . It gives me pleasure.'

One might conclude that only a masochist could enjoy the company of such a man. But hordes of beautiful young women go to great lengths to seek Mike Tyson's affection. Rose Trentmont, a member of the New York State Athletic Commission, says: 'Tyson is a ladies' man . . . Tyson had girls around him like hungry mosquitoes.' The blood-sucking mosquito is a perfect symbol for some of the women who have sought Tyson out. There have been several attempts to sue Tyson for fantastic amounts of money by women who claimed sexual harassment.

The most blatant attempt to bilk the former world champion out of millions is the $11 million paternity suit brought by Ms Natalie Fears of Los Angeles. Filed last October at the Californian Superior Court, the suit alleges that: 'In May 1989, plaintiff and defendant Tyson entered into an oral agreement whereby it was agreed that plaintiff would act as defendant Tyson's companion, confidante and social partner and defendant Tyson would then and thereafter provide for the complete support and maintenance for the rest of her life.'

Ms Fears based her claim on the assertion that Tyson is the father of her son, D'Amato Kilrane Tyson, whose first name was given to honour Cus D'Amato, Tyson's revered trainer and surrogate father, who passed away a few years ago. However, a blood test report this month concluded that Mike Tyson was not the father. This must have come as quite a shock to Mike because, according to bank records made available to me, Tyson gave Fears $100,000 on August 27, 1991, and three days later an additional $15,000 as three months' support for the child. He also displayed the child before the press and confessed to TV boxing pundits that siring an heir was 'the proudest moment of my life'.

Whatever problems Tyson may have had with women previously, present events do not offer much hope for improvement in the near future. In fact he recently said: 'Every time I get close with a woman something weird happens.' These days he seems bewildered by the number of women out to get a piece of his hide. So many are filing suits charging that they were violated by Tyson's roving hands – one Connecticut woman is suing him for $100 million – that the promoter of the Miss Black America pageant, J. Morris Anderson, labelled him 'a serial butt fondler'.

Yet in a letter to Tyson, written in her own hand, Natalie Fears paints a quite different picture of Tyson. Dated September 12, 1991, less than a month before she slammed him with the $11 million suit, it says: 'Maybe a lot of people think that you don't live your life right or you're insensitive, wild, crazy, manic depressive and so on. It really doesn't matter what they think. I think you're doing a damn good job, believe me.' Then she tells him: 'Mike, keep your head up high, because even though I never tell you, you have been very good to me, Monique [her daughter] and D'Amato and I'll always love and respect you for that.' This is a strangely moving tribute from a woman who then tries to get millions out of him to endow the future of a child whose paternity remains a mystery.

But the two things that are most essential to understanding Mike Tyson's character are neither in dispute nor difficult to comprehend: his early childhood and his phenomenal success in the square ring of combat.

By all accounts Tyson had a difficult childhood. As one of three siblings in an impoverished family which was abandoned by his father, Tyson grew up quickly. Born and raised in Brownesville – the Brooklyn neighbourhood that produced Meyer Lansky, Bugsy Siegel and Murder Incorporated back in the good old days before the neighbourhood went downhill – Mike became a tough guy in order to survive. When he began school, he was a chubby kid in glasses whom the other kids taunted, taking his glasses and hiding them. Tyson decided to fight the bullies. He soon discovered he had a devastating punch that could put most guys down. Soon he developed a reputation as a tough guy with miles of heart – and then he became the bully.

According to his sister Denice, Tyson was arrested 40 times before he was 12. That's easy to believe when one becomes acquainted with the facts of his life on the streets. Early on Tyson joined a gang and he tells us: 'After word spread throughout Brooklyn that I had kicked butts for fun, everyone wanted to be my friend. I felt good and special.'

By the time he was 10, Tyson says, 'I used to drink . . . heavy stuff, cheap stuff, gasoline.' And there was no absence of role models: 'We thought that the pimps, the thieves, the drug dealers were cool.' While other kids were partying and having fun, Tyson recalls the activities of his street crew. 'We'd ride through these parties very slow and we checked for gold chains, watches and money and usually there was a lookout, a black guy. If he sees something wrong happening, he'll come and then there was a crowd and we would pull the guns and start shooting.'

Had he not been rescued from the streets and sent upstate to Spofford, a juvenile detention centre where he was brought to the attention of Cus D'Amato, Tyson might well not have survived his childhood. D'Amato, a former tough street kid himself, was past 60 when he met the 12-year-old Tyson and had already produced two world champions: José Torres and a former juvenile delinquent named Floyd Patterson. D'Amato established his credentials as a professor of pugilism when he took Patterson in 1950 and trained him well enough to win the Olympic gold in 1952, and the world heavyweight championship in 1956. After observing Tyson in one sparring match, he observed: 'This kid can become the heavyweight champion of the world.' And he did; the youngest ever.

I must confess that I was not immediately a Tyson fan. I remained sceptical long after the pundits had declared him boxing's next great superstar, an invincible warrior. It was not until he fought Spinks that I conceded the possibility that 'Iron' Mike was not a paper tiger. Spinks was a truly great fighter with a flawless record. He had gone undefeated in a decade while taking allcomers. I knew Tyson could punch but I thought he would be dog meat for a great boxer/puncher like Spinks. But in his finest performance in the ring Tyson demolished Spinks in 90 seconds. It was the shortest heavyweight championship fight in history – and the most lucrative. Spinks received $13 million and Tyson $21 million, which averaged out at $145,000 per second for Spinks and $221,000 a second for Tyson. The battle of the Mikes was an unforgettable night. All the doubting Thomases disappeared as quickly as snowflakes in a microwave oven. We all had to concede that 'Iron' Mike was for real.

If the Spinks fight was Tyson's finest moment in the ring, the bout with Buster Douglass in Japan was his worst. Dismissed by the boxing élite as a bum-of-the-month charade, Tyson was expected to toy with Douglass and then dispatch him early on in the bout. But, at 6ft 4in and 230lb, Douglass was in the best condition of his career. A skilled fighter, he could box and punch in beautiful combinations. He also had great lateral movement, could lead with his right or left and throw punches from all angles, landing hooks, jabs, uppercuts, and body shots with equal skill. It was one of those rare moments of pugilistic poetry that true fight fans are always seeking but seldom find. And it proved disastrous for 'Iron' Mike as he wilted under Douglass's steady fire.

It ended with a stunning knockout in the 10th round. Douglass had shocked the world; Tyson's invincibility had been exposed as a myth. Tyson had come into the fight as the world's most celebrated athlete, entering the ring with a perfect record of 37–0, 33 KOs, nine successful title defences. At the final bell he was just another contender for the crown.

Few knowledgeable fight fans doubt that Tyson will one day be a champion again, if he remains a free man. Indeed, dethroning the reigning king of the heavyweight division, Evander 'Real Deal' Holyfield, would be child's play compared to his struggle to beat the rap in Indiana. For the outcome of that fight is out of his hands and depends upon whom the jury chooses to believe.

Will the jury believe a lovely middle-class young lady of

sterling character who was just 18 years old at the time, or Mike Tyson, whose background is, at best, shady? For, as José Torres reflected: 'Maybe there were really two Mike Tysons. One who laughed, hugged and kissed and was sensitive and compassionate; and one who enjoyed the sight of pain and hurt in others.'

Even those who know him best don't seem to know the answer to that question. And that's the trouble with Mike Tyson.

Mike Tyson was later found guilty and sentenced to six years in jail.

March 30, 1992: Martin Walker

Old Irish

There are golden moments when a legend does more than live up to its advance billing, but exceeds it. And rather like a sceptical child learning that there is a Santa Claus after all, I was flooded by a glorious feeling of completion as I stood in a polling station in a solidly Irish ward of Chicago and watched Tommy Hands run the last, silky remnant of one of the great American political machines.

The voters came in, some escorted, all appearing at the expected time like visitors to a doctor's appointment and were greeted by name. After some brief patter from Mr Hands about their families and the splendour of recent wakes, they were handed a small card, which began with the name of Bill Clinton and went down through the list of the approved slate of candidates for the Illinois primary election. Approved, that is, by Mr Hands and his hundred-odd precinct captains.

In they dutifully trooped to cast their ballots, and one saw the last beating of the wings which had once carried off the Cook County vote each time Major Daley commanded. There were wards here which produced electoral results that Stalin might have envied, 95 per cent turnout, 95 per cent for the machine. Who was the original craftsman of this organisation, I asked? Who drew up the blueprints for the machine Mayor Daley ran so well?

''Tis on the tip of me tongue,' responded Mr Hands, and smote his forehead like a man who had just lost a heavy bet. 'Faith, I'm gettin' the Irish Alzheimer's. I can only remember the names of me enemies.'

I laughed out loud in pure joy at the perfection of this performance. The foreign journalist wanted his colourful taste of the old Irish politics, and Mr Hands is too courteous and thoughtful a man to deny another such a simple pleasure.

We all know that the old Irish and Polish and Czech wards of Chicago have changed, that the old beer halls now boast the words *cerveza* and *bodega* to attract the new Hispanic customers, and that the black machine is close to dominance in the old precincts that Mayor Daley ruled.

But you would hardly think so when you penetrate the stocky and taciturn plain-clothes Chicago cops who guard the way to the new Mayor Daley's office in the original City Hall that you could never beat. It is a splendid building for this city-state, which announces firmly over its front door that there is a Chicago city ordinance that forbids the manufacture, transportation, assembly or ignition of any nuclear weapon within the city limits. Any infractor has to answer to the mayor.

'I still live in the precinct, just a block away from the house on the South Side where I grew up,' says Mayor Richard Daley II. 'The Irish all moved out. My neighbours now are Poles, some Lithuanians, Italians, and now more and more Chinese. It's a great mix, good neighbours.'

He looks like a younger version of his famous father, with the same flat and growling voice, the same intense local patriotism about the city of Chicago that is honestly surprised when a presidential candidate tries to tempt him with the offer of the vice-presidency.

'I wouldn't accept the veep job. I don't wanna play golf, go to the Winter Olympics. Who wants to go to Washington, DC, where they're all generals and no privates? I don't know that I could take that city,' he says, shaking his head. 'You know what we need for a vice president? A businessman, not someone for international funerals.

'Let me tell ya about Washington. It's like Russia. The federal government is archaic and bureaucratic. It's a mess, delays everything. They have rules there, it takes me three years to get money outta them to pave a street in Chicago. Three years for a sidewalk. Listen, the public is outraged by Washington. Outraged.'

The body language of Mayor Daley is poetry in the raw. The shoulders hunch, the head comes down like a boxer, the hands drift into a feline shrug, the jaw thrusts into a prominence as sudden and as sharp as his city's skyline sheers up from the shore of the lake.

'I want to build a new airport. Eight billion bucks, would create 250,000 jobs, fill in those wastelands of America between South Chicago and Gary, Indiana. This is ghostland, polluted land, you buy it for $10 millions and it costs ya $50 millions to clean it up. Nothing is gonna get built there for 500 years unless we do it. Ghostlands.

'You gotta go to Washington, DC, on your hands and knees, get the money. Forget it. They should be begging me to build. I got respect for the Germans, the Japanese. They get things done. Our Feds can't. They put it in a file, talk about it a few years. Hey, we're bankrupt. The US is bankrupt, a debtor, just like Donald Trump. It frightens me.'

The Mayor summons a photographer, clasps shoulders for the commemorative snapshot and gestures to an aide. A small box is brought, a souvenir of Chicago.

Inside is a felt-wrapped package, and inside that a

handsome case for carrying business cards. Its cover is black lacquer, bearing the seal of the city and the Mayor's boldly etched signature.

'Hey, this is Chicago. We do all right,' he says, brushing away a polite word of thanks. 'You know how we win this election? We take all their nasty ads of the last campaign, Willie Horton, Boston Harbor and play it right back at them. We say: Hey, remember this. Remember what they sold you last time. Now you know.'

May 21, 1992: Maggie O'Kane reporting from the war in Yugoslavia

Goodbye, Sarajevo

Jordi had his doubts on Sunday morning. He wanted to leave. At 12.10 on Sunday afternoon a mortar bomb dropped out of the sky like a shot putt and killed him.

He was from Barcelona, 25 years old and wore his thick black shiny hair in a pony-tail. It was his first job and he told his friend, Santiago, who had a bit job with Associated Press, that he wanted to be a war photographer. His newspaper had put up $1,000 for the trip. $100 for each picture. His last picture was a shot of a man fishing in the river in the centre of Sarajevo with a burnt-out building rising above.

The mortar bomb came as mortar bombs do in Sarajevo, falling out of the sky from no particular place with no particular logic except terror. David Brauchli, the 27-year-old photographer, had a bullet-proof vest. Jordi had none.

'Fuck, I've been hit,' he said. 'The blood is coming out of my chest.'

David crawled into a doorway with shrapnel in his groin and leg. 'Help us,' he shouted.

Jordi died quickly, losing consciousness on the pavement. David Brauchli was operated on immediately and survived. The city had been under blockade for six weeks and the hospital had run out of oxygen so there was no general anaesthetic. The local anaesthetic did not work as it should so the nurses tied his hands to the edge of the operating table.

The men in the beds beside him and the nurses kept asking: 'When is the Sixth Fleet coming to help us?'

On Monday they took Jordi's body to the mortuary and laid him down beside a woman who had turned black. 'These days people just can't get to the hospital to collect their dead,' his doctor said.

For the last month the siege of Sarajevo has been covered from the outside, from the Bosnia Hotel six miles from the city. Last Thursday it was hit by mortar bombs. The BBC were leaving, ITN telephoned London – they were leaving too. The television teams left at five on Friday morning and the rest, led by Tony Smith and David Brauchli of Associated Press, moved into town.

On Monday afternoon the Red Cross convoy winding along a small country road was hit by mortar bombs. White plastic ducks in a shooting gallery. Frédérique Maurice, the Swiss leader of the convoy, died from wounds to his face and neck on Sunday night. His two companions were seriously injured and the medicines and food they brought went up in flames as a rocket sliced through their white lorry with its red cross.

Sarajevo is surrounded by hills, held by the Serbian militia and what remains of the Yugoslav federal army. Being in the city is like being in a doll's house whose roof has been lifted off by a giant. Running past the Bristol Hotel had been the worst. The road is filled with holes that look like great splashes of ink where the mortar bombs have hit. We hear the bullets. Perhaps for us – perhaps not. At the crossroads a van had been hit by a rocket and as it burst into flames the men inside tried to crawl out. One had lost a part of his leg and as he dragged himself away from the van the snipers picked him off. One bullet, then another until he finally lay down on the pavement and died.

The Belvedere Hotel became our haven, hidden under the poplar trees in a side street. The owner, Druskic Suleyman, had played centre-forward for Udinese in northern Italy and earned $3 million.

A Muslim, he had returned to Sarajevo, his home town, to get married to Branka, a 20-year-old Serb. Their son was born in Croatia and was called Ricardo in honour of all the money his father had made in Italy. Druskic set up the Belvedere Hotel with a bar and a pizzeria, decorating it in the pinks and blues of neapolitan ice cream. 'I know this will all go up in smoke some day soon,' he said.

After Jordi Puyol died and David Brauchli was wounded we decided it was time to leave.

In the distance there was the thud of mortar bombs but in our street the smoke was only the piles of rubbish burning. Three jets swooped low overhead. We felt like flies waiting to be swatted. We needed another car to take Jordi's coffin and someone suggested we try the presidency.

The presidency in Sarajevo is death row. All the president's men will be the first to die when the Serbian militia take the city. They know it and are resigned to it.

On the mauve-coloured carpets of the Austro-Hungarian corridors people wander aimlessly in and out of offices tinkling with five telephone lines to the outside world, where nobody is listening.

The presidency has no cars. A civil servant, who like all the men is trapped in a city encircled by Serbian militia checkpoints, has no need of his.

'How much?'
'$1,000.'
'Petrol?'
'Yes, do you want to see it?'

'No, just bring it to the Belvedere in 10 minutes.'

'The UN protection force is a bad joke,' the former footballer said. 'If the international community cared about Sarajevo they would send in 5,000 troops. The UN is impotent; the EC is impotent; and Alija Izetbegovic [Bosnia's Muslim president] is impotent.'

Across the road from the Belvedere is the polyclinic hospital where 500 corpses are piled in the mortuary. Space is scarce and they have begun to dig a mass grave in the grounds to take the rotting bodies.

At the gatehouse the remaining French United Nations soldiers in their blue helmets shifted restlessly foot to foot. Could they escort Jordi's body? Could they take David, the injured American photographer, in their smart white armoured-personnel carrier?

No, they needed authorisation but the radios were out of action. Could they come in and ask permission on our satellite phone? No, the commander said, he could not leave his men.

So someone lied and told the commander that there was a call for him on our telephone. He came and talked to the UN headquarters in Belgrade, but he spoke to a Canadian.

No, he, the French soldier, could not take authorisation from a Canadian in Belgrade. Afterwards the French commander admitted: 'We have been reduced as a protection force to trying to protect our 12 observers and 70 soldiers.'

In the UN building the corridors echoed to the occasional sound of army boots. Almost everyone had gone. In the front hall where the UN guards used to stand to attention behind their royal blue designer sandbags there were only two young French soldiers sitting slumped and smoking in armchairs.

In the end we took the coffin in the civil servant's chugging blue Zastava, laying the rough brown chipboard from the passenger seat into the back of the car. At 2.30 a Catalan journalist, Eric Hanck, pulled away from the Belvedere Hotel on a 12-hour journey from Sarajevo to the coast with the naked body of his dead photographer and friend, Jordi Puyol, wrapped in plastic and sprayed with formaldehyde.

On the road out we passed the burnt-out trams in Titova Street, where the corpses of nine soldiers had rotted for four days, then passed the crossroads and the burnt-out electrical switching station.

On the road from the city the first of the women and children from the children's convoy trying to escape from the city were turning back. They knew it was hopeless.

She was in her middle thirties with two children, walking back to the city along the main road in the rain. She had two brown-paper bags and the children were carrying blankets that dripped on to the wet pavement. The children's convoy had been stopped at the Serbian militia checkpoint.

No way out.

There were 3,500 women and children in the convoy. The mile-long queue would wait all day in the rain to be turned back as night fell. In the back of each car were children sitting amid bursting suitcases. Round the cars the Serbian militia in blue uniforms and green camouflage carried Kalashnikovs and strolled up and down past their little hostages.

It took 12 hours to get to the coast. Tony Smith of the AP in a smashed-up car led us through the checkpoint saying: 'We have one wounded and one dead.' The coffin was our passport.

In the morning we woke in a hotel by the sea. Jordi's father was coming to take his son's body back to Barcelona, and Eric wanted to buy clothes for the corpse. We thought about a suit but decided on a white T-shirt and denim trousers.

October 9, 1991: Ian Black

The price of collaboration

Ramzi will never forget the moment they told him to leave town: it was late in 1989, two years into the *intifada*, and he drove from Hebron to Tel Aviv, very fast and without stopping, as if his life depended on it. It almost certainly did.

The order came from his controller in Israel's Shin Bet security service, Captain Elias. A tip had come through that Ramzi was about to be killed – the mutilated corpse of a fellow Palestinian informer had just been found.

Ramzi did as he was told and made his way to a small hotel on a seamy stretch of the Tel Aviv waterfront. Outside, its faded stucco was peeling, eaten away by the salt air. Many of the rooms were let hourly to prostitutes and drug addicts.

For a veteran collaborator, used to easy money and secret power, it was a painful come-down. 'I didn't think it would be the Sheraton,' he says with the easy smile that softens his sordid tale, 'but this was really too much. All the scum of the earth were there, and that's where they decided to put us. I still had my gun and walkie-talkie, but I had no money. I couldn't even feed my children or buy them clothes for the winter.'

Eighteen months after leaving the hotel, Ramzi's lot has improved. The ministry of defence pays the rent on his flat and a little shop in Jaffa. No one in the rundown Arab neighbourhood knows his real name or exactly where this likeable young man in jeans and T-shirt comes from. Physically, he is fairly safe, but like hundreds of other Palestinian collaborators from the West Bank and Gaza Strip who have been resettled under new identities inside Israel, his long-term prospects are bleak.

Burned-out cases like Ramzi are the human detritus of

the *intifada*; fear and secrecy combine to keep them out of the public eye. Slowly though, loathed by their fellow Arabs and discarded by the Israelis, they are becoming a problem that will not go away.

Whatever else happens, Ramzi can never go home again. In Hebron he is a dead man. His mother and sister are boycotted and do their shopping in a nearby Jewish settlement. When Ramzi's father died, only immediate relatives came to the funeral. He has been denounced as a spy on PLO radio.

His story is typical enough. As a young man working in a café and living on the edge of respectability he was an obvious candidate for helping the Israelis, one of a clandestine army of informers who kept the occupation running smoothly.

It was fairly low-grade stuff at the beginning. 'I used to go round town and maybe see a crowd of people gathering for a demonstration, so I'd phone my controller. Or I'd write down the car numbers if I saw someone distributing leaflets or painting slogans.'

His vegetable stall in the local market was a useful point for discreetly observing activity in the streets. Meetings with the Shin Bet were held in a safe house in Jerusalem.

Life became more difficult when the *intifada* began in December 1987. Many Palestinians who were too close to the authorities repented publicly in mosques. Since then, over 450 people suspected of collaboration have been killed.

Ramzi came under pressure to stop selling Israeli produce and took to hawking his goods around nearby villages. In one of them he was attacked and had to be rescued by the army. His cover clumsily blown, the Shin Bet gave him a pistol and a regular salary, starting at 500 shekels per month.

'After that,' he recalls happily, 'if someone threw stones at me, I'd just shoot at them.' But the danger had increased: he surrounded his house with guard dogs. The

Shin Bet encouraged him to supplement his earnings by collecting fees from other Palestinians who needed permits from the civil administration. He still has the laminated plastic pass – signed by Captain Elias – that identified him as a collaborator and allowed him to move freely even during curfews.

By now he was aiding the Shin Bet in their hunt for the core of desperate young militants who emerged from the grassroots to dominate the *intifada* as its mass character waned under Israeli pressure and internal exhaustion.

Several of his fellow-informers lost their lives, cruelly, to masked men with names like the Blue Falcon or the Red Eagle, who found collaborators an easier target than the Israelis. Shortly before he quit, Ramzi found his own death sentence scrawled on a wall near his house.

He tells his story with pleasure, his Arabic peppered with Hebrew words. Like an Israeli, he uses the acronym Shabak instead of the more formal Shin Bet. He even relishes the paranoia of a hunted man who sees death at every turn.

Ramzi is strikingly untroubled by his conscience. Fate and character – not politics – determined his course. He could, he admits, in a moment of reflective candour, equally well have become an *intifada* activist, on the payroll of this or that Palestinian 'front'. It is a point that he turns to his advantage when arguing that his former masters owe him and others like him a better deal. Ramzi is demanding a house registered in his name, a car, and his gun back. Occasionally he glances nervously towards the front of the shop. If he does not get what he wants, he warns, he will demonstrate outside the Knesset.

He is luckier than most. At camps near the West Bank town of Jenin, and in the southern Gaza Strip, hundreds of other blown collaborators live in miserable poverty behind barbed wire. In Jaffa, some ex-informers are forced to seek shelter in cemeteries. Only a few have been given the Israeli identity cards they need to get medical care or send their children to school. Ramzi's neighbour, Ali, crippled by a bullet wound he received when working with the Shin Bet, says he is considering suicide.

More embittered and frightened Palestinians are waiting to start their new life in the same seedy Tel Aviv hotel that so shocked Ramzi. It is a continuing problem; earlier this year, the defence ministry appointed a lieutenant-colonel to co-ordinate the rehabilitation of former collaborators.

'It's true that some of them are living in harsh conditions,' the officer told the *Yediot Aharonot* newspaper. 'Some of them get money and some have been given pistols, but you can't expect us to give a gun to a drug pusher or someone with a criminal record. Some of them are simply trying to blackmail the defence ministry.'

July 29, 1991: Martin Woollacott

The Iraqi precedent

As the anniversary of the invasion of Kuwait approaches, it is an easy piece of irony to point to the fact that Saddam survives and the West is again threatening him with both economic sanctions and bombs. That could suggest we have got nowhere after the dispatch of great armies, the spending of much money, grave damage to the environment and the killing of many people.

Twelve months have passed since that mad act of invasion, five months since the end of a dangerous war – and, while Saddam is out of Kuwait, he still rules in Baghdad, still terrorises his own people and, outrageously, he shuttles his nuclear devices from hole to hole as if playing some devilish shell game.

And there is still no actual progress on the Palestinian problem, no visible 'democratisation' in the Middle East, no arms control and no plan to tackle the grave economic problems of a region split between poor and populous republics and rich and selfish kingdoms.

But while there have been mistakes in Western policy – stupidities and mistakes that have allowed Saddam to hang on – the decision to act against Iraq undoubtedly will be seen in the future as constituting a great watershed in world affairs, perhaps as the first serious intervention aimed at heading off that era of international unmanageability, of potential chaos, that peeps at us ominously from the next century.

We have to say 'perhaps' because the intervention in Iraq cannot be fully judged until it is complete and until further interventions allow us to understand in which pattern it belongs. Is it to be part of a pattern of enlightened action by the world's more powerful states, now freed of the exigencies of the East-West conflict, to spread democracy and justice in those large parts of the world where they emphatically do not prevail at present? Or is it to be part of a pattern of intermittent, ill-judged and mainly military coercion of the poor world by the rich world, in the rich world's interests, dressed cynically in a few rags of democratic rhetoric? Was the United Nations cynically used and abused by the coalition powers, or was the failure to employ the relevant UN mechanisms and institutions, except for the Security Council, forgivable because of the extreme urgency of the situation and the extreme creakiness of those mechanisms?

More simply, we still wait to see whether the Iraq intervention will succeed in its primary, although not formally declared, purpose of destroying Saddam and whether US efforts to 'match' it with a breakthrough on the Arab-Israeli conflict will bear any fruit.

Although the Iraq intervention was a response to an act of international aggression, it had from the beginning that other objective of bringing a tyranny to an end, and was, and is, a drastic interference in the internal affairs of a sovereign state. From Tiananmen to Yugoslavia, a single thread connects modern tragedies and crises of varied types and origins, which is that they take place behind the 'wall' of classic national sovereignty but are an affront to the international community and a threat to international order, seem to demand international action and yet have led to little such action, beyond partial and usually ineffective economic sanctions or, sometimes, feeble arbitration.

In the past, the cold war both prevented most interventions and imposed its own, imperfect discipline on some states. Now, the question of what devices and rules can be created to vault the sovereignty wall when necessary is one of the most important we face.

The Iraq war is part of the answer. In particular, the US and European response to the flight of the Kurds resulted in an extraordinary operation in Northern Iraq in which a handful of professional soldiers and some tough-minded aid-agency people 'made policy with tents', staking out an allied enclave by moving their camps well into Iraqi territory and later seizing control of a string of towns. They did so without the approval of their governments, especially in the American case, and were only justified retrospectively, by their success in moving refugees back to their homes. Whether this Western protectorate can be maintained at one remove, by stationing a deterrent force in Turkey, is another question.

The US mania for extrication, its neurosis about leaving troops in any situation for any length of time, its quick-fix 'in and out' mentality, is what lies behind what could turn out to be too early a withdrawal. But the essence of the operation was that Saddam's reconquest of the north was halted and, in order to do this, Iraqi sovereignty was cavalierly and, most people would agree, rightly ignored. A precedent has been laid down for similar actions in the future.

Of course, similar conditions would have to prevail: the offending state's crimes would have to be great, while at the same time it would have to be weak enough to make interference relatively risk-free. The very issue that has led to new threats of bombing – Saddam's attempt to preserve Iraq's nuclear weapons potential – underlines the fact that the period in which delinquent states can be reasonably easily coerced could be a short one. The opportunities to set right what is wrong or dangerous in the world's unstable regions are greater now than they will be when more states have acquired usable weapons of mass destruction.

The Gulf war set the seal on an American ascendancy in the Middle East more total than that of Britain in the aftermath of the first world war. That predominance had already been established as Soviet power in the region slipped away, while European influence remained secondary and usually supportive of Washington. When the USA, with a minimum of courtesy, ignored Soviet efforts at mediation towards the end of the air war, the Soviet Union's eclipse as a Middle Eastern power could be said to be complete. We wait to see if this ascendancy will be used by the USA in a responsible or, indeed, consistent way.

The signs have been mixed so far. There was, first of all, the silly retreat from policy objectives when, confused by uprisings in Iraq that it had not expected and irritated and disappointed by the failure of the Iraqi armed forces to stage a coup, the USA decided to leave rebel Kurds and Shi'ites to their fate – when it had the means, by forbidding Iraqi air activity, of materially assisting at least the former. That decision in late March led to many thousands of deaths, propped up Saddam and had to be reversed, in the case of the Kurds, almost within days.

The USA may have flirted briefly with the notion that a weak Saddam in power was preferable to a 'Lebanon' or a Shi'ite revolutionary state. It now seems to be understood in Washington that anything is preferable to Saddam but that, in any case, both the Lebanon and the Shi'ite revolutionary projections were based on false assumptions.

The centrality of the question of Iraqi democracy to the future of the Middle East does also seem to be better grasped. Iraq's combination of wealth, education, population and secular tradition makes it the most favourable society in the region in which to establish a democratic system. Decades of dictatorial politics are admittedly a factor against, which is one reason why many opposition Iraqis unrealistically hope for a period of Western tutelage after Saddam, something equivalent to the democratisation programmes in Germany and Japan after the second world war.

Whatever the difficulties, once democracy was established in Iraq its influence over its neighbours to the south and west would be likely in time to be profound. Washington's determination to bring Saddam down has been re-affirmed during the confrontation over the country's nuclear programme. Its readiness to look beyond Saddam's fall to a democratic future for Iraq is far less assured, particularly given the fears of conservative Gulf allies, but at least it is no longer insisting on a non-democratic army–party succession.

Meanwhile the most recent evidence shows us that Washington is pursuing the Arab-Israeli question with some seriousness. The revelations from Damascus about US assurances that, once under way, negotiations between Israel and the Arab states and the Palestinians would have to include land for peace are hardly surprising. They indicate a strategy of pushing Likud into such a tight corner that it must either make territorial concessions or declare itself utterly unable to make such concessions, even for large gains. That would put Likud between a rock and a hard place, as the Americans say.

This is a strategy which, if taken to its limits, is likely to result in the destruction of Likud, either in its break-up after territorial concessions, or in its defeat at the polls. If we reach that point, and there are many stations on the way where America could allow itself to be bested by Likud delay, procrastination and obfuscation, that would presuppose a degree of deliberate US meddling in Israeli politics that would be a parallel to what we have seen in Iraq.

US power, supported by European influence, and with the acquiescence of the Soviet Union, is the commanding fact in the Middle East today. We may squirm at the neo-colonial aspects of the use of such power, but that it ought to be used is undeniable. The gravest danger is not of US bullying but of US (and European) neglect, a falling back on the old regional system – the alliance with Israel, the Israel-Egypt axis, the uncritical bargain with the oil kingdoms, the procedural playing around with the Arab-Israeli question to conceal the lack of real progress, and the almost racist assumption that democracy is not for the Arabs and the Arabs are not for democracy. Even, perhaps, a readiness to leave the Iraqi people in an awful limbo while Saddam's half-life slowly decays.

A year on from Saddam's challenge, it is still not possible to say whether the USA and the rest of us can live up to the great responsibility which victory in the Gulf war has brought, but there are signs that the effort is at least beginning to be made.

March 28, 1992: David Hirst

Men who would move mountains

Every morning at eight o'clock, knots of young men and women in battle fatigues make their way through corridors in the high-piled snow to a bleak, unheated 'classroom' in a remote and stony wilderness close to the Lebanese frontier with Syria. They shiver – this has been the coldest winter in living memory. But they rejoice, too. There are dozens of such training camps scattered through the Syrian-controlled Beka'a Valley and its surrounding heights. Most are Palestinian. But this one, the Mahsum Korkmaz Academy, is Kurdish, and its occupants rejoice because these fearsome conditions are perfect preparation for those they will encounter on their return to their 'homeland' as nationalist guerrillas in the mountains of eastern Turkey.

Their encampment is guarded by watch towers flying the green, yellow and red flags of Kurdistan. Its buildings are dispersed across the craggy terrain because the Kurds believe there is a risk that one day the Turkish high command might order a bombardment. For it is here that for years the Kurdistan Workers' Party, or PKK, has been turning out new recruits for its separatist insurrection at the rate of three or four hundred every three months.

That insurrection has brought new levels of violence to Turkey in the past week. During the Kurdish new year last weekend protests and fighting between PKK supporters and Turkish forces exploded in south-eastern Turkey, killing more than 75 people. Sixteen died in one town, Cizre, where a 24-hour curfew was in force until yesterday and where police detained 71 people after finding hundreds of rifles and pistols, as well as rocket-propelled grenades and explosives, in an arms swoop.

Emergency rule is in force in the mainly Kurdish area and night-time curfews have been clamped on PKK strongholds. The violence reached Istanbul yesterday with two attacks in which gunmen opened fire on an army bus and a police patrol car, wounding two soldiers.

Kurdish protests disrupted several European cities during the week, including London where the embassy was the target of Kurdish demonstrators. On Thursday, an additional international dimension emerged when Germany suspended arms supplies to Turkey and halted military co-operation – until reports that German-supplied weapons and vehicles, including tanks, had been used against the Kurds had been clarified.

International concern after the Gulf war concentrated attention on the Kurds living in Iraq, but Kurdistan also sweeps across parts of Iran, Syria, Armenia and, particularly, Turkey – home to nine million Kurds. The PKK is clearly intent on stepping up its fight, and on drawing international attention to its particular rebellion.

At 8am up in the craggy terrain of the Beka'a, the youngsters in the guerrilla camp have already completed two hours of military training; now they head off to a much longer period of political education, which is apparently held to be at least as important, if not more so. For they are learning to change their whole outlook and personality as well as to fight the Turks.

The classroom walls illustrate an ideological time warp which these Kurds still inhabit. Unmoved by events in the ex-communist world, the walls are adorned with pictures of Marx, Lenin and Che Guevara.

The morning session begins with a common ritual: a passing-out ceremony. One by one, a dozen or so graduates come to the front of the class and address their comrades in a virtually identical formula. They do so – oddly – in Turkish. There are Kurdish-language newspapers lying around the camp; these are the product of the modest cultural reforms introduced in Turkey, permitting some 15 million or more 'mountain Turks' – as they have been called since Ataturk's time – to call themselves Kurds and to use their own tongue. But Turkish is the only language which all are sure to understand.

'My name is . . . ' the graduates intone, 'and I wish to say that when I came to this Academy I suffered from shortcomings of personality, from bourgeois habits, but now I have corrected them. I promise the Leader, the prisoners of the resistance, the Kurdistan people, that I shall struggle to the last drop of my blood.' Polite applause.

After a few hours at the Academy one ceases to be surprised at such ritual tributes to the Leader. To a man, the academicians are persuaded that, without the 44-year-old Abdullah Ocalan, there would be no Academy, no rebellion, no future for the Kurds. Some of his followers prophesy that he will become far more than just a Kurdish champion. And there can be no doubt that if, under his leadership, Turkey's Kurds continue to challenge the state on a growing scale, this still little-known guerrilla chief will emerge as one of the principal actors in a region whose existing order is under increasing strain.

Ocalan has come a long way from the days when, as a political science student at Ankara University, he had what he calls his 'radical new idea', one which, in retrospect, has taken on something of the aura of prophetic revelation. This was his realisation that the only way the Kurds could achieve self-determination was to aim, from the very outset, for the maximum. This meant eschewing minimalist, fragmentary solutions of the 'autonomy-in-one-country' type which have been the ambition of the best-known Kurdish leaders, the late Mullah Mustafa Barzani and his son Masud – and to make Turkey's Kurds the base for the eventual establishment of a Greater Kurdistan, one and indivisible.

He would not define the precise boundaries of a state that would rank as the largest and most strategically located in the Middle East. But an artist's exuberant fantasy, on a wall behind him, has it running from western Iran to Alexandretta on the shores of the Mediterranean. The 'homeland' breaks into four segments: Turkish Kurdistan being the 'north-west', Iranian Kurdistan the 'east', Iraqi Kurdistan the 'south' and Syrian Kurdistan the 'south-west'.

'It was my idea alone,' Ocalan says. 'At first there were no sympathisers with it, even among the Kurds.' For years he struggled to promote his idea by word of mouth. The Turks decided he was no threat 'because only crazy people could follow such crazy ideas'.

In the 1920s, Ataturk had put down Kurdish uprisings with great cruelty. Since then, 'the Turks have been thinking that Kurdistan is in the graveyard, that the Kurds have no history,' says Ocalan. And even the Kurds were apt to think like this too. Turkish 'colonialism' and oppression had so thoroughly penetrated the Kurdish mind and personality that they no longer saw themselves as Kurds, no longer believed in themselves, he goes on. And that was why Ocalan – though he himself gave this interview in Turkish – saw the changing of the Kurdish personality as an even greater challenge than the physical liberation of Kurdistan.

Therein, he suggested, lay the true originality of his leadership and revolution. One quickly senses that, where qualities of leadership are concerned, it would be unwise to venture any comparison between himself and the Barzanis. When the subject does come up, he can barely disguise his contempt for such backward, tribal, traditionalist lackeys of regional and imperialist powers. For eight years, he said, his own partisans had fought off one of the biggest armies in Nato. But Barzani's Peshmerga found life in the mountains too hard, so that 'when [he refers to the flight of Iraqi Kurds after the Gulf war] Saddam launches a few bombs, they run away'.

But what did his unique leadership really consist of?

'For the English that would be very hard to understand. If, for 20 years, the Turks haven't been able to do so, how can you?' Was this not rather mysterious? 'Lots of people have wanted to find out about this. But I told them they could not grasp it. You should have someone qualified to do that.'

Was he a Marxist-Leninist? 'Yes, but of a kind that has not been seen before. You would need a thousand witnesses to understand what kind of Marxist I am – or Muslim, or patriot.' His was an 'historic' revolution – especially in building the new Kurdish man – of a kind that Lenin or even Mao had not attempted.

These large claims seem all the larger in that, physically at least, there is nothing particularly impressive or commanding about this corpulent, moustachioed offspring of south Anatolian peasants. A Turkish official says he 'has neither the brains nor the education' to lead an insurrection on such a scale. It is not to lend any support to this contemptuous opinion to say that Ocalan does not come across as a man of particularly impressive intellect.

Whatever his secret, the upshot was that the Kurds, instead of collaborating on a large scale with the Turks, were now flocking to his banner 'with all their heart'. He declares: 'The Turks are very frightened. They are afraid that they are going to lose completely. That is why they are now bombing us almost every day. But we don't think that.' This year, the rebels would set up a parliament in the most rugged and mountainous corner of 'north-west Kurdistan', close to the Iraqi border.

It would take time before the revolution, spreading beyond the mountainous heartland, embraced all Turkish Kurdistan. Three-quarters of the groundwork had been done. The remaining 25 per cent could suddenly be speeded up with 'the collapse of the Turkish state'. That 25 per cent could also prove very nasty indeed. Some of Ocalan's entourage speak openly of meeting terror with terror, of countering anti-Kurdish death squads with bombs in Turkish cities. He, personally, distances himself, if only slightly, from such tactics, attributing them to 'sympathisers'. But 'we could do 50 such operations a day if we wanted'.

As for the 'south-west' in Syria, was there not an intriguing contradiction in President Assad's tolerance – in spite of repeated Turkish protests – of an organisation whose ultimate aim is to detach more than a million Kurds from his state? Ocalan pointed out that Syria had its quarrels with Turkey, not least over water resources. Assad knew that 'when we are a state it is we who will dispense water to Syria'.

The greatest gain for the Kurds, Ocalan concluded, would be for the West to stop supporting Ankara, without which 'we would have won our freedom and independence a long time ago'. Unfortunately, however, his 'message' could not be conveyed by a Western newspaper because the Western system was 'very closed'. Still, he was happy, out of friendship, to give interviews like this, even if he set little store by what Western newspapers wrote about him. At least the Leader can be sure his interview will be added to his collected works, and, as such, become part of the required reading of future students at his Academy.

June 13, 1992: John Hooper

Olympic shadows over Barcelona

By any standards, the opening ceremony of the 25th Olympiad on July 25 will be an extraordinary affair. Never before can a Games have begun a few javelin throws from a mass grave, let alone one filled with the victims of a movement served by the incumbent President of the International Olympic Committee.

Anyone queueing to enter the Olympic Stadium on Montjuich – the Jew's Hill – is bound to notice a line of what look like battlements on the crest of a higher outcrop overlooking the stadium. They are burial niches, marking the farthest limits of Barcelona's chief cemetery.

Just over the hill, where the VIPs' cars will be parked, is a burial ground without niches, much less tombs. The Fossa de la Pedrera is so perfunctorily signposted that it would be easy to walk past the steep incline, planted with cypresses, which leads to it, without noticing it. At the top stands a row of square columns, engraved with dates and names, most of which come from the years immediately after General Franco's forces overthrew Spain's democratically elected government in 1939.

Beyond the columns, fringed by a gravel path, lies an immense expanse of grass dotted with wild flowers and sheltered by the craggy sides of what was once a quarry. These towering walls create a sensation of tranquillity which can only be disturbed by the loudest of noises.

On July 25, it will no doubt be possible to make out the sounds of music and hubbub from the other side of the hill, where Juan Antonio Samaranch – formerly unelected president of Barcelona's provincial council, erstwhile member of Franco's rubber-stamp parliament, and the dictator's one-time junior minister for sport – will preside over the biggest event in Barcelona's recent history. Samaranch will share the limelight with Jordi Pujol, the Catalan president who was imprisoned and tortured under Franco, and the mayor of Barcelona, Pasqual Maragall, whose sister was imprisoned under the dictatorship.

Numerous questions will be raised. How, for example, did the IOC elect as its leader a man with Samaranch's past? And how could the Catalans have expected to stage the Olympics without a controversy such as the one that has blown up over the book, and film, *The Lords of the Rings*, an exposé of the commercialisation of the Olympics?

The second question is perhaps easier to answer than the first. Franco's dictatorship was not overthrown but gradually and peacefully transformed. Recriminations were avoided because they might have led to a backlash from the armed forces. Modern Spain is a society built on communal, voluntary amnesia, and today's Spaniards are often genuinely startled when foreigners refuse to respect the taboos which have served them so well.

Another reason is that the Barcelona Games mean so much, not only to the city but also to that 'nation which is not a state', as the Catalans sometimes describe their country. So another sort of taboo has come to affect everything connected with the Olympics, including several controversial planning and development decisions.

Pep Miró, head of the Federation of Barcelona Neighbourhood Associations (FAVB), admits that 'when Barcelona was chosen, none of us dared to say that we'd end up paying for it dearly'. This may explain the absence of debate in the city. What it does not explain is why the transformation of Barcelona – and particularly the construction of its Olympic village, a project that bears strong resemblances to the development of London's Docklands – should have received such unquestioning praise from foreign architectural critics and planning specialists.

Barcelona is the nearest thing on earth to heaven for the design-conscious. 'This is a city with bus shelters which do not keep out the rain but which look absolutely sensational,' jokes Albert Alós, the editor of FAVB's bulletin. It is also a city with a strong sense of public relations, and visiting journalists are subjected to an intense propaganda offensive. HOLSA, the body which oversaw the infrastructure work connected with the Olympics, will drive them round the city's new ring road laying repeated emphasis on the fact that, in parts, more than 60 per cent of it is covered over so as to reduce traffic noise and avoid splitting neighbourhoods.

It is only when you talk to someone like Miró that you hear, 'This was a struggle that took years. The town council said it was only going to cover 30-odd per cent.'

In his otherwise excellent book *Barcelona*, Robert Hughes gives an outstanding example of how critics can cheerfully apply different standards between countries. The Olympic village, he writes, is 'the kind of urban clearance project that in the United States today would bog down in the courts for years, as one special interest group after another whittled away at it. In Barcelona it was pushed through fast . . . '

Or, to put it another way, it has been steamrollered into existence without the consultations normal in a democratic society. No inquiry was ever held into the Olympic village and its surroundings, even though objections could be made on various grounds.

The first is aesthetic. The two 42-storey tower blocks that have been erected on the waterfront beside the village can scarcely be said to blend in with the low-rise area. The village itself is an extraordinary hotchpotch of styles, but then it was designed by no fewer than 19 architectural partnerships. The city administration says this was to avoid favouritism. Opponents claim it was done to ensure there was no criticism from within the profession.

The Olympic village also covers an area which the city's 1976 plan had intended as a green belt and which had to be re-zoned before the project became legal. Its 1,800 flats will merely add pressure to Europe's most densely populated city.

But the outstanding reason an inquiry would have been embarrassing as well as inconvenient is that the Olympic village project is so ideologically incongruous. Built under a socialist-run council with £100 million of public money, the athletes' accommodation is not destined to become public housing, but is being sold off at prices which only well-to-do professionals can afford. A three-bedroom flat overlooking the sea would set you back about £170,000. This is in flat contradiction to undertakings given by the city's administrators. Hughes quotes the mayor, Pasqual Maragall, as promising in 1986 that the flats would be sold at 'low, competitive prices'.

In addition to tax breaks from the central government, buyers will get the benefit of some exceptional infrastructure created with ratepayers' money. The lighting in the Olympic village, according to Albert Alós, has cost £275,000 more than usual to install and will cost £275,000 a year extra to run.

The deputy mayor in charge of planning, Lluis Arnet, insists that the project is 'terrifically socialist'. He points to features that will benefit the whole city.

Besides the housing, 40 hectares of park are to be created; the shoreline will have four new beaches; and, most importantly perhaps, there has been a massive investment in sanitary engineering to ensure that waste is carried away from the coastline. Low-cost housing 'wouldn't have been able to pay for the green spaces, the marine promenades and the spending on sewerage,' Arnet says.

The result, though, is that the Olympic village is a ghetto, a middle-class enclave within a working-class district. Poble Nou, on the other side of the wire fences surrounding the village, used to be known as the Catalan Manchester. It is where the textile factories that created much of Barcelona's wealth were concentrated. Its population of 50,000 are mainly descendants of the Aragonese and Valencians who, at the turn of the century, flocked to the city to work in them.

Jill Morrell, founder of the Friends of John McCarthy,
hearing that her man had at last been freed after he had spent
over five years as a hostage in Lebanon (August 9, 1991:
Graham Turner).

Which one has the short fat hairy legs? John Prescott and John Smith at the upbeat Labour Party Conference (October 1, 1991: Martin Argles).

Polls apart . . . Chris Patten and John Major at a downbeat Tory press conference as Labour appear to have the election won (April 1, 1992: Martin Argles).

concert in Sheffield, featuring Neil Kinnock and the entire Shadow Cabinet, that assisted Labour on the road to electoral defeat (April 2, 1992: Don McPhee).

Will there be a successor to provide them with a living? And should they have built it anyway? VSEL workers watch the emergence of Britain's first Trident nuclear submarine, HMS *Vanguard*, from its construction hall in Barrow-in-Furness (March 5, 1992: Denis Thorpe).

Cockspur, cockscomb, and fishtail jets on display at the opening of the National Gas Gallery at the Museum of Science and Industry in Manchester (December 14, 1991: Don McPhee).

Children at a meeting seeking voluntary-aided status for an Islamic school in Dewsbury (March 10, 1992: Denis Thorpe)

...he International Balloon Fiesta at Bristol (August 10, 1991:
...rank Martin).

Middlesbrough . . . designated Environmental City of the Year (December 20, 1991: Don McPhee).

Two of the two million visitors a year who follow in Izaak Walton's footsteps in Dovedale, on the Derbyshire–Staffordshire border (October 19, 1991:

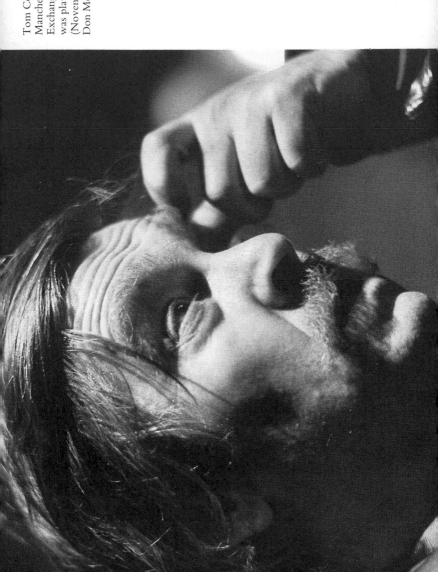

Tom Courtenay at Manchester's Royal Exchange, where he was playing The Miser (November 29, 1991: Don McPhee).

The chippie, Todmorden, West Yorkshire (February

a second successive Olympic giant slalom gold medal (February 19, 1992: Frank Baron).

Wade Dooley's dominance in the lines-out contributed to England's Rugby Union victory over France – though on this occasion he was receiving a little illegal help from friendly hands (October 21, 1991: Frank Baron).

George Noble jumps in anger at missing a hoop in the British
Open Croquet Championship at the Hurlingham Club
(July 22, 1991: Frank Martin).

Alós, who lives there himself, compares it to London's East End. 'Socially and geographically, it remains cut off from the rest of the city. People often talk about "going to Barcelona".'

But, as a direct result of the Games, Poble Nou is unlikely to retain its unique character for long. The Olympic village development has unleashed a classic process of gentrification. HOLSA officials admit, indeed stress, that there is more building work in Poble Nou than in any other part of the city. Individual and corporate speculators are reacting not only to the creation of the village itself, but also to plans to redevelop a much larger area farther north.

According to senior town-hall officials, the scheme would involve 3,700 flats, shops, offices and a hypermarket. It depends on a sale of land the council owns to private developers, but this is almost certain to go ahead because the expected profit of some £40 million has already been written into the council's books.

HOLSA has overshot its budget by more than £100 million. Since the council has a 49 per cent stake, it has to meet a deficit of £50 million. 'If we don't sell, then the deficit will be even bigger,' Arnet says.

'With a conservative ruling group, all this would be normal,' says a local property lawyer, Eduardo Moreno. 'In London's Docklands, they've done much the same. But that was under Mrs Thatcher.'

The only undeniably socialist aspect of the Olympic village is the name it will bear when the Games are over. It is to be called Nova Icária in memory of a Utopian committee founded by the proto-communist Etienne Cabet.

Even for admirers of the project, this has proved a bit too much to take. 'You might as well call an upscale condo block in Berlin the Rosa Luxemburg Tower,' Hughes writes, apparently unaware that a semi-detached house in

the Rosa Luxemburg Estate in fashionable north-west
Madrid would currently cost you about £165,000.

November 23, 1991: Richard Gott

The UN corridors of bumbledom

Just in time for evening drinks, the 15 members of the
United Nations Security Council file out from their private
sanctuary into a corridor where tradition allows them to
be waylaid by journalists. They might have been debating
Yugoslavia today or Cambodia. Or perhaps Central America. Or the Western Sahara. All are items on the current
autumn agenda. But on Thursday afternoon, they had
participated in yet another meeting to discuss who should
be the next Secretary General. When they voted, they
produced – to everyone's surprise – a conclusive and
disastrous result.

This is the staged bit at the UN, for the corridor is a
carefully constructed semi-public space through which
the delegates trail, between the potted plants and the bar.
The television cameras are kept behind a metal crowd-
control barrier, but the journalists are permitted to leap
about, notebooks and tape recorders in hand. They try to
ambush their favourite ambassador, preferably in their
own language. Some of the diplomats look around hopefully, anxious to be interrogated. Others stride past without a sideways glance.

Five of them in this exclusive club represent the Permanent Five who wield a veto on all substantive decisions.
Ten come from the countries that are elected to sit on the
council for a brief spell of two years.

Although mandated by their governments, and not therefore completely free agents, this is the group that makes decisions that can affect the world. Like priests, they are not unconscious of their power. In the last two years, unimpeded by cold-war divisions, their power and arrogance has grown dangerously.

The small man over there must surely be the ambassador from the Yemen, the only member of the council (apart from Cuba) to oppose the war in the Gulf. He always likes to stop for a chat. The large towering figure talking to the *New York Times* is presumably Thomas Pickering, United States ambassador, a man more popular in this gathering than the country he represents. And the debonair, balding man hogging the camera limelight can only be Sir David Hannay, the ambassador who fronted for Britain's Conservative government during many of the difficult moments of the Gulf war.

A natural actor, Sir David needs no prompting to speak. Waltzing into the corridor like Olivier playing Archie Rice, you half expect him to be twirling a cane. He talks fluently to camera, answers questions with the icy politeness that British diplomats reserve for the fools they are enjoined to suffer gladly, and disappears as if in a puff of smoke.

His is a much appreciated ritual, and it gives added weight to Britain's claim to retain its permanent seat on the Security Council. The specific gravity and expertise of the Foreign Office, rather than Britain's intrinsic economic or political significance, is what has allowed the British to keep this important perk for so long. Diplomats and the BBC World Service are our gift to the world. *Timeo Danaos et dona ferentes.*

Within minutes the show is over. The lights are switched off, and the chief participants are whisked away in their stretch limos into the New York gridlock, with the cheerful prospect of cocktails and canapés to come. The journalists scratch through their notes, the agency reporters put a useful quote from Sir David on the wire, and another exhausting day at the UN in the service of world peace grinds to a close.

Quite suddenly, the 10 turbulent years of the Pérez de Cuéllar era begin to look exceptionally bright. The unimaginative choice of the ageing Mr Boutros Ghali to be the new Secretary General throws into doubt all the radical plans that have been brewing to reform the world organisation. It suggests that the great powers who run the Security Council will be quite happy to allow it to bumble on in the old way without any important changes.

If so, it seems that whatever form the new world order eventually takes, the United Nations will play no significant part in it. With a man at the helm who will essentially be a caretaker Secretary General for the next five years, the organisation is now in danger of drifting back into the state of obscurity and irrelevance from which Mr Pérez de Cuéllar had rescued it. This may be exactly where the great powers would like it to be.

As usual, the member states have no one but themselves to blame. The old Third World majority in the General Assembly shouted vociferously for an African candidate – though it would take a perverse supporter of the *Black Athena* thesis to characterise an Egyptian Copt married to a Jew as an African – and the great powers sat back and allowed it to happen.

Those chiefly at fault are the British, the Americans, and the French. They had the opportunity to make a better choice, but they bungled the footwork. The Russians have other things on their mind at the moment, and the Chinese play their traditional low-profile role.

Even the Surrealists, with their childlike delight in parlour games, never dreamt up anything quite so foolish as the system for choosing the new Secretary General. At regular weekly intervals throughout October and November, the 15 grown men who comprise the Security Council have been meeting in a small room, writing down names on pieces of paper, and marking their preferences.

In the course of their games, sometimes with white paper and sometimes with blue, a list of a dozen illuminati eventually emerge. While most were well known at the UN, many would have been unfamiliar to the world outside.

The folkloric details of the selection process would not matter much were it not for the fact that the UN is supposed to be entering an exciting new era in the aftermath of the cold war. Innumerable plans had been drawn up to take advantage of the apparently favourable climate for reform. Meetings were held, study groups organised, and the strenuous endeavours of the Nordic countries and the Australians were deployed in support of change, seemingly with the support of the Security Council.

Top of the list was the reform of the way that the Secretary General is chosen. Clearly, the Security Council should have undertaken to find someone everyone would have regarded as the best man (or woman) for the job. In an era of great-power unity, this task should not have been too difficult for trained diplomats.

They were said to be looking for a young, dynamic diplomat and manager, someone capable of presiding over a major overhaul of the UN Secretariat and a dramatic change in the way the UN conducts its business. Yet there was no such person on the list of names produced when the Security Council was paying its variant of blind man's buff. So, even before this week's vote, there was some feeling here that the prospects of reform had fallen at the first hurdle.

Many found the candidates so unsatisfactory that they hoped a second list, with more promising names, was being prepared. It was not to be. It turns out that the great powers are not in fact committed to the reforms by which everyone had set such store. Those who favour inertia have won the day.

Debate about what is needed for the job inevitably

begins with a discussion of the qualities of Javier Pérez de Cuéllar, now coming to the end of his 10 years' stint. A distinguished Peruvian diplomat, plucked from obscurity in 1981 when the Chinese (and probably one or two others as well) could no longer stomach the oleaginous Kurt Waldheim, Pérez de Cuéllar has presided over two dramatic periods in the UN's history.

During the first, in the days of President Reagan and Jeane Kirkpatrick, it appeared that United States hostility to the UN was so great that the organisation might founder under the weight of great-power disapproval.

During the second, after President Gorbachev's epochal speech in New York in 1987, it seemed as if the UN might blossom anew in a fresh atmosphere of great-power friendship and amity. More peace-keeping operations have been launched in the past year than in the entire history of the institution, though many of them have been a cleaning up operation after the cold war.

To have bridged these two eras, and to have survived a Gulf war during which many members of his Secretariat felt that the UN had been hijacked by the United States (and to which he personally was opposed), remains a considerable feat. And, unlike Kurt Waldheim, who sought a third term, Pérez de Cuéllar had the good sense to make a timely withdrawal, refusing to accept any notion that he might stay on.

That is all on the plus side when his biography comes to be written, but any list of what is now required for a modern Secretary General inevitably emphasises the characteristics that Pérez de Cuéllar lacks. The depressing aspect of this week's decision is that Boutros Ghali has the defects of Pérez de Cuéllar in spades.

'What we need now is a strong managerial hand,' says one prominent reformer. 'Pérez de Cuéllar was a skilful political operator and he recognised the importance of reforming the Secretariat – but he did nothing about it.' It is unlikely that Boutros Ghali, a glad-handing politician, will feel able to take on this difficult organisational task.

'We need a powerful communicator,' the reformer continues, 'someone who can deal with the press and the non-governmental organisations. Pérez de Cuéllar was essentially shy and withdrawn. He hated that side of things.' Ghali will be no better, though he likes the sound of his own voice.

'We need someone who is economically literate. Pérez de Cuéllar was a traditional diplomat with no training in that area.' Boutros Ghali, with a background in international law, is similarly ill equipped.

The task of adapting the UN to the post-cold-war era is not just a matter of reforming the Secretariat. The General Assembly, where the erstwhile Third World still holds sway, is also a mess, endlessly preoccupied with trivia. There are too many agenda items, says one senior and influential Western critic in the Secretariat. 'A large proportion of these are stupid, trivial, and self-serving.' The same is true of the economic debates at the UN, once a crucial battleground between north and south. 'There is the problem of escaping from the rigid pattern of decades, with interminable discussions of no significance, full of rhetoric and cliché.' Even the participants don't seem to enjoy them much.

The situation with regard to the UN's own finances is no better. 'Everything is organised in a hand to mouth fashion with the organisation permanently on the brink of insolvency.'

Nor is this all. At the back of everyone's mind is the future of the Security Council itself, this historically self-appointed would-be ruler of the world. No one expects it to be changed in the near future, but the composition of the Permanent Five is unlikely to be acceptable over any length of time. The Japanese and the Germans, the two largest contributors to the UN after the United States and the Soviet Union, cannot be excluded indefinitely.

A huge question mark now hovers over the Soviet Union. Will this one significant veto-wielding ex-super-power be around in a year or two? And if not, who will inherit its veto? And where will that leave the British and French?

The Italians have suggested that a European veto should replace that of the two west European nuclear powers – not a notion that appeals much to the British Foreign Office in the current neuralgic state of the European debate. Sir David Hannay's days in front of the camera may be drawing to a close.

To confront these problems in the nineties, the Security Council in its unwisdom has presented us with Mr Boutros Ghali. He looks ready made to preside over the decline of the organisation rather than its revival.

Criminal practices

July 17, 1991: Melanie Phillips

The public prosecutor

The most intriguing question in criminal justice is this: why is the Director of Public Prosecutions always so cheerful? Or, to put it another way, just what has Sir Allan Green QC got to smile about?

Look at his record as a crown prosecutor. Randall and Pottle? Failed. The prosecution of the Guildford Four policemen? Thrown out. The case against 14 police officers arising from the Wapping disturbances? Abandoned. The criminal justice system of which he is a lynchpin? A public confidence disaster. Leave aside perverse magistrates or stroppy juries. The Crown Prosecution Service, understaffed and overstretched, has not had an easy time since it was launched and its public image is not, shall we say, heroic. Yet just look at Sir Allan. Always beaming, always twinkling, always unflappably happy.

A state prosecutor is potentially a threatening, oppress-

ive and secretive figure. Sir Allan is not like that at all,
except possibly for the secrecy, of which more anon. He is
that most improbable animal, a highly popular prosecutor. His staff think he's wonderful. Even defence lawyers
concede that he is rational and reasonable. It is impossible
to feel threatened in his presence. He is not stuck-up or
shifty or remote. When you remark on his phlegm in the
face of adversity, he beams again and then tries to look
grave. Up and down the country, he says, cases are being
handled perfectly properly and fairly and well. Critics of
the service lack a sense of proportion. And of course he
does go home and worry about things; it matters a lot to
him that the CPS should be well thought of; but he just has
a buoyant temperament and he really enjoys his job. 'It's
never dull,' he said. 'When I was at the Bar the adrenalin
flowed, you'd make your opening and closing speeches,
then you'd sit down. Other barristers would address the
jury and it would take *days*. For hours and days on end
you'd be becalmed.'

So the Bar was boring. But his earliest legal inspiration
had been somewhat idiosyncratic. His maternal grandfather was a persistent litigant who had a remarkable
record. 'He never ever won a case, whether he was
plaintiff or defendant. He was always on the wrong side.'
As a child, Allan Green accompanied him to one of these
doomed cases, in which his grandfather was being sued –
successfully, of course – by a firm to whom he had sold
some defective barrage balloons. Leonard Caplan QC
appeared for him and the 13-year-old was smitten by the
barrister bug. 'I thought he was absolutely marvellous. He
was very fluent, incredibly tenacious; the judge was
obviously against him but he stuck to his guns and I
thought he was quite magnificent.' Magnificent – but he
lost! Whatever does this tell us about the future DPP?

At the Bar, he quickly got into criminal prosecutions,
working the Essex courts and then moving to the Old
Bailey where he became Treasury Counsel. There are

some barristers who won't ever prosecute because they think the system is weighted against defendants. Sir Allan, by contrast, was never at ease when defending. 'I never turned down a brief for the defence, but I always used to go into court with something of a sinking feeling because the territory is quite different. If you're prosecuting you make the running, you make the opening speeches and if you're defending it's a totally different approach. The relative informality of it was something I found unsettling.'

To an untutored lay person he appears extraordinarily detached, even by the standards of a profession for which emotional detachment is a prerequisite. As a prosecutor, he is not as committed to getting a result as defence barristers are to getting their client off. 'The defence does everything he can within the rules to secure an acquittal. The prosecution is not there to achieve a conviction at all costs; he's there to put a case fairly and the vigour with which he puts the case will depend on the circumstances, the weight of the evidence available. He's a minister of justice and he should not press the case more forcefully.'

So much so, in fact, that he doesn't actually want people working for him who will do the job too well – a curious concept for a lay person to digest. 'On occasion we've looked at candidates for Treasury Counsel and rejected them on the grounds that they were too prosecution-minded and they would prosecute too rigorously, that the boot would go in. That can be unfair and bad advocacy.' So it would seem that all these high-profile prosecution failures may be embarrassing public-relations fiascos but according to legal principles they demonstrate the system is in rude health.

As a barrister, he prosecuted Dennis Nilsen, the Muswell Hill multiple murderer whose defence was based on a plea of diminished responsibility. To prepare for his cross-examination of scientific witnesses, Sir Allan studied the prosecution tactics in the case of Peter Sutcliffe, the

Yorkshire Ripper, who had employed a similar defence. 'After conviction, Ivan Lawrence (Nilsen's counsel) went to see him and he came back and I said how was he. He said he was very pleased with me, very pleased with you, very pleased with the judge and he thought we'd all played our parts admirably.'

But surely on any reasonable analysis someone who did what Nilsen did, or Sutcliffe, or Mirella Beechook who strangled her little daughter and her daughter's friend and whose similar defence was also demolished by Sir Allan, *must* be of diminished responsibility. 'In Nilsen's case I think the motivation was obscure. He was obviously a very, very curious person because he cut off a young man's head and boiled it in the kitchen.'

Curious? A man boils someone's head and Sir Allan describes him merely as curious? 'He would pick up these young men and take them back to his flat and ply them with large quantities of food and drink. Not surprisingly they would fall asleep and this would enrage him. His mind was bizarre but his responsibility wasn't diminished. He was cunning.'

But just because someone is cunning, does it really mean they are fully *compos mentis*? 'The psychiatrist who gave evidence for the crown didn't think he was suffering from diminished responsibility. He gave compelling evidence that he wasn't.' So if those people who boil heads and murder their children aren't mad, what are they? 'I certainly believe that some people are evil, yes.'

Sir Allan found the transition from boiling heads to heading the CPS a bit of a strain. He'd had no experience whatsoever of administration, politics or Whitehall. 'On one occasion we were discussing with Tony Hetherington (the previous DPP) someone who was acting up, and I said why don't you get rid of him; it was explained to me that he was on temporary promotion and the last thing they wanted to do was get rid of him!' Of course, most interest centres not so much on the staffing difficulties of his service as the apparently 'political' decisions he often has to take where his reasons are often obscure. 'Public-interest decisions are often very difficult because there are public-interest factors that conflict with each other. You have to weigh them up and strike a balance.'

Why didn't he prosecute Sonia Sutcliffe for alleged perjury, or Khalim Siddiqui for incitement to murder Salman Rushdie? He refuses to discuss his reasons, one of the rare positions with which he is clearly uncomfortable. 'If detailed explanations were made public, that might reflect on the integrity of particular individuals and I would be seen to be condemning them in a particular way, indicating they were untruthful or untrustworthy.' But why not say more in those cases where this danger didn't exist? 'Probably because that would create a great deal of speculation in relation to cases where I *was* inhibited.'

But surely public suspicion of a fix was a very serious consequence of such secrecy? 'Oh, yes, but it's a question of the public interest. You can't win on this. It's a difficulty. The public interest is very difficult to define; it's a bit like defining an elephant.'

So what kind of an elephant would a war crimes prosecution, for instance, have to be? 'One will want to satisfy oneself that a defendant can have a fair trial; his health will be a factor, the availability of witnesses. The decision will be taken by the Attorney General and not by me. If I ever advise proceeding on war crimes I would want to be satisfied that the case was a *very, very* strong case indeed; I would set a *very, very* high standard of proof.' Clearly, this would be one case the detached public prosecutor most definitely would not wish to lose.

Sir Allan Green resigned on October 3, 1991, after police observed him approaching prostitutes in a red-light district in London.

July 27, 1991: Nick Davies

Crimes of passion

It was a Tuesday morning. As soon as the bus stopped in the middle of Twickenham, she hurried out along the pavement with her bag on her arm, down towards the river, to the darkness of the ladies' toilet there. The shops were full of people, most of them women, just like her.

Inside the cubicle, she started pulling everything out of the bag: the notebook, the dark glasses, the Sainsbury's carrier bag and her husband's old clothes (for some reason, it seemed right to dress like a man to do this). She was still calm as she changed, and wrote the note, and combed her hair and clamped the blue and white sunhat on her head with the brim down over her eyes. But as she walked back out, she began to seethe with fear.

She started to shake and then to cry, and she had to duck back into the toilet to throw up. Slumped in there, sobbing, she started arguing with herself, spurring herself on, mewling, 'You're a failure at everything.'

Somehow, she walked back out again, back along the pavements full of ordinary people, through the heavy glass door of the Chelsea Building Society, and straight up to the counter where, without a word or a pause for thought, she pushed her note under the glass screen. 'This is a hold-up,' it said (she had borrowed the wording from an episode of *The Bill*). 'Stay calm. Don't panic. I've got a gun. So just do as I say. Put all used notes in plastic bag and pass back to me. Wait five minutes before raising alarm.'

The truth was that she had no gun, only a little brown-paper bag which she had stuffed with toilet paper in the ladies' a few minutes earlier so that it would make the right sort of bulge under her jacket. She pushed her crumpled Sainsbury's carrier bag across the counter and half a minute later, she was walking out again with £405 in cash. She had to hurry. She had to get to the playschool to pick up Elizabeth and Clair, but when she checked her watch, she couldn't see the time. She was crying again.

Until that Tuesday morning in September last year, Sue Jones had never knowingly broken a law in her life. She lived quietly in a neat little house in the red-brick maze of Hampton, west London, devoting her time to her four-year-old twin girls and to her husband, Keith, who worked for British Rail at Feltham where he was in charge of drawing up duty rosters. They were the model of a stable, suburban family.

Yet Sue Jones's life had fallen apart for the simplest of reasons: she did not have enough money. She had twisted and turned in search of help but there was none. She had tried pawnshops and bookies; she had contemplated suicide and prostitution. She had worked and saved and stalled and, in the end, she had run out of choices. So she got on the bus to Twickenham to steal the money she needed to keep her family fed and clothed. In the next three months, she committed seven robberies, stealing a total of £7,020.

Looking back now, she can see that the tide of debt had been sweeping up around her for years. In the hope that she can help other women, she has written her own account of what happened. It is the story of a family that started to drown and found there was no one to rescue them.

Sue Jones, who is now 37, had always lived a most ordinary life. She grew up in a one-bedroom flat over a dry cleaners in Battersea opposite the old Granada cinema; her father cleaned windows; her mother kept house for her and her two sisters, Maureen and Debbie. She left school at 15, worked as a telephonist and a secretary until she was 21, when she met Keith, who called the numbers at the local Casino bingo hall. He was clever, confident and a bit of a rebel. And when he took her out walking one evening and draped his jacket round her shoulders to keep her warm, she felt better and safer than she ever had in her whole life. They married a few weeks before Christmas, 1976.

They did well. Keith was marketing director of a building company. Sue had office jobs. They moved away from Battersea to a bigger house in Hampton. They went on holiday to Greece and talked about having children. Then, in the autumn of 1983, it all started to fall apart: the government forced the economy into recession; the building industry collapsed and Keith was made redundant. He was so shocked that he developed a nervous illness, Bell's Palsy, which paralysed one side of his face and kept him off work for 15 months. Sue was working in Sainsbury's, filling shelves, but they had to borrow from the bank to stay afloat.

Then Sue's mother developed lung cancer. On her last night at home before she went into hospital, her mother sat up in bed and took Sue's hand: 'Sue, I know I don't have to ask. You will take care of Dad and Debbie for me?' So when she died, in May 1984, Sue's father, who was no longer working, and her 14-year-old sister Debbie, came to live with them. To cover the extra cost, Sue took on a night job, cleaning railway carriages, from 11 at night until 5.30 in the morning. And she borrowed a little more.

By chasing every vacancy he heard of, Keith managed to find himself a new job, with British Rail. During his illness, Sue had taken over the household finances and she knew that they were sinking further into debt. They owed the bank £6,000 and they had fallen behind with their rent, but she did not want to worry Keith and risk bringing back his illness, so she kept it to herself and tried to get by. Then she became pregnant with the twins. Now she could work only part time.

By the beginning of 1990, Sue Jones knew she was in trouble. 'I had got our bank account overdrawn, mainly with a credit card. Bills, standing orders, direct debits, cheques were not being paid, and everything was in a complete mess. I began to hide demand letters in plastic bags and put them in the wardrobe upstairs. "Out of sight, out of mind" became my motto. I wouldn't answer the phone, took it off the hook.'

Keith was bringing home £745 a month from his work at British Rail. And Sue got £50 a month in Child Benefit. But it seemed to vanish: £200 on rent, £80 on poll tax, £170 to pay off the bank loan, £50 in rent arrears. She had barely £60 a week left for gas, electricity, food, and clothes for herself and Keith, her father, her sister and the twins, Elizabeth and Clair. More and more bills went unopened into the little bags in the wardrobe.

One morning, Clair tore open a letter before Sue had a chance to hide it and showed it to Sue's sister. It was a repossession notice from the landlord. Still hiding the truth from Keith, Sue begged and borrowed £800 to keep the house. Desperate to turn back the tide, she started an evening job, cleaning offices for £3 an hour, and then added a second, late-evening job in a nursing-home, putting old people to bed. Her goal was to save enough to pay for a week's holiday in a caravan at Great Yarmouth, so that she and Keith could relax and enjoy being with the girls alone.

But before she had a chance to save anything, British Rail cut back Keith's overtime and then, in June, they told him they were closing his office in nine months and that he might be made redundant. Within days, he was suffering from Bell's Palsy again. Sue began to despair. 'Everything was now in turmoil. If he was ill again, like before, there wouldn't be any job. There wouldn't be any holiday. No escape. And now I thought: "Please, whoever you are, don't do this to me. I'll do anything. Just don't take this away from me."'

Keith got himself back to work very quickly, but before Sue had a chance to feel relieved, her cleaning company made her redundant and the nursing-home, which had promised her a permanent job, told her that they no longer needed her. 'My immediate thought was: no job, no money, no holiday, no escape. The feeling of being trapped was overwhelming.'

She was still stuffing official letters into the wardrobe without opening them, hoping that somehow she would find a solution before the bills caught up with her. Then a neighbour showed her a letter she had just received from the council demanding her poll tax and threatening to send in the bailiffs. 'I just froze. I had had the same letter, which I had hidden upstairs.'

Just as she felt she had nowhere to turn, fate seemed to offer her a solution. Her father had won a little money by betting on a dog race and he asked her to go into the bookies to pick up his winnings. The bookie was a friendly man, quite charming in his way. Why didn't she try a little bet herself, he suggested. Her dad was a winner. Maybe she would be, too. As a favour, said the bookie, he would let her have a little credit. So she tried it. And she won. Looking back, she wonders whether she really won or whether the bookie was just baiting his trap. But she went home with £60 in her pocket and a bright light at the end of her tunnel.

For the next few weeks, she became a regular punter. The bookie gave her a telephone account and she would simply call up from her home, place bets and hope. She lost, but it was all on tick. She bet some more in the hope of covering her losses. She lost more. She lost track of how much she owed – until one morning, when one of the bookie's friends came round to her house. He was not at all friendly and he made it very clear that if she did not pay off her account, there would be trouble. She gave him her £50 child benefit and pleaded for time. But he kept coming back. The bookie had added interest to her debt and he was now asking for £2,300.

Still, Sue would not tell her husband for fear of driving him back into his illness. Once, Keith came home just as the bookie's debt collector was leaving with another bundle of scarce cash in his pocket; Sue told Keith he was just a passer-by asking directions. She went to a money lender in Battersea but he refused to lend her anything without Keith's signature on the paperwork. She went to a pawnbroker and sold him everything: her earrings, her cross and chain, even her engagement ring.

A few days later, the bookie's man came back. He barged into the house, shouting and threatening, pushed past Elizabeth and Clair and pinned their weeping mother against the kitchen wall. He wanted more money and he threatened to go to Keith if she failed to pay. She bargained for one more week.

'I was now desperate. Time was running out. I had to do something. I couldn't let Keith find out. If he found out about this, he'd find out about the poll tax, the rent, the overdraft. He'd find out everything. What would he do? Would he leave me? Would he take the girls? I couldn't stand it. Everything was in a spin. It was my girls' birthday that week. They were to be four years old. I had no money for a birthday present, no birthday party, nothing.'

That Saturday morning, she told Keith she wanted to visit her mother's grave on her own. Instead, she walked along the edge of the river. 'I needed time to think. Everything was catching up on me. I started to think as I stared into the river. I had tried to work. I had tried to get a loan. I had pawned everything of value I had. None of this had worked out. What could I do? I stood there thinking. I thought about prostitution. Where could I go? King's Cross – that was the place they all went. But how could I get there during the night? I had never left my little girls at night-time. Then I laughed out loud: "My God, who'd have me?"

'I began to walk along the river, around the back, by the church. Should I go in? No. What's the point? He didn't help me before. Look what He did to Mum. I carried on past the new council office, along the shops. As I came to the building society, a lady came out. She held the door open for me. She must have thought I was a customer wanting to go in. As I looked in the open door, I saw a girl sitting there and she looked up and seemed to smile.' An idea began to take shape.

On Monday, the bookie called to say her time was up. On Tuesday, she collected Keith's old jacket and his gardening shoes, the pair of sunglasses she'd worn on holiday in Greece, a notebook and a Sainsbury's bag. She took Elizabeth and Clair to playschool and then she caught the bus to Twickenham.

After the first robbery, she found, to her amazement, that life went on. She went home and hid the money in the wardrobe, cooked lunch, played with the girls, cooked the evening meal. The only problem was that she had not stolen enough to pay all the bills.

Ten days later, she did it again, this time in Clapham, where she came away with £980. She told Keith that she had won some money at bingo and they agreed they could afford their week in a caravan at Great Yarmouth. The truth was that she was still nowhere near to paying off the bookie's debts, the poll tax, the rent arrears and the bank loan. When they arrived in Great Yarmouth a week later, Sue had only £37 in her pocket to pay for the whole week.

'We were all sitting on the grass verge feeding the swans. I told Keith that I had left my building-society book at home, so we would have to be careful that week. He said not to worry, he'd go along with me and sort it out at the local branch and if there was any problem, he'd ring up our bank and ask for a small overdraft. He wasn't angry at me. He was trying to be helpful. I just kept thinking: "If he goes to the building society, he'll find out. Oh, my God, what am I going to do?"'

The answer was that while Keith and the children walked along the beach, Sue said she had to go shopping and went instead to the Cheltenham and Gloucester Building Society in the market place with her usual note and stole £500. Back in London, still fending off debt, she stole again and again. As the robberies continued, she found herself consumed by guilt and fear. She ceased to care whether she was caught or not.

She committed her fifth robbery, in Richmond Road, without any attempt at disguise. Afterwards, she slumped down on a park bench around the corner with the bag of money between her feet. 'I just sat there. I heard the police cars go by. I didn't move. I was glad. I thought they would come any minute now and it would all be over. I waited and I waited, but no one came. I sat there saying to myself, "Why are you so upset? It's no different than usual. Here you are, all alone. Even the police don't care." '

She began to worry that she was frightening staff in the building societies and started apologising to them while she was robbing them. The girl behind the counter on her sixth robbery reminded her of one of her nieces and she thought of how angry she would be if someone treated her niece like this. 'I ran and ran: I just had to get away from that young girl's face. It seemed to chase me along the street. I don't know how I got there, but somehow I made my way to the cemetery. I fell on to the grass by my mum's tree and cried and cried and cried.'

After seven robberies, in which she stole £7,020, she had still not paid all her debts and she was finding it almost impossible to hold together her normal life. Then the world closed in on her. It was a Thursday night, November 29. The phone rang and Sue heard her older sister, Maureen, tell her that her husband had brought home a copy of the *Sun*, and it had this story about a woman who had been robbing building societies – and there were photographs. They had been taken by security cameras and Maureen said they looked just like Sue.

Sue persuaded Maureen that it must be her double, then she called the Samaritans, who advised her to go to the police. On Friday morning, she went to a call box and telephoned Scotland Yard and told them that she would give herself up on Saturday morning. Then she went to the playschool to pick up Elizabeth and Clair.

'I spent extra time with them. I bathed them, washed their hair, read stories, played, made cakes – all those wonderful things you do with your children. That night, I pushed their beds together and got in bed with them. I told them stories, tickled their feet, kissed, cuddled and fell asleep with them.'

The next morning, she took the girls to Maureen's house, where they were putting up Christmas decorations, hugged them and turned away. She asked Keith to drive her to the shops but at the railway station she suddenly got out, leaned back through the open car door and told him: 'I did it. Go back to Maureen. It's in the paper. Maureen will tell you.' Then she ran.

At Scotland Yard, she told the Flying Squad everything. Detectives could see that she was no hardened criminal. A psychiatrist said she was an unselfish and highly moral person. Her family were told that she would be given probation. But at Kingston Crown Court on April 26, Judge Wakley told her she was guilty of 'wicked crimes' and sent her to prison for four years, tearing her away from the family she had been so desperate to protect. Now she is in Holloway Prison.

On Monday her lawyers will ask the Court of Appeal to cut her sentence. Her solicitor, Brian Raymond from Bindman's, says: 'The normal sentencing tariff is meaningless in cases like this. We shall be asking the court to treat her as an extraordinary case, arising out of exceptional circumstances and demanding a special response.'

At Sue Jones's request, the names of her children have been changed. On July 29, 1991, the Court of Appeal released Susan Jones from prison and put her on three years' probation.

August 16, 1991: George Delf

Mock ·justice for Sara Thornton

Entering Durham Prison's 'H' Wing for the first time was a chilling experience. Britain's only maximum security unit for women contains around 40 inmates. It stands, grey and gaunt, alongside the main men's prison, wrapped in its own tight metal embrace of high fencing and razor wire. Clutching the visitor's order sent by Sara, I counted the gates and electronic doors that confronted us. There were eight of them. My prison officer escort, a silent woman with set face, seemed bored. As we passed alongside a section of the men's wing, I glanced up at the huge stone wall dotted with tiny barred windows. There were faces behind the bars, hundreds of pale, silent prisoners, eyeing our progress.

As we entered the final narrow corridor, lit with bright fluorescent light, I was tense. Would she be wearing uniform? Would guards stand close by? Would we have anything to say to each other? I was ushered into a small room, an oasis after our desert trek. Wall-to-wall carpeting, curtains, pictures, coffee tables and low chairs. A small, trim woman rose to greet me. Dressed in pink, brown hair neatly curled, with the broad smile I was to get to know so well, Sara shook hands with me and we sat down.

Our introduction began with her letter in August 1990 to a national newspaper. Concise, it detailed the lack of effective intervention by helping agencies in the months leading up to the stabbing of her violent, alcoholic husband. I wrote to express interest and she invited me to visit. It was her first visit since she had arrived from 'grisly Risley' three months earlier, and six months since her conviction at Birmingham Crown Court. Her defence plea of diminished responsibility had failed and she was given the mandatory sentence for murder, life imprisonment.

Sara laughed when I commented on her smart appearance. 'The girls were almost as excited as I was by your visit,' she told me. 'They tried to get me into high heels, but I thought I'd fall down the metal stairs.' The hairdresser, she told me, was one of two young IRA prisoners. Sara had a quick-witted, often humorous way of talking which reminded me of women I had met in New York.

As we went over the basic facts of her case, I was immediately struck by the contrast between the unpredictable drunken violence of her husband's last month and a defence of diminished responsibility which centred on Sara's emotional history.

Her defence lawyers, David Barker QC and Graham Buchanan, had tried to hit that elusive moving target between the law's 'reasonable person' and the candidate for Broadmoor. They had to prove to the jury that Sara suffered from 'substantially impaired responsibility' and 'abnormality of mind'. They failed.

At the end of that visit, I told Sara I thought she should be free. She wrote to me next day to say that our meeting had 'unlocked' something in her. She had returned to her cell and cried for hours. It was the start of an extraordinary year, for both of us.

Soon after we met, Sara was granted leave to appeal. We examined her appeal papers. The main ground for appeal was the comment in court by the prosecution that if she suffered from incurable abnormality of mind, and if she received a manslaughter verdict, then this would amount to 'a licence to kill'. Further grounds consisted of the blatant sexist innuendo so typical of our courts where women are concerned.

We were both uneasy with this appeal. It followed closely on a defence argument which made little sense to us. And although the prosecution comment was clearly in error, because sentencing is a matter for the judge alone, the remark had been withdrawn and the judge in his summing up had warned the jury to disregard it. It could be said that the line of defence precipitated this comment by presenting Sara as abnormal.

The jury had been left with a disturbing picture of her. They heard little about her patient efforts to rescue her husband from an accelerating spiral of drunken violence, by getting him into a London clinic, by hiding drink, by cleaning up the vomit and chaos left in his wake, by bringing him home off the street. A few months before his death, Malcolm Thornton was found drunk on a motorway. He lost his job as security manager with a national company.

As Sara began to lose her fight to preserve some semblance of a normal home, her 10-year-old daughter Luise was becoming increasingly agitated. It was then that Sara appealed for help, to the police, to the Church, to the social services, and to Alcoholics Anonymous. As an ex-policeman, Malcolm Thornton was well known to the local Midlands police. Some were drinking partners. On five recorded occasions, the police were called to intervene. Warnings could not affect a man engaged on slow-motion suicide. Each of the agencies expressed concern and made suggestions. None responded at the level required. Sara, tired, frightened and demoralised, finally admitted defeat. She went to the nearest police station and charged her husband with assault. The case was due to be heard a few days after his death.

It became clear to both of us that her appeal was misconceived. It did not reflect her experience, and it did not go to the heart of the matter: brutal, cumulative provocation. What was hoped to be her best defence in fact turned out to be the most effective prosecution. We decided to change the defence and find new lawyers to argue provocation.

This was much easier agreed than done. Sara wrote to

the Registrar at the Court of Criminal Appeal, Master Mackenzie. For weeks there was no reply. Finally he wrote, ignoring her decision. She wrote back announcing that she would conduct her own appeal if she could not have new legal advice. Stung into action, he phoned Sara to say she could seek new lawyers.

We found new lawyers, Lord Gifford QC and Edward Fitzgerald, who quickly sought to realign the appeal along the lines of provocation. Ignored by the original defence as not being pertinent to the case as put, expert evidence of the unbearable stress suffered by any spouse of an alcoholic was provided for the Court of Appeal by Dr Glatt, an international authority. He had treated Malcolm Thornton, and wrote of the devoted concern of Sara. He stated that her behaviour was entirely consistent with that of a normal person reduced to utter despair. He made it clear that 'abnormality' should be identified in the alcoholic, not his victim.

True to form, Sara's appeal began on July 19 in a shambles of the Appeal Court's making. Despite all the relevant papers being made available to the court several days earlier, there were 10 cases down to be heard in Court Seven. Sara's was the eighth. Her case was reached at 3pm, far too late to be completed that day. Whispered consultations ensued. Lord Justice Beldam announced that they faced a major problem because the court was due to be reconstituted the following week, but that they had agreed to alter this arrangement. He and Mr Justice Buckley would hear Sara's appeal the following Monday with a new judge, Saville, replacing Rougier, who had other commitments. Relatively trivial in itself but indicative of the general attitude.

Lord Justice Beldam made a brief apology to Sara, who had been woken at 5am for the journey to London, waiting in the basement for most of the day in order to have five minutes in court. All her belongings had been brought with her, in case she was freed. For the QCs, the barristers and solicitors, all funded by the taxpayer, there was no audible apology. For the well-wishers who crowded the public gallery, many of whom had travelled hundreds of miles and taken time off work, not even a glance.

The appeal hearing itself proved that it is not only evil which can be banal. Even at the highest level, our law contrives to wring boredom out of personal suffering. As if to symbolise her irrelevance, Sara was almost invisible behind the high walls of the dock. Her curls lined up in our view with the neat wigs of the men in judgment. During the lunch-break I complained, and she was raised on cushions so we could see her face. She listened silently for hour after hour as the melodrama of her disintegrating marriage became abstract debate for minds as far as Mars from her experience.

Her appeal was dismissed the following week, with the same careful absence of feeling as characterised the whole proceedings. Ensconced above us in wigs and robes, the three judges seemed figures from an 18th-century play. Lord Justice Beldam presided with pink-cheeked calm. The expression with which he refused Sara the right to appeal to the House of Lords will remain with me for a long time. Mr Justice Buckley, with his sharp, small, pale features, stared down without expression, saying little and nothing encouraging. Mr Justice Saville, the replacement, was direct, concise, alert, seeming to draw out Lord Gifford QC with leading questions. Our hopes centred on him. But during the final judgment he looked down at his hands, his tanned face blank.

Mock justice seemed to mimic the shabby mock-Gothic of Court Seven, with its high ceiling, dusty windows, creaking benches, silent microphones and obsequious officials. Power of a sort, but little humanity.

Sara was silenced, her child ignored, the responses of a woman trapped with a violent alcoholic examined with disdain. The law as currently interpreted, the judges implied, was perfectly satisfactory. Sara was not. 'Thank you,' she told them quietly, as she left the court under escort, to return to prison with her belongings, for the third time in a week.

Resilient as ever, Sara seemed to overcome this bitter setback. But when she phoned and I told her of the Birmingham McGrail case she broke down and cried. Demoralised by his alcoholic wife, Joseph McGrail had finally snapped and killed her. He walked free with a suspended sentence. The contrast was brutal. Sara meditated during the night of August 2–3. The next morning she phoned to say she would not eat until she received the same understanding and justice.

The British people care little about law and understand less. They have an instinct for justice and it is alive and well. Probably no hunger strike since that of the suffragettes has caused so much concern among ordinary men and women. It is as if the anaemic body of British law has received a massive blood transfusion. Our task is to translate this vital energy into permanent gain.

What are the main lessons to be learned? It is too early to be sure, but among them are: law without justice is state brutality; justice requires the law to absorb modern insight rather than hire it; psychiatric science is even more fallible than physical science; the medieval pomp of British justice is a dusty and decrepit relic; without feeling and mature emotion, something women tend to know more about than men, our law will remain sterile and justice crippled.

Calls to change the law miss the point and waste time. The English language, even when reduced to legal jargon, is flexible, open to modern interpretation. What is missing in the system, and absent at the Court of Appeal, are minds and hearts with an instinct for justice in the light of modern understanding.

One day soon, if the people of Britain insist, Sara will walk free to greet her daughter. She will have good cause to say to them, without irony, 'Thank you.'

September 28, 1991: Nick Davies

Granny gets her man

There is only a handful of ways by which an ordinary life can suddenly become flooded by limelight. One of them is murder. Another is scandal. Florence Siddons's family has suffered both.

It is the nature of ordinary families that they are caught off balance by these kind of catastrophes. Suddenly they are dealing with lawyers and policemen and journalists and they make mistakes and lose all control of events. But Florence Siddons is naturally fuelled by so much bloody-minded determination that, from the very beginning, she has failed to succumb.

Disaster enveloped Florence Siddons 13 years ago in the spring of 1978. She was then aged 64 and living in a council house in Sinfin, a working-class suburb of Derby, where she had been since the war. She worked in a shoe factory. Her husband, Fred, a bricklayer, had died the previous summer and her four children had long since left home, but she still cared for her 16-year-old grand-daughter, Lynn, who had been raised by her and called her Mum.

On Monday morning, April 3, 1978, Lynn said, 'Ta-raa, see you later,' and went off shopping. When Lynn had not returned by four o'clock, Mrs Siddons went off to look for her. She remembered that Lynn had talked about visiting a boy down the road, Roy Brookes, a shy frail 15-year-old. Roy Brookes told her that he and Lynn had gone walking but then Lynn had vanished while he was peeing in the woods. She thought that sounded odd. When Lynn had still not returned by 10 o'clock, Mrs Siddons called the police, but they said it was too dark to do anything and, anyway, Lynn was probably just stopping out late with a boy. She told them they were wrong.

The next day, two things happened that were to colour the rest of her life. First, Roy Brookes and his mother came to see her and told her that Roy had seen a strange car up by the woods at the same time that Lynn had vanished. Florence Siddons knew there was no road anywhere near those woods and, full of suspicion, she called Roy Brookes a liar.

Then the police came back and said they had looked in the woods and there was no sign of anything and Lynn had just run away. Florence Siddons knew Lynn better than that, so she decided to do the police's work for them; she called her four children and they started their own search.

For the rest of that week, while the police shook their heads, the Siddons scoured the woods, poking under hedgerows, using their family dogs and metal detectors to help. They went to the Easter fair and showed Lynn's picture. They even persuaded Derby County to appeal to fans for information at their game on Saturday. And when Roy Brookes's stepfather, Mick, tried to tell Florence Siddons that Lynn often spent the night in derelict buildings, she knew that was nonsense because, since her husband's death, Lynn had been sleeping in the same bed as her, so she called Mick Brookes a liar too.

On Sunday, they found Lynn's body, stuffed under some bushes down by the old Trent and Mersey canal about 20 minutes' walk away. She had been stabbed too many times to count. Within 48 hours, the police had charged Roy Brookes, but even though Florence knew the boy was a liar, she told the police they had the wrong person.

The police said Roy had confessed. She tried to tell them that Roy was too puny to have killed Lynn or to have dragged her body into the bushes. Then, at the inquest, she discovered that, although Lynn had been stabbed more than 30 times, the thing that had actually killed her was asphyxiation, and she knew Roy had not mentioned that in his confession. By now, Florence Siddons had another suspect, and a few months later, on the eve of his trial, Roy gave a psychiatrist a new version of events which confirmed her view. Roy Brookes blamed his stepfather, Mick. He said Mick was always talking about Jack the Ripper and about stabbing women and he said his stepfather had told him to get Lynn on her own down by the canal. Then he had followed them down there, grabbed Lynn from behind, stabbed her, then stuffed her mouth with mud and water to finish her off and threatened Roy that if he told anyone, he would kill Roy's mother, too.

The police arrested Mick Brookes. He denied everything and was released. But at Roy's trial, in November 1978, the stepfather was accused in the witness box of murder and produced an alibi which collapsed to the point where he was accused of talking nonsense. The jury said young Roy Brookes was not guilty of murder. The judge said he agreed. Florence Siddons no longer had any doubt that Mick Brookes was the real killer. The police said they could do nothing, so she set out to prove it herself.

She needed evidence. She did not even have a phone or a car to work with, but she teamed up with her two daughters, Cynthia and Gail (who was Lynn's real mother) and the three women started to rummage through Mick Brookes's past, sifting his life for clues that would put him behind bars. They began to find things. There were fragments of his personality: the woman who had known him as a child and said that from the age of ten he had been fascinated by knives; the teenage girl who had been to wild parties at his house; the remains of burned pornography they found when they searched his garden in Sinfin.

And there was direct evidence. One Sunday afternoon, his wife, Dot, called Florence Siddons and told her that Mick had run off to a caravan site in Skegness with a 16-year-old girl and that she was ready to talk. Later that week, Dot Brookes spent four hours with the Siddons' family lawyer describing, first, how their sex life was dominated by Mick's fantasies about stabbing, then how she had found Mick burning a knife and a pair of trousers on the evening of Lynn's murder and, finally, how, after months of anxious questions, Mick had turned on her and shouted: 'If you must know, I did kill Lynn – and I fucking enjoyed it.'

All this time, a deep hatred was stirring in Florence Siddons's heart. One Christmas, she was in Woolworths in Derby with Lynn's mother, Gail, when she saw Mick Brookes. She started shouting at him, calling him a murdering bastard and chased him out into the street. Sometimes, she simply stood outside his house and stared while he hid behind the curtains. Her family and friends felt the same. They pushed messages through his letter box, some of them anonymous, calling him a murderer, warning him that someone had been hired to kill him. They painted 'murderer' across his front path. He moved to a secret address on the other side of Derby. Within two weeks they found him and broke his windows and shouted through the letter box that they would burn him out. He moved again. They found him again.

Florence Siddons went public with her campaign. She wrote to MPs and newspapers. She organised protest marches to Derby police station and she and Gail gathered 6,000 signatures on a petition to reopen the case. She produced a car sticker – 'Who murdered Lynn Siddons?' Then she handwrote posters that answered the question. A local MP warned her she might get into trouble naming Mick Brookes. 'I don't mind,' she said. 'I'm doing it for Lynn.'

She and her two daughters kept trawling for clues. When Mick Brookes abandoned his young girlfriend and went home to Dot, they persuaded her to hide a tape recorder under the marital bed in the hope of recording a confession. But then Dot decided she loved Mick after all and went to the Siddons' lawyer and withdrew her statement. Undaunted, the women appealed for information in a local newspaper and two men came forward to describe how they had met Mick Brookes in a pub during the trial of young Roy in November 1978. They had known him for years and he had confided in them that he was worried about going to jail. They had asked him why he should worry, since it was his stepson who was on trial. 'Well,' he had replied, 'we are both involved.'

As the evidence accumulated, Florence Siddons twice persuaded the police to file new reports with the DPP, in 1980 and 1982. But each time the DPP refused to order a trial: Brookes's stepson was an accomplice and, therefore, an unreliable witness; his wife could not be forced to testify against him; the evidence of the two men in the pub was only hearsay. Florence Siddons said this was all legal loopholes; murder was murder and she was not giving up.

Every week, she went to the cemetery and put fresh flowers on Lynn's grave. Every night before she went to bed she thought about Mick Brookes and how she could put him away. She carried a knife in her handbag in case she met him. When her daughter Cynthia saw Brookes and his wife walking in the street, she drove straight at them and sent them running for cover as her car mounted the pavement. She was fined £100 for reckless driving.

In 1983, Mick Brookes tried to escape by changing his name to Mick Goodwood and moving to Peterborough. Florence Siddons traced him. She and her two daughters drove down to Peterborough and sat grimly staring at his new hideaway.

To keep the case alive, she filed for criminal compensation. She was awarded £27. In 1984, despairing of ever persuading Derby police to do justice, Florence Siddons secured an independent inquiry by officers from Mersey-side. By now she was armed with still more evidence: an old friend of Brookes had described his obsessive stabbing of photographs of naked women; the man who had moved into Brookes's last house in Derby said Brookes had confessed to him, 'I did it but they will never get me for it'; and Brookes's own brother had told the police Mick had burned a pair of trousers on the day of the crime.

But when Merseyside police produced a report, recommending that an outside force should start a new murder inquiry, their advice was ignored, and Florence Siddons adopted a new tactic which is now poised to make legal history: she and Gail sued Mick Brookes for damages for the murder of Lynn.

It has been a long struggle. They were granted only limited legal aid and had to organise a sponsored walk and open a stall selling second-hand clothes to raise money. A High Court judge then ruled that they could not sue because too much time had passed. They appealed and won with a judgment that added that one or both of the Brookes was certainly guilty. Then Mick Brookes got legal aid and appealed, saying they had no right to sue him, but he lost. Finally, in July this year, Florence Siddons and her family arrived in the Royal Courts of Justice with their witnesses and their unblunted determination. This Monday, the court will announce its decision. At home in Derby, Florence, now aged 77, has still not succumbed: 'I would never forgive him. You read about people who talk about forgiving but I couldn't. When I think of what he did to Lynn – for nothing, for fun – it makes me sick. Lynn's not here and he's got away with it. It's bad enough when you don't know who the murderer is, but when you know him . . . It's such a waste of life.

'It was the police who messed it up. I'm not saying all policemen are the same. There are some good ones but there are some who have made a lot of mistakes. If I had sat down and thought about how long it would go on, I wouldn't have started. But if I start something, I like to finish it. Perhaps when it's done, Lynn will rest.'

On December 11, 1991, in the High Court, Michael Brookes was ordered to pay £18,600 in compensation to the family of Lynn Siddons for her murder. But he said he was unable to pay, and the family was unlikely to receive the money.

February 19, 1992: Leader

The ordeal of Stefan Kiszko

In a sense, the absence of any political dimension makes it worse. The débâcles of the Birmingham Six and the Guildford Four twisted our system of criminal justice in a gale of public outrage. That outrage had political force. The police bowed, unforgivably, before it. But, whatever the natural anger in Rochdale 17 years ago when 11-year-old Lesley Molseed was brutally murdered, there was no seemingly irresistible pressure to find a culprit – any culprit – at the double. What happened to Stefan Kiszko was without possible excuse.

Yesterday, after 16 years in prison, many of them in solitary confinement, Kiszko was a free and totally innocent man – broken by his experience, secluded in hospital, his life a wrecked victim of a system which failed him. If there had not already been a Royal Commission in being to examine tattered British justice, the plight of Stefan Kiszko would have made one necessary.

The things that went wrong form a dismally familiar litany. Mr Kiszko was held for seven weeks without access to a solicitor. The charge against him was based on his own, uncorroborated confession. The police thought they had the right man: they did not pause to question their own assumptions. And then, utterly dismayingly, the evidence that might have set him free 16 years ago – and which did set him free yesterday – was never produced in court. Mr Kiszko was, is and always will be infertile. The semen staining Lesley's clothing never could have been his. And Kiszko's lawyer – David Waddington QC, who went on to be Home Secretary – was forced, or elected, to run an argument which conceded that the police had caught the right man.

There's naught for anyone's comfort here. Redeeming features come much later: the devoted campaigning of Stefan Kiszko's mother: a hearteningly thorough re-opening of inquiries by West Yorkshire police: the generous, open sympathy of Lesley Molseed's family yesterday. But there is little in this to acquit the system – and even less when you consider that the real turning point in events was a stroke of simple luck. When all else had failed, Mrs Kiszko managed to attract the attention of a solicitor, Campbell Malone, who became absorbed in her fight for justice. Without him, she might still be battling in vain today. And, as Mr Malone himself asked yesterday: what are the chances, as legal aid funds shrink, of anyone finding the time and the resource to keep on fighting? Uncorroborated confessions; forensic evidence not made available to the defence; the luck of the single champion. We have been here before, far too often. The coming Royal Commission has crucial surgery to perform.

March 14, 1992: David Pallister

One year after the Six were thrown out on the street

Paddy Hill woke up on his first morning of freedom and heard his family talking and laughing in another room. He looked at the closed door. 'It was the first time in 16½ years that I had been in a room with a doorknob on the inside,' he recalled yesterday. 'I stared at it for 45 minutes. I was paralysed.'

It has been a traumatic and bewildering year for the Birmingham Six. One minute they were mass murderers, the next internationally famous and free wronged men. They came out to face a regiment of television lights and then, after all the public palaver and curiosity, came the painful process of trying to re-establish the family life they left behind nearly 17 years before.

Only three marriages have survived and there have been nearly 60 children and grandchildren to rediscover between them, as well as the experience of daily life in a changed world.

The six did not have the benefit of pre-release counselling or home leave that prepares prisoners for the outside world. Unlike the Beirut hostages closeted at RAF Lyneham, the nearest they got to some peace and quiet was a couple of nights in a hotel courtesy of Granada TV. 'We were just thrown out on to the street,' says Paddy Hill.

Neither the men nor their families had contemplated life much beyond those first delirious moments of freedom. But they are surviving and all of them, in different degrees, have become involved in other campaigns about miscarriages of justice. As soon as they stepped out of the

court, the names of the Tottenham Three, the men convicted of the Carl Bridgewater murder, and Judith Ward
were on their lips.

That commitment has taken some of the six around the
world speaking about injustice. John Walker has talked to
dockers in Sydney; Paddy Hill has toured 15 US states and
Gerry Hunter met relatives of prisoners on death row in
Jamaica. Billy Power and Hugh Callaghan are on the Irish
Commission for Prisoners Overseas sub-committee dealing with the welfare of prisoners and their families.

None of them returned to Birmingham where they had
all lived for years. There, news of their release was tinged
with a public resentment at the way the celebrations had
overshadowed the other victims of the two pub bombings
in which 21 people died in 1974. The six were jailed for
life.

Some people just could not accept what had happened
at the appeal. Gerry Hunter's two sons, Tony and Gerry –
one working at a vehicle plant, the other in a paint spray
shop – experienced it first hand. On the day of the
acquittal some of their workmates started muttering about
the six being IRA. They left and have not worked since.

John Walker joined his wife, Teresa, in his home town of
Derry where she had brought up their six daughters.
There were also seven grandchildren to get to know and a
stream of commiserating neighbours. 'I could have been
killed with kindness,' he says, recalling the drinks that
piled up before him when he first ventured out to the pub.

With the first £50,000 tranche of his compensation, the
Walkers bought a new neo-Georgian house on the out-
skirts of town, although Teresa was unhappy at the move.
He rowed so much with his youngest daughter, then 18,
that she moved out. Walking to the corner shop was an
ordeal. He sometimes wakes up in a panic, imagining he is
back in jail. 'That scares the life out of me. It can unsettle
me for a long time afterwards.'

After so many years in prison, concentrating on the

single issue of getting out, the strain of finding how to live together has proved too much. The Walkers are now living apart, each with some of the family. 'We are still the best of friends and talk every day,' he says. 'There is no animosity.'

At first John thought it would take a year to get the past out of his system. Now he thinks it will take another, and then another. 'I don't suppose I'll ever really be over it.'

Gerry Hunter and his wife Sandra, who had three children, separated after about three months. Gerry lives in south London, although they keep in touch. Sandra knew it was not going to be easy. 'You've got to fall in love again after so much sorrow.'

Gerry says: 'We were complete strangers, different people, getting at each other's throats. And it was difficult getting to know the kids. You're supposed to take a fatherly role but after being in prison with people telling you what to do that was pretty hard.'

The pace of life was so fast that the first five months seemed like five years. Like the others, he was confused by the volume of London traffic and repelled by the fumes. Being a celebrity ('it's not a word I like') was at once reassuring and trying. 'People meant well but after a while it began to pall.' Still, Gerry Hunter, who became withdrawn in prison, talks like he's on a high. 'Life is good. It's nice to wake up in the morning without prison bars.' Tomorrow he takes off for New York and St Patrick's Day.

The couple thought least likely to get back together have now remarried. Nora Power was a robust and cheerful campaigner even though she divorced Billy in April 1990, a year after their first appeal was dismissed by Lord Lane.

It was something he, as a practising Catholic, never accepted. 'We were back together within a week of coming out and it was the most natural thing in the world. So we went to the registry office. We've had a few arguments but that's how you know you're married.'

Billy, who was the most relentless analyser of his own

case, has been one of the most active supporters of other controversial cases. He makes regular prison visits and he has a job, of sorts, as press secretary to the Judith Ward campaign.

He says he has had few problems in coming to terms with freedom. 'Unlike the Guildford Four, we were mature people. I adjusted to life inside and I was level-headed enough to be realistic about what might happen when we 'came out. The attention from the media was probably the most overwhelming thing. There we were, six uneducated working-class Irishmen and people expected us to be orators with views on everything.' He has started to think of work. 'That's a must for your psychological well-being.'

Another formidable champion was Kate McIlkenny whose forthright handling of the media won her affection and respect. She, too, was under no illusions about the future with Richard, having also seen six children grow up and produce 17 grandchildren.

'He can go off on his own and come back when he's ready,' she told me in the final days of their appeal. She stayed on in Birmingham after the bombings, but they have since bought a bungalow near Dublin. Richard, who studied languages and liberation theology in prison, has also involved himself in the Judith Ward campaign.

Hugh Callaghan, the oldest of the six at 61, and his wife, Eileen, who are still together, have had a tragedy. The husband of their only daughter, Geraldine, was recently killed in a car crash. Geraldine was expecting her second child.

Paddy Hill's wife Pat divorced him several years ago. In a television programme on the wives before the six were released, Pat was unapologetically frank about the emotional and sexual strains of separation.

Paddy had a reputation as a bruiser in 1974, though it was difficult to see in the slight, wiry man who emerged from the Old Bailey the chubby pugilist that went behind bars. After his brutal treatment at the hands of the police, he set his own ground rules in prison. 'I told them, "Your regulations don't apply to me. I'm an innocent man. If you screws give me a hard time I'm going to get a big blade and stab the fuck out of you."'

He is today probably the most fearless about recognising the extraordinary strains of the last year. 'A lot of people think that when you get out all your problems are solved. I wish that were true. Sometimes I'm in a pub, in the best of company, and it's like you're outside your body looking down. You don't feel part of anything.

'Sometimes I feel like bursting out into tears or I have just to walk away. But I'm fortunate that I have a few friends who understand just how emotionally hard it is. There are times,' he says, his voice falling to a whisper, 'when I wish I was back in jail. I mean it.'

He, too, has been a tireless campaigner for other prisoners. 'I promised the first year of my life outside to the lads in prison. I'll tell you why, because I remember lying in that poxy cell wishing somebody would do it for me.'

He still seethes and rages at the system that put him behind bars – much about which is being put in a book which he expects to finish next month. 'This is one of the dirtiest, evilest, corrupted, perverted systems in the world.'

Paddy lives in west London with a son who works as a chef, but he has had little time to see his other five children and grandchildren. 'I don't feel like a father.' He has a girlfriend whom he met at a football match three weeks after his release. 'If it wasn't for her and another good friend I would have cracked up. They've kept my feet on the ground.'

He remains involved in Ireland. 'I'd love to see my country free – a united Ireland. They talk about the IRA as if it was something new. The IRA have been going, under different names, ever since England set foot over there. As

long as there's a Brit uniform there's always going to be an
Irishman or woman prepared to pick up a bomb or a gun
to remove them. English governments have tried everything except withdrawal.'

The search for individual identity has meant that all of
them dislike being collectively described as the Birmingham Six. But the ramifications of the case have been so
great that that is one thing from which they will probably
never be free.

May 12, 1992: Leader

The Holloway One

Unlike other miscarriages of justice against IRA suspects,
Judith Ward had no campaign group. In her own wry
words: 'After the Birmingham Six and the Guildford Four,
the Holloway One does not have much of a ring.' But
eighteen years ago, there was a lot which should have set
alarm bells ringing over her prosecution for three IRA
bombs including the horrific M62 coach bomb which
killed 12 people. If the police, lawyers and doctors had
responded to those bells in 1974, yesterday's decision by
the Appeal Court to free her on all charges would have
been unnecessary.

The latest miscarriage is an indictment of three separate
services: medical, legal and investigatory. Just a month
before her trial, she was considered 'unfit to plead' by
prison doctors. Yet this never emerged at her trial. Not
only was she known to be unstable and prone to fantasise,
the RUC in Ulster had refused to take her seriously. Here
was someone who was not just open to suggestions, but
had a record of invention, insecurity and mental illness.
When she tried to commit suicide, her family was not even
informed. Her confessions were full of holes. When these

were discovered by the investigating police, she changed her story to make it more credible. Finally, when the prosecution was ready to go ahead, five 'inconvenient' and inconsistent elements were not passed on to her defence team.

There are common themes here from earlier miscarriages: a false confession, vulnerable witnesses who need more protection, the prosecution's reluctance to pass on inconvenient facts plus the involvement of the now discredited Home Office forensic scientist, Dr Frank Skuse, who claimed to have found traces of nitro-glycerine on her hands. These answer several questions. Why didn't her defence team do more? The forensic evidence looked damning. Why wasn't psychiatric evidence produced in court? This was an era in which courts refused to listen to talk of 'suggestibility', vulnerability, or neurosis. Why was there no campaign? Here the Home Office played an inglorious role by persuading the prisoner that a campaign would be counter productive.

Several important reforms have introduced more safeguards since Judith Ward took the stand in 1974. The courts have become more sceptical of suspect police evidence: 38 people have had their convictions quashed since the Guildford Four were released 30 months ago. The Royal Commission on Criminal Justice, set up after the release of the Birmingham Six, is already investigating most of the issues raised by Judith Ward's case: interrogation, police supervision, legal advice, the degree to which the system can be 'bounced', plus the invidious temptation in an adversarial system to bend the rules.

Yet the Ward case does raise a new issue: the speed with which courts are ready to accept breakthroughs in medical understanding. Institutional conservativeness has a role. The courts have to protect themselves from false prophets. If they accepted every fad and fancy, there would be even more chaos. But the present delay between new psychological insights and their acceptance by the courts remains far too long.

May 20, 1992: Clare Dyer

Death in the desert

For Sergeant Trevor Smith, a dedicated career soldier, the day he was awarded the Queen's gallantry medal for bravery in the Gulf war should have been the proudest of his life. Smith was in one of two armoured personnel carriers blown up in an aerial attack in the closing days of the war. The citation says: 'Having received shrapnel wounds to his legs, burns to his face and hands and temporarily blinded, he escaped from his turret. Whilst crawling from his vehicle, another wounded soldier stumbled into him as a secondary explosion occurred from both vehicles. Showing great courage . . . he pulled the soldier to the ground and placed his own body over the soldier. A few seconds later as the explosions subsided he continued to crawl forward pulling the injured man with him until help arrived.'

But the medal is poor consolation for Sergeant Smith, whose injuries brought his army career to an abrupt end. For nine of his comrades – boys on the brink of their adult lives – that blast on the afternoon of February 26, 1991 spelt oblivion.

Anyone reading the citation would imagine that the British troops sustained their deaths and injuries under enemy fire. The truth, which it carefully avoids spelling out, is that the fatal missiles were fired by planes of the US Air Force, in the worst 'friendly fire' incident of the war. In what the Americans describe as a 'fratricide incident', two pilots flying A-10 jets each launched a Maverick missile at what they thought were Iraqi vehicles.

How did they come to make such a devastating mistake? The US forces carried out no formal inquiry and the Ministry of Defence refuses to publish the report of the British board of inquiry into the tragedy. For the dead soldiers' parents, the coroner's inquest, which ended this week, seemed their only hope of reaching the truth. But as the evidence unfolded it quickly became apparent that their hopes were to be dashed. Whatever really happened on that February day last year, it was not going to be revealed at Oxford County Hall.

It was always unlikely that an inquest without its key witnesses – the A-10 pilots – could ever arrive at the truth. The coroner has no power to compel anyone outside his jurisdiction to come. But it was only at the weekend, with the jury due to go out on Monday, and after strong pressure from the families' lawyers, that he agreed to send a formal request to the Pentagon asking for the pilots' attendance. The answer, to no one's surprise, was no. Barbara Thompson, whose 19-year-old son Lee died in the attack, said: 'We were told lies right from the beginning – it was in a sandstorm, in the heat of battle. It wasn't until the day before my son's funeral another soldier who was there told us it was in the afternoon and clear and they were resting.'

Unexpectedly, the families got the verdict they wanted – unlawful killing – but along the way, the system put every possible hurdle in their path.

Uniquely among English courts the coroner's court adopts an inquisitorial fact-finding approach, designed to get at the truth, rather than the traditional adversarial stance, where parties line up against each other and one emerges the winner. The system dates back to the 12th century, when the crown had a financial interest in sudden or violent deaths because the land and goods of a convicted felon, and objects which caused death, were forfeited to the crown. In most cases, which are uncontentious, the system works perfectly well. But for the highly charged cases which provoke public anxiety, where relatives are ranged against large institutions with an interest in covering up their errors, coroner's courts are ill-equipped to deliver 20th-century justice.

Parties to a court case are normally entitled to legal aid if they pass the means test, and have the right to call their own witnesses. There are no parties to an inquest – families may be represented, but have no right to legal aid, and the coroner alone decides which witnesses to call. Defendants in criminal cases, and to a large extent litigants in civil cases, have the right to see opposition witnesses' statements in advance, so they know the case they have to meet and can prepare questions to ask in cross-examination. Coroners are not obliged to provide families with any documents in advance. Their lawyers can question witnesses, but not cross-examine as in court: they may not, for instance, accuse a witness of lying. Any points they wish to make will have to be brought out through questioning, because they may not address the jury or suggest possible verdicts – only the coroner can do that.

The friendly-fire inquest lasted six days. Barrister June Tweedie, co-director of the campaigning group Inquest, said it would have been a much more perfunctory affair if the families had not managed to secure the services of a leading QC, Geoffrey Robertson. 'The coroner sometimes tried to stop Geoff, but he just ignored him. You couldn't do that unless you were pretty senior.' Robertson and a solicitor, Mark Stephens, took on the case free of charge. Ms Tweedie said: 'This is a high-profile case which high-profile lawyers are prepared to get involved in. When you get deaths in hospital, deaths in custody, you're not going to get lawyers who are prepared to do it for nothing.' More typically, institutions are represented by large legal teams at public expense, while families – if they're lucky – may get a junior barrister from the Inquest Lawyers' Group to represent them for a reduced fee.

The families' lawyers threatened to take judicial review proceedings against the coroner, Nicholas Gardiner, unless they got witness statements in advance. 'We argued that it was impossible to have effective representation without the papers in advance,' said Stephens. 'We said we needed to speak to air-traffic controllers and ballistics experts. We also said if we were unsuccessful in the judicial review we would publicly withdraw legal representation from the families and indicate that it was not appropriate for us to partake in the legal process when we could not sensibly represent the families.'

In the event, one bundle of statements arrived late on the afternoon before the inquest started and another on the second day. The families had to disclose all their evidence to the Ministry of Defence in return and their lawyers were forbidden to show the statements to their clients or to experts who might have helped frame questions for witnesses. They were fortunate to get advance disclosure at all, said Ms Tweedie: 'Normally the legal team representing the institution has a big bundle of documents and the family has nothing.'

Families may suggest witnesses to be called, but the coroner alone decides who to call. Stephens flew to the USA to obtain evidence about the Maverick missile. Its suitability for use near friendly troops, because of problems in target identification, has long been questioned. But no evidence about the Maverick was called.

The key issue comes down to a conflict of evidence between the A-10 pilots and the British air liaison officer responsible for directing them to the Iraqi target. Flight Lieutenant Fergus McSkimming told the inquest he had given them the right grid reference, but couldn't recall exactly how they had confirmed it. The pilots, in written statements supplied to the coroner, said they had been given no grid reference, but relied on an assurance by the air liaison officer that there were no friendly troops within 10 kilometres, and a description of the target from a departing F-16. The inability to question the pilots leaves a gaping hole in the evidence.

Even where the evidence is clear, inquest verdicts may not point the finger of blame at any individual (until 1977 they could return verdicts of murder, manslaughter or infanticide). Juries' power to attach riders to their verdicts attributing blame for a death was abolished in 1980 after the Blair Peach inquest, which cast blame on the police.

John Spencer, lecturer in law at Selwyn College, Cambridge, and a critic of the inquest system, said: 'I'm not at all impressed with the Government nibbling away at the right of the jury to say anything critical of authority. Every time a jury has produced something critical of authority, the law has been changed and then they say something subtly different and the law is changed again. We need to sort out what coroners' inquests are expected to deliver – are they supposed to be a public clearing of the air or simply deciding the cause of death? I'm not sure the public hasn't got it right in expecting more of them than the law allows at present.'

Coroners are appointed by local authorities and, as Spencer points out, 'there is little or no quality control.' In country areas, many are retired solicitors; in cities, coroners are often doctors without detailed knowledge of legal procedure. The law-reform group Justice recommended in 1986 that each area should have a senior coroner to whom the more difficult cases could be referred. Inquest, which is pressing for an official review of the role and operation of coroners' courts, suggests a supercoroner, with the status of a High Court judge, to handle complicated cases.

Mrs Thompson simply wants to know how her fifth and youngest son met his death. 'All we want is the truth – why this happened. I don't know if we'll ever get at the truth.'

February 1, 1992: Hugo Young

Juror's indictment

Barrington Lee Smallin is a dangerous young man. Not long ago he appeared at Wood Green Crown Court charged with assault, aggravated burglary, theft and unlawful wounding with intent to cause grievous bodily harm. I was a juror in his case and helped decide that he was guilty.

But being on a jury is not just an experience in judgment. On that level my week in court confirmed most of the good things ever written about the jury system. But sitting there offers a much wider canvas to explore. I've listened to parts of cases often enough as a journalist, but never had to stay from start to finish. Whatever else jury service does or doesn't do, it keeps you pinned to your seat for the duration. You're a captive audience for the whole panoply of the law.

This proves to be a more ambivalent experience. It's at the heart of the work of a new Royal Commission, chaired by Lord Runciman. Is the process working? Through questionnaires on thousands of cases Runciman is hoping to build a picture of how the judicial system is assessed by those (excluding defendants, it seems, but including everyone else) embroiled in it. After R v Smallin, a typical mundane, unglamorous, unreported though bloody case, my ratings of the players may seem, given the verdict, a perverse indictment: Judge 7 out of 10, Defence Counsel 5, Police 2, Prosecutor 1. The jury, I am quite certain, deserves 10 out of 10.

The Wood Green Crown Court is in north London, seven stops up the Piccadilly line from King's Cross. With a single, flagrant exception, being a juror there was an acceptable experience. The massive Victorian building has been refurbished at a cost of £8.7m, and both the courts and the juries' quarters are well-designed for the long haul. The chairs are comfortable and the light is good. Naturally it's a great bore to be called, disrupting all other plans. And it involves being plunged into a life of regimentation, herded in and out of different rooms at the lawyers' convenience. But as a herd, you're treated with decent respect. You, after all, have the decision to make. There was no hanging about. And after a case was over, the telephone hotline saved you a futile journey to court next day, telling you when you were not needed.

But there was this grave deficiency. In the morning, the train to Wood Green is always emptying, and by the time it gets there most of the occupants are black. It's the Brixton of the north. Yet in the jury assembly hall, with a hundred or so people waiting to do their citizen's duty, not one black juror was present.

This fact struck several members of the Smallin jury, since Barrington Smallin is a 17-year-old Black. How can it have been? It plainly wasn't a calculated piece of racial discrimination. Among court officials the explanations ranged between poll tax-inspired non-registration to vote – the electoral register is the source of jury lists – and offhand insults about 'literacy tests'. When I later rang the jury summoning office, the spokesman said: 'I'm surprised. Our system is totally random. I would certainly expect some coloured people to have been there.'

In court, however, the point occasioned no remark. Since the case turned in one way on an aspect of blackness, this came to me to seem doubly unfortunate. It could surely never have happened in New York City. Is it a reflection of British maturity, or of an innocence that can hardly last much longer, that almost every person in that court room seemed to think nothing of it? At any rate, 11 white men and one white woman, chosen at random from this random herd (other Wood Green juries that week had a female majority) took their place to try Barrington Smallin.

The charges, though numerous, related mostly to a single incident. Smallin was alleged to have burst into a flat in Hornsey last April, beaten the two young Whites who were there, tied them up, slashed one of them with a knife, stolen the usual gear (bikes, video, camera etc) and removed £500 from a bank cash dispenser having extracted the relevant PIN code from its terrified owner. Smallin, if it was he, was accompanied by two other Blacks, neither of them named at any stage, and both presumably still at large.

There was never much doubt about the law. On this kind of joint enterprise, as far as guilt goes it is all for one and one for all. The prosecution did not need to prove that it was Smallin rather than one of his accomplices who actually did the GBH. All they had to show, as was admitted by both sides, was that he was there. The case turned entirely on identification. Was this black youth, looking like so many other black youths, correctly identified by one of the two young Whites?

In support of this, an earlier episode came into play. Smallin was also charged with attacking the same man five months earlier at another flat. It was someone, it turned out, who had been fleetingly at school with him. The recognition witness was unshiftably firm. The same Smallin he knew from school five years before had done both the attacks.

No other witness, however, could put a name to the face. This was the police and prosecution's problem. How, by the most elementary incompetence, they very nearly failed to resolve it was the issue that dominated my own instructive baptism as a functionary of the English legal process.

The prosecutor was a barrister named Williams, although this detail was not easily discovered. A feature of jury trial is that while the jurors' names are read out loud and clear twice, those of counsel are confined to episodic mumbling between them, and that of the judge is never mentioned at all. It can be discovered from the lists posted on a noticeboard, but otherwise judicial majesty evidently guarantees exemption from the Citizen's Charter: no name tags for these officers of the state.

Mr Williams, it emerged from further inquiry, was a Mr O. Williams, or Owen W. A podgy man with a fruity voice, who looked around 40 beneath his wig, he was of that school of oratory in which the double-breasted suit plays an important histrionic part, the elaborate procedure of buttoning it up being called into service as some kind of visual aid to authority. Unfortunately, in Williams' case, his smooth way with a double-breasted was not enough to conceal a half-arsed forensic performance.

He kept getting the names wrong. At one stage he was persistently referring to the defendant when he meant the victim. Quite often the judge had to ask him to reframe his question, and each time Mr Williams conceded his error without a blink of embarrassment. He seemed quite used to it. 'Haven't you read your papers?' the judge tetchily inquired after one especially egregious omission. Maybe he'd only just got them. It was hard to know whether the sluggard pace at which Mr Williams examined his witnesses owed more to some special cunning he sought to invest in them or to the possibility, as he perused the texts of the statements they'd given the police, that he had forgotten what they were going to say next.

In fact, where Mr Williams met his Waterloo was not entirely his fault. Besides the single witness's evidence against Barrington Smallin, the prosecution's prize exhibit consisted of his finger- and palm-prints on pieces of newspaper strewn around the flat and photographed by the police at the scene of the crime. Plainly, if these were proved, Smallin's defence – that he was never there, that this was a case of mistaken identity based partly on the fact that white witnesses tend to think many Blacks look alike – collapsed. It was the defence's contention that although Smallin's prints were incontestably on the newspaper, the relevant pieces were not the ones in the pictures but had been planted later among the exhibits, having been seized from one of Smallin's places of abode after the pictures were taken.

This argued for an elaborate conspiracy. It put the police in a disgraceful light, having taken a risk for which they needed, among other things, a strong motive. The defence decided to supply this in the form of Smallin's past record, which would normally, of course, have been withheld from the jury. But the defence produced a litany of brushes with the law, some of them serious, showing Smallin to have been a hardened juvenile criminal – but one who had sometimes escaped the penalties the police thought he deserved. This, the defence implied, was the big one: the moment the police thought they could nail Barrington Smallin and put him away for a long time.

Repudiating this subterfuge, however, was not assisted by what happened next. A crucial piece of evidence was mysteriously missing. One of the newspapers most plainly visible in the police photographs suddenly turned out to have gone astray from the bag of evidence supposedly being kept in a secure place before the trial. Although this was not the incriminating item with prints on it, it was the salient piece that would most cogently attest to the claim that the papers in the picture and the papers presented as exhibits in court were the same papers: i.e. that the police were honest and the defence case was a pack of lies.

For the police, therefore, to have mislaid so vital an exhibit was a serious misfortune. The young detective constable in charge of the case, a Scotsman, DC Neil Murray, had no explanation for it. The solicitor from the Crown Prosecution Service – 'if service is the word,' the judge fumed – was absent from court at the moment when Mr Williams needed to produce the crucial newspaper. But it never appeared, even after a night to search for it. The defence counsel did not miss his moment.

Mr Philip Levy was a reassuring specimen of the kind of

legal service available among the advocates hacking round the unchronicled crown courts of London. One must assume that, in keeping with the cab-rank principle of the Bar, Mr Levy does prosecution as well as defence work, but his demeanour on this occasion was that of a hardened defender. It is doubtless possible that DC Murray will some time find himself in court among the officers Mr Levy is leading rather than opposing, but one would have to assume that their professional relations might be a little strained in view of the disdainful manner in which counsel put it to the detective that he had cooked up the whole case of R v Smallin, culminating with this mysterious loss of a vital supportive piece of evidence.

Mr Levy, a small man, with an interrogating style even slower than that of prosecutor Williams, none the less had an air of menace about him. Although his cross-examinations sometimes seemed forlorn, they carried a sense of heavy, if impenetrable, moment. When it became clear what he was seeking to show, his delivery accelerated and his lucidity became unmistakable. By the end of the evidence and the closing speeches, the weight of probabilities seemed to hang puzzlingly in the balance.

It was the judge's turn to hold the floor. Judge Jarlath John Finney. A circuit judge, *Who's Who* reveals, since 1986. Born in 1930, an habitué of the south-east circuit, as barrister, recorder and judge for more than 35 years, and according to one of the middle-aged lady ushers whose job is to keep this show on the road, their steady favourite among the judges at Wood Green.

Judge Finney had thus far been a swift and vigilant presider: helpful to the witnesses, exigent towards the barristers, unpatronisingly courteous in his remarks to the jury as they were shuffled in and out of court while points of law were decided in their absence. He had his ways of lightening the wearisome days, revealing, for example, a Mastermind's ability to convert any imperial measure into metric equivalents in his head. This head, moreover, proclaimed a desire to escape from the imposed anonymity of his profession. Beneath the depersonalising wig and above the uniform robes, Judge Finney cultivates a rich growth of facial hair suspended from his cheeks and tonsured at the jaw-line.

His address to the jury was a model performance. Since the law involved in the case was neither complex nor disputed, he had less to do than usual. By far the judge's most useful function is to remind the jury of the early evidence. He has taken a copious note, and can therefore recreate on the last day what is easily forgotten from the first. Judge Finney was good at this, in a calm and unloaded way. The only deviation that might have been held against him occurred when he was dealing with the plausibility of the defence's dramatic accusation, and in the course of this described one of the police witnesses, a civilian scenes-of-crime officer, as 'an independent expert'. This was not the most credible depiction of a man who, while not in uniform, works day after day alongside police officers. But this was a blemish. For the rest, Judge Finney dispatched us to decision with a clear and balanced remit.

At this point my story must become more obscure. So far everything I've written derives from being a mere observer, albeit one who was concentrating more than usual, in a public court. It would be open to anyone who turned up to make the same report. Once in the jury-room, however, the law intervenes. Not only must jurors refrain from discussing the case with anyone while it's going on, but what is said in the jury-room is protected by the Contempt of Court Act. I do not intend to break it by describing the course of our deliberations.

Some impressions can be conveyed, however. The first and overarching one is of our almost agonising honesty. We were together for more than five hours, isolated from the world until we finished. At the start, there was a wide variety of opinion about the charges, the resolution of which was not assisted in any way by the inadequacy with which the police and prosecutor had presented their case. A finding of not guilty would have been crippling for the police. Although it could just about have been brushed aside as merely a technical failure to meet the normal test of guilt 'beyond reasonable doubt', the message shining more luridly out would have been that this was another frame-up. To a remarkable extent it was the jury, making its own examination of the evidence, including the exhibits and the photos sent in with it, who saved the police from this humiliating outcome and decided, unanimously, that there could be no trace of a doubt about Smallin's guilt.

This jury conformed to few of the familiar caricatures. Everyone could read and write, all without exception paid close attention to everything that was said, each one of us was palpably anxious to do our duty. Newspapers on display ranged from the *Sun* to the *Guardian*. In five hours of intensive discussion, it becomes pretty clear what people's arguments are made of, and in all that time not the faintest trace of racially-based opinion entered anyone's discourse. What people wanted was certainty and more. Even after certainty became clear, no hypothetical possibility was left unexamined, however outlandish, to test the possibility that Barrington Smallin might indeed, despite everything, have been framed.

Two thoughts especially impressed me as the court process neared its end. The first was that we were fortunate to be conducting it in the perfect laboratory circumstance: when the case started, we knew nothing whatever about Mr Smallin or any details of his life and work. This was the situation jury-trial aspires to, where no pre-existing prejudice pollutes the course of justice.

The rules of court designed to this end often seem irksome. Not only does the jury come with empty minds, the way the case develops often contrives, especially at the start, to leave them confused. This is not a straightforward unfolding of the story, but one which is marked by obscure silences and mysteriously unput questions. Slowly you sense you are getting a case from which the procedural formalities exclude the search for total truth. At moments one wants to scream at the barrister to ask the obvious question, and one could never be sure in this case why he hadn't asked it. All the same, this sense of watching a case from a position of fresh innocence, through a glass that filters out some of the surrounding 'reality', is an aid to judgment. It made me look with new respect on the problems that must confront everyone concerned in any case where, through prior publicity, it is impossible to assemble a jury guaranteed to know nothing more than it hears in court. That seems to me, by definition, a seriously different trial experience even though the law does not say so.

Secondly, an invaluable accessory before the fact of jury-service is television. It was slowly borne in on me that we English probably make good jurors partly because of the diet of whodunnits that contributes to so much of our television intake.

The law, in this respect, is quite different from politics. Take 12 good persons and true, and you couldn't rely on getting a decent political discussion going between them. Many would not even want to begin. But offer them witnesses to believe, facts to sort out, policemen to suspect, a judge to be wary of, barristers to scorn, evidence to examine, and you find that inside the skin of the average Englishman and woman there runs the blood of a meticulous, undeceivable descendant of Sherlock Holmes.

This was a case of Sherlock multiplied by Twelve: each recalling different parts of the evidence, each assisting the others to piece the bits together, each displaying a mind ready to be persuaded of the truth. It was the most serious Platonic dialogue in which I have ever engaged.

What it did not do, however, was to determine the final fate of Barrington Smallin. Finding him guilty was not quite the end of the story. He then had to be sentenced, which was where Judge Finney contributed his own lapse from perfection in my book, and called to mind another set of the problems to which Lord Runciman's Royal Commission should be addressing itself.

How and why judges pass sentence the way they do is already the subject of an abundant literature. In David Hare's marvellous play, *Murmuring Judges*, which no one interested in these matters should miss while it's in repertory at the National, the debate about sentencing policy comes out of the mouths of a High Court judge and the Home Secretary, perambulating in their black ties before a grand dinner at one of the Inns of Court.

Judicial independence, ventures the judge, is part of an infinitely precious tradition. The Home Secretary agrees but tentatively suggests there is always time to change. Picking his way delicately round the subject, he finally lets rip. 'To be frank,' he gasps, 'we're reaching the point where we'll run out of ways of requesting the judiciary to be less *trigger-happy*. We've nowhere to put these bloody prisoners you keep sending us,' he finally explodes. To which the judge retorts with a smooth well-honed speech about how judges must decline to become 'an instrument of government convenience'. It is a telling scene, full of the velvety dialogue of the British establishment classes.

Barrington Smallin's crimes were serious, with grievous violence done. Moreover, he had been violent before and had not responded to non-custodial sentences with which he was favoured as a juvenile. All the same a certain shock attended Judge Finney's abrupt exercise of his independence, compared with any number of other sentences handed down for offences involving as much or greater violence. With a five-minute lecture, he sent Smallin to prison for nine years.

Minding their business

December 6, 1991: Ben Laurance

The week the Maxwell scandal broke

At 8.25 on Monday morning, investors were perplexed when Stock Exchange information screens broadcast the news that shares in Robert Maxwell's two public companies were being frozen.

It was less than four weeks since Maxwell had died off Tenerife, prompting the *Sun*'s front page to ask the question: Did he fall or did he jump?

It was clear that his private empire was swamped in debt. His sons Kevin and Ian were looking gaunt from the strain of trying to keep their father's corporate creation intact. Rich men around the globe were weighing up whether £750 million was a reasonable price to pay for the glory of becoming proprietor of Britain's second-largest selling newspaper.

Until that morning, only a tiny coterie of City accountants and merchant bankers knew the ghastly truth that was to unravel over the coming days.

Post-Tenerife reporting of the Maxwell business saga had been confused. Newspapers, radio and television had repeatedly muddled the distinctions between the private and public sides of Cap'n Bob's business empire.

It was an easy mistake: Maxwell's global operations were of byzantine complexity, using off-shore funds, charitable trusts and every tax-avoidance device known to accountants and lawyers.

Professional investors knew that Maxwell's personal empire was in a mess. But they also knew that the Mirror group, MGN, was safe. Maxwell's family controlled 51 per cent of the shares, but there was a water-tight barrier between the Mirror group's finances and those of the Maxwell family.

After all, MGN had been floated on the stock market only six months earlier. Its accounts had been crawled over by an army of financial experts; everything had to be tickcty-boo.

The other quoted company, Maxwell Communication Corporation, was trickier: it was known to have lent to and borrowed from the private empire. It also had heavy debts of its own, most of which had been acquired in 1988 when it paid $2.6 billion for the Macmillan publishing giant in the USA.

But it, too, was a stock market company with accounts which had to meet the standards laid down for quoted groups. The Maxwells owned two-thirds of MCC, but the collapse of the family's finances need not spell the end for the publishing group.

Hence Monday's sense of shock when the stock market was told that shares of MCC and MGN were both being suspended because of the need to clarify the position of the family empire. The media might have got it wrong, but the City knew where the distinction between the private and public companies was drawn.

Over the previous seven days, Kevin and Ian Maxwell and Sir Michael Richardson of the merchant bank Rothschilds – friend of Margaret Thatcher, newly-appointed adviser to the Maxwell sons and one of the Square Mile's most powerful and influential figures – had been discovering that not only had the media muddled the distinctions, but so too had Robert Maxwell.

Sir Michael and two senior colleagues from Rothschilds had been delving into the family empire. They worked with accountants Coopers & Lyband Deloitte, who had for years audited the accounts of many Maxwell family companies. 'The further we dug, the more awful it became,' said a source yesterday. 'The inkling that there was something seriously wrong came within a day or two. It just got worse and worse and worse. If you have a complex spider's web of transactions you don't just discover it in 10 minutes.'

By last weekend, the appalling truth was becoming clear. Rothschilds and Coopers had found that in the last months of his life, Maxwell had: dipped into the Mirror group to finance his private businesses; borrowed heavily from MCC; ripped off funds held on behalf of thousands of pensioners and employees of the *Mirror*, and the small British arm of MCC and private Maxwell businesses like the European and market research company AGB.

The Maxwell brothers and the inner sanctum of bankers and the accountants from Coopers kept their secret. But by Sunday, it was clear that lenders to the private companies would have to be told.

A meeting was hastily convened on Sunday evening. Rothschilds and Coopers spelled out the discoveries to a small group of bankers. They agreed two things. First, they would say nothing to anyone else. And second, shares in MCC and MGN would have to be suspended the following day.

Following the Monday announcement, financial journalists faced a wall of silence. Sir Michael, whose City reputation usually gives him the confidence to give away a few morsels to appear in print, was as charming as ever, but firm. 'I would love to help, but we have agreed to say absolutely nothing.'

Sir Michael, and the Maxwell brothers themselves, held the line. But by late afternoon, news was percolating through the banking establishment.

A source said: 'When this business about the pension funds comes out, the whole thing could blow.' Yesterday, he was proved right when the accountancy firm Arthur Andersen were called in to pick up the pieces.

A group of about 30 banks owed money by the family empire was to meet the following day. They were to be addressed by the 'steering committee' of their peers, which had told Coopers to pin down how much Maxwell owed to whom. The steering committee wanted to hold back all the bad news until that Tuesday meeting but by late Monday evening, the story was seeping out. First editions of the *Guardian* reported that the accountants had found a huge gap in pension funds linked to Maxwell. At the centre of the scandal was a tiny and little-known offshoot of the private family companies, Bishopsgate Investment Management. Robert Maxwell had been in charge of BIM: that much was clear. But how could an offshoot of a family company have become involved in the misappropriation of assets held on behalf of pensioners of public companies?

And were the Maxwell sons linked to the scandal?

On Tuesday morning, Kevin and Ian met their bankers at the Chartered Insurance Institute in the City.

Richard Stone from Coopers stood up to speak. When the assembled bankers heard the gravity of the situation – and realised how much of their money they might never see again – an audible gasp went round the hall.

But they were prepared to give the Maxwell brothers a

further three days. They agreed not to pull the plug before Friday. But unless Kevin and Ian could come up with hundreds of millions of pounds by then, the empire would crumble.

Kevin held out the hope that a mystery investor might be found. Even the men from Rothschilds looked worried. Few of the men in pinstripes at the Tuesday meeting seriously believed that a saviour could be found.

Shortly after midday, the Maxwell brothers left. Ian, who had taken over his father's stewardship of the Mirror group four weeks before, returned to the MGN headquarters at Holborn circus.

Kevin went next door to Maxwell House, the headquarters of the group created by his father. A meeting-room was packed with newspaper reporters and television crews.

Under the glare of television lights, Kevin smiled, sat down and calmly announced that he was giving up the chairmanship of MCC. David Shaffer, from the company's Macmillan US offshoot, took over control as group managing director.

Kevin Maxwell said there was a conflict of interest between his role as inheritor of the private companies and his chairmanship of the public publishing group.

It was a masterly performance. When asked to speak in French for a Paris TV crew, he did so. When asked if money had vanished from the pension funds, he unhesitatingly replied: 'I can't say.' Without blinking an eyelid, he revealed that the family companies had borrowed hundreds of millions of pounds from MCC itself, not just the pension funds.

He remained polite and composed. The journalists, too, showed remarkable lack of hostility. They had yet to discover what Rothschilds had known for two days. They were unsure what questions to ask. (Later that day, Sir Michael rang the *Guardian*. He was still refusing to comment but about one thing he was certain: 'Wasn't Kevin brilliant!')

In the *Mirror* building, Ian was facing persistent questions from increasingly anxious staff worried about their pensions.

There was pressure for him to resign. One by one, fellow directors were called into his office. Joe Haines, the *Mirror*'s veteran political columnist and respectful biographer of the 32-year-old's late father, urged him to stay. One further *Mirror* director said likewise. The remaining nine told Ian Maxwell his time was up.

They, unlike most outsiders, knew that both Kevin and Ian sat as directors of BIM, the investment company which had handled most of the *Mirror* pension money. The company's press office was told that the following morning's *Guardian* would publish details of BIM, its directors and its role as manager of money which was meant to be for the benefit of staff retiring from the *Mirror*, MCC and AGB. Much of the money had gone in the pet projects of Robert Maxwell.

That evening, the Mirror group confirmed that its pension funds had been plundered. It put no figure on the shortfall. Ian Maxwell had decided to quit. A terse statement from the group said that he, like his brother, faced too great a conflict of interest to continue.

In the *Mirror* building, sub-editors who four weeks before had prepared a front page to report dramatic news from the Canaries with the huge headline THE MAN WHO SAVED THE MIRROR, set to work. They agreed on a similarly stark approach. Two days ago, the tabloid proclaimed: MILLIONS MISSING FROM MIRROR.

The affair had become a full-blown scandal. Just 24 hours before, on Tuesday morning, people close to the Serious Fraud Office had admitted that it was not keen on having to investigate the Maxwell empire. It feared that it had too few staff to cope, given the huge burden of its existing workload.

But by Wednesday, the pressure for a fraud investigation was irresistible. The SFO – working with detectives from the City of London police – launched an inquiry.

The full extent of the gap in MGN and MCC's finances was becoming clearer, but there was still a fog of ambiguity around the size of the sums which had gone walkabout.

As late as Wednesday this week, even Ernie Burrington, the ex-editor of the *People* who had agreed the previous evening to become chairman of MGN, admitted that the position was uncertain. 'The quantum of the problem we are looking at appears to vary from day to day,' he said. That morning, there had been reports that MGN itself – as opposed to its pension funds – was owed £50 million.

A few hours later, the picture had changed. A senior *Mirror* figure admitted: 'It seems it could be twice that.'

Nominally, the SFO investigation was into the affairs of the *Mirror* pension scheme alone but the City's investment fund management watchdog IMRO pointed a further finger. It announced its own inquiry into BIM – and into a further Maxwell-controlled company, London & Bishopsgate International Investment.

The investment company had changed its name just two weeks ago to Maxwell Central and East European Partners. This seemed curious – until yesterday, when it emerged that the tycoon had used the Partners name to buy assets in Eastern Europe.

Mirror pensioners and staff were more interested in how much money had vanished than in where it had gone.

By late on Wednesday, the picture was clearing. It was estimated that: perhaps £350 million or more had gone from pension funds; around £250 million had been borrowed from MCC; a further £100 million had gone from the Mirror group.

That night, a further *Mirror* front page was assembled. It

suggested an improbably precise number. The headline ran: £526 MILLION IS MISSING.

Burrington said the sordid affair of his late boss's finances suggested 'the increasingly desperate actions of a desperate man'.

Everyone who had anything to do with the Maxwell family companies was told to sever their links with the remainder of the pension funds. New, squeaky-clean trustees were sought to oversee what remained.

'I take the point that there is not enough worker representation,' said Burrington. Control of the funds would have to be done 'in a way which was impossible when Robert Maxwell held all the aces'.

From next spring, the Government will put a 5 per cent limit on the amount which a pension scheme can invest in its sponsoring company. Labour's spokesman Michael Meacher rightly pointed out that this would not have stopped Maxwell. Most of the missing money went into his private companies, not the public ones. The BIM-run fund held only a relatively small stake in MCC, for example – about 25 million shares.

And yesterday at 11 o'clock, one month to the day since their father tumbled from his yacht *Lady Ghislaine* into the Atlantic, the Maxwell brothers admitted that the private empire was bust.

There was no white knight, no new funds – just a gaping financial hole.

An international network of firms built up by a man with a liking for gambling, bow ties and large cigars fell under the control of John Talbot, a taciturn accountant with a passion for snooker. The family group owed £1.4 billion, said Mr Talbot.

In yesterday's *Mirror*, Haines admitted to being shocked. It was 'an awful week, the worst I can remember'. But even though he now knew that Maxwell had plundered the funds of pensioners, Haines retained some loyalty to the publisher whom he served for so long. He called him 'the man who once genuinely saved the *Mirror*'.

Maybe so. But few *Mirror* pensioners will celebrate.

December 6, 1991: leader

No surprise about Cap'n Bob

Students of the human comedy will smile a bitter smile. The script is fit for Ben Jonson. The canvas belongs to some modern Hieronymus Bosch. One moment, last month, Robert Maxwell was dead, and the world teemed with uneasy eulogy as the great man was laid to rest on the Mount of Olives, below the pink ramparts of the Intercontinental Hotel; one moment, this month, there is a black hole in the pension fund, an edifice in ruins, and the tributes turn suddenly to gall.

All manner of lessons, of course, are there for the learning. Pension-fund lessons, with mandatory legislation attached. Lessons of corporate governance and ineptly trusting regulation. Lessons for mighty banks, who dozily thought they could manage a cad, but never dreamed they were handling a bounder. Lessons for the conscience of lawyers brandishing a law that made them fat, but which hides rather than reveals malfeasance. But no one, in this first flush of indignation, should expect too much to happen; for such lessons, every last one of them, in detail, were there for the learning in the Department of Trade report on Robert Maxwell decades ago. He didn't change his spots; human folly and forgetfulness merely allowed him to repeat his exercises on a grander scale, spreading wreckage and destruction. Outrage is out of place; it is embarrassment that rules the day.

Such lessons, anyway, are not really the point about Captain Bob; and there is no single stable door to be bolted forever aft on the *Lady Ghislaine*. His story, suddenly spilling forth, is far from complete; his self-appointed role as saviour of and publisher to the old Iron Curtain dictatorships, his path across further continents, barely yet begun. But, no matter how great the surprises to come, they will not be at root so very surprising. The point about Robert Maxwell was that anything was possible. There's no single word to describe him. A crook? That's a narrow, petty little word. Maxwell built things, saved falling enterprises, pounded on. He created more than mayhem. A bully? A megalomaniac? The words do not suffice because he was all of these things and more: a monstrous, innovative ego who – that DTI report again – had boundless, heedless faith in his own abilities, and acknowledged no rules but his own. And that's inevitably a complex mix: brilliance and malevolence intermingled. Pension-fund rules can and must be strengthened. Executive directors ought to have their backbones stiffened. But that will only curb the pinstripe spivs, the smaller fry of fraud and deceit. For another Maxwell, there are no rules that cannot be broken.

The real reflection, then, is over how a booming, buzzing, blustering personality – a balloon of certitude – can dwarf and cow the judgment of ordinary mortals. And here, queasily, there is a lesson. Life occasionally throws up such men; and women. In all shapes and sizes. (One such, more benign, left Downing Street a year ago.) They fill a seeming need. We perennially clamour, in every walk of life, for leadership and bow in its shade: a servile deference. But beware. Robert Maxwell, on any stage, is the man to remember: a case study in the suspension of judgment.

Hindsight, and revelation, bring many humiliations.

The managers who leapt to attention when he beckoned, or stood outside when he shut the door, look puny and bemused. His eager hagiographers seem absurd, the groundlings of Bartholomew Fair. And, dismayingly, those politicians who paid him court are diminished too. There is now a great Labour Party wailing (reflected in our letters today) about the role of the *Mirror* and the party staunchness of Captain Bob. With respect, that is perspective gone topsy-turvy. Some Labour leaders – Neil Kinnock – kept their distance. They felt – because they sought to lead – that there was some company not to keep. They sensed a disaster waiting to happen. They were not prepared to mingle for favours, as though the fate of the party depended on fawnings. It is a deeply held article of Walworth Road faith that the *Mirror* is important because it is the one true friend of the party. Well, perhaps: though a theory much overblown. But, in truth, the *Mirror* is and will surely remain a Labour paper because that is the character its readers want and buy: not because of cosy canapés and confidences with the Captain. Social democratic parties all over Europe have a bad, salon habit of getting into bed with the rich and cynically compliant, as though such encounters bestowed special power. The Maxwell experience, at least, should send them scuttling towards the exit.

Hour by hour, now, the empire destructs. In the end, many banks will be poorer: and their shareholders ought this time to demand heads on platters. In the end, there will be new laws, to be policed by larger, tougher teams of regulators. In the end, we guess and hope, there will still be a *Daily Mirror*, still voting Labour – and paying its pensioners from squeezed profits. In the end, there will still be many good businesses that Maxwell bought or founded, flourishing alone. In the end, too, there will be a trail of failures and sad redundancies and betrayals for time to erase. But pause over a haunting question: *if* he had not died off Tenerife, the abrupt puncturing of the balloon, would any of these things be remotely clear or suspected or published beneath the familiar, ordurous mountain of writs – or would Mr Maxwell, with familiar aplomb, not this morning have been launching the *Mirror*'s Christmas Bingo for the cameras? It was the man who hid all and kept all together. We shall surely see someone of his like again. Beware.

August 8, 1991: Catherine Bennett

Treasure island

Discretion is guaranteed. Confidentiality is assured. In a small, sweaty room in the Cayman Islands, two American tourists are being soothed by a video made by a local bank. Over and over, at twice daily showings, the video tells tourists why they should put their money in the Cayman Islands.

Why? Well, for one thing: 'The Caymanians are renowned for their honesty and integrity.' For emphasis, the film shows you devout Caymanians spilling from a Sunday service. But most banks in the Caymans are not owned by members of the Grand Cayman Presbyterian Church. They are not even owned by Caymanian atheists. They are owned by foreigners. They were put there expressly for foreigners in the 1960s, when the Cayman Islands were discovered for the second time and turned into a 'tax haven', or privy piggy bank.

Until then, no one had bothered much with the Cayman Islands, three rocky, swampy, mosquito-infested blobs of land in the Caribbean, 180 miles north-west of Jamaica. Christopher Columbus discovered the islands in 1503 but no one attempted to settle them until they were acquired by Britain in 1670 (as part of a job lot with Jamaica) in the Treaty of Madrid. They were not much of a prize. All you could do for a living there was kill turtles, barter with passing ships or go to sea. When the islands became a dependency of Jamaica in 1863 no one seems to have missed them. The inhabitants carried on fishing for turtles, going to church and mingling genes.

Then, in 1962, Jamaica became independent. The Caymans chose to stay British. Almost overnight, the Caymans moved up in the world. They got a government and a constitution. The mosquitoes were exterminated, making life more agreeable for the tourists. And the new government invented special banking laws, to make things inviting for foreign bankers. The bankers came, and the population grew from 17,000 to its current 28,000, a little smaller than that of Bury St Edmunds.

The result is now a country-sized version of Dickens's Veneering family. A brand-new population, in a brand-new town, in a brand-new quarter of the Caribbean. The Cayman airport, cars and shops are new. Their buildings may look as if they were designed and built by concrete-happy amateurs but they are new. Their crimes are new. Their drug problem is new. Their Burger Kings and Pizza Hut are new. They didn't have a carnival, so they invented a new one – Pirate's Week!

Every day, the Cayman Islands get newer and newer. Every day more tourists arrive, off cruise ships, off aeroplanes. Dressed like giant toddlers, in shorts and pumps, they burn in the sun, disport themselves in the duty free shops and pay $25 to watch the video telling them why they should invest yet more money in the Caymans.

'Most of us,' the video tells the toddlers, 'have worked very hard to accumulate various assets.' And, it says, there are two views about assets. One view, clearly defective, holds that your assets should be public knowledge. This view is favoured by many tax inspectors. The other view, preferred in the Caymans, says that 'the individual has a right to financial privacy'. This right the Caymans will, if not fight for, at least legislate for. The islands have

stringent confidentiality laws, which forbid financial institutions from supplying information about their clients.

Better still, the Caymans demand no personal taxes, no
company taxes, and they have no exchange controls. So
why not set up a totally secret, untaxed trust? 'Trusts need
not be registered with the government, thus enhancing
the confidentiality pertaining to your personal assets.'
Why not set up a totally secret untaxed company? 'The
actual beneficial owners of a corporation need not be
disclosed.' You don't even have to go there. 'We can
provide directors, offices and nominee shareholders.' Put
your money in the Caymans, and nobody, and especially
not that nosy parker, the Inland Revenue, will ever know
what you're worth. 'Have you ever wished to have any of
your assets held in a corporation where no one could
determine who was the absolute owner?' Of course you
have. Just choose your management company. Or
approach one of the 535 banks.

Until July 5 there were 538 but now three Cayman
branches of the Bank of Credit and Commerce International are in the hands of liquidators. Injunctions have
been served on eight affiliated companies. The bank's still
there in the phone book: 'A Special Commitment to
Service . . .' Fountains are still spurting outside its ostenta-
tious flesh-pink and white headquarters but no one wants
to know them any more.

'The action we are taking is making it perfectly clear that
we do not want bad banks here, so in a sense it is good
news to us, we are getting out what has been a very black
sheep,' said Alan Scott, the British Governor of this briny
quag, a cheerful friend to tax avoiders. Although Scott
would shrink from the word *evasion*. 'There is a difference between tax *avoidance* and tax *evasion*,' he said.
Avoidance and evasion mean exactly the same thing in
plain English if not in legalese. But no matter. In the
Caymans the distinction is daintily maintained. 'That's
from the point of view of the other jurisdictions,' said the

Governor. 'From our point of view there can be no offence because we don't have tax.'

British tax laws are of no importance in the Caymans, which are, however, dependent on Britain for defence, security, external affairs. Britain's real significance in the Caymans is as a guarantor of 'stability', evidence for investors and tourists that they and their money are safe from revolution, disturbance or any sudden, fiscal change born of envy or local discontent.

Photographs of the extended Royal Family are strewn around government offices, heavy hints that this tax haven is *respectable*. No one could be primmer than the Caymanian politicians and financiers, with their framed certificates, empty desks and rows of gold pens, their laborious denials that anything could be improper about secreting money away from the proper authorities, their pride in a brand-new Mutual Legal Assistance Treaty with the USA, which allows the secrecy laws to be lifted if the American authorities can prove that funds were raised illegally. It does not, naturally, cover tax enquiries, from the USA or anywhere else.

'I mean,' said Norman Bodden, Minister of Tourism, 'if the UK has laws and they cannot control their own citizens, why should they expect *us* to control their citizens?' He remembers people arriving with suitcases of money but that was *long* ago. Back in the 1970s. 'Maybe during those days we did have crooks and people but, sister, we don't want them here. The banks and their systems have long been removed from that sort of scene.'

'It must be established that we are an important international banking centre,' said Jennifer Dilbert, the Islands' deputy Inspector of Banks, who sniffs at 'tax haven' and even attempts to deny what the bankers proclaim – that confidentiality is a powerful attraction.

Dilbert's office gave BCCI a licence when it opened in 1975 and has been earnestly checking its accounts since. Were they satisfied with what they saw? 'We weren't satisfied, looking at BCCI as an individual entity, no. We were asking questions about large loans and things we had seen in the Cayman Island books,' said Dilbert. But the Caymanians had joined the Bank of England's college of supervisors in 1989 and were prepared to be patient. 'We were satisfied to wait for the college to work it out. It didn't make any sense for us to act on our own, because we knew the restructuring package was being put together.'

So the bank continued to trade, to hold lavish Christmas dinners and to attend the lunches of the Cayman Islands Bankers Association. 'They were doing nothing wrong – publicly,' said Rosaleen Corbin, president of the association. 'If it is, as has been said, an out and out deception to the auditors, well, how could the public be aware of anything?'

Well, they might have read about BCCI's role in the Tampa cocaine-money laundering case in 1988, to which the Cayman subsidiary later pleaded guilty. 'That doesn't mean, because they are doing something wrong in one country, you don't even talk to them, or you throw them out of your association,' said Corbin, illuminatingly. 'They hadn't done anything to break the laws of our country.'

In her deserted but prosperous bank, where she accepts only deposits of over $10,000, Corbin was resolutely unconcerned about the effect on the Caymans' reputation. 'Why should it worry people?' she said, all at once deciding that the Tampa case *should* have warned people off. 'If anyone put their money with BCCI since that date, they did it with their eyes open. If you still, after reading those reports, put your money there, who are you going to blame? The Inspector of Banks? He didn't force you to put your money there.' Could it be, she suggested blandly, that these late investors had been motivated by *greed*?

Perhaps these greedy people had missed, like the Bankers Association, the rumours about BCCI, which, according to some residents, had long been circulating in the Caymans' distinguished banking community. One prominent expatriate deliberately kept his distance. 'We all knew there was something but nobody could put their finger on it,' he said. 'It's just the way they cultivated politicians and people in power.'

Alan Ratcliffe, former Deputy Chief Constable of Cambridgeshire, became the Caymans' Police Commissioner in 1989 and from the start refused invitations to BCCI social events. 'By that time it was clear that their people up in Tampa were going to be indicted. To me, in my position, there was an obvious danger and I'd heard stories about how they liked to cultivate various people, and I don't want to be cultivated.'

Ratcliffe's reservations apparently came as something of a shock to Roy Bodden, one of the 12 elected members in the Caymans' tiny legislative assembly and manager of a car dealership. 'If the Chief of Police had that knowledge, why did he not circulate it?' he said. 'Certainly that was news to me.' Bodden worries about the banks. 'This is going to negatively affect us, because this was a vast financial empire and we were the second most important outpost in the organisation. And to hear now that we are the source of the secret billions being stashed away – oh my God! And we are professing that we are so clean, and we are so tight! How do you explain *that*?'

For a group of Caymanian backbenchers, who for the last two years have been agitating against the Governor and the finance committee, the BCCI débâcle is a tempting opportunity for attack. They do not, they insisted, have anything against capitalism. They don't want any destabilising independence – 'Don't mention that dirty word!' But there is an increasing sense, they said, as the numbers of foreign workers threaten to outnumber the indigenous population, that the bankers, 'the mercantile people', have somehow taken over, developing what they needed for business in Georgetown, the capital, and ignoring the rest of the islands. 'The Caymanian people virtually have no control over what happens in the banking world here,' said backbencher Gilbert McLean. 'They are foreign banks, so in effect we are simply the pawns and the location where they are set up.'

They are also, of course, the beneficiaries. The Governor likes to recite the triumphant statistics: 'Electricity consumption has tripled since 1980! They have 40 per cent over employment! You have to be careful not to boast but things are very prosperous *indeed* here. I think, per capita, we've gone over $20,000.'

But there are 'growing pains'. The children are spoilt. They can afford to buy drugs. Nothing too worrying. Nothing that could affect *stability*. 'They really are immensely commonsensical people.' Even when the backbenchers are fractious, it doesn't really signify. 'Don't bother talking to them,' he said, amiably. 'It's a very small place, you just have to bear this sort of nonsense . . . and they lie like troopers. The issue is power, it's as simple as that.' The backbenchers retort that Scott is autocratic and interfering: 'It's his ways that infuriate.'

Behind their noisy conflicts, business goes on as usual. New banks and companies set up their stalls outside other companies and other banks. More and more of the island is parcelled up and sold off to foreigners. Things are going swimmingly for the right people. Along the island's one good beach, even plots of sea are being roped off, for tourists.

'Caymanians are very complacent,' said Consuelo Ebanks, who recently lost a campaign to stop yet another condominium with its own private slice of beach. 'I sometimes think, "How can people sit and allow these things to happen?" They refuse to look into the future. They squeal about the foreigners owning all the land but who sold it to them? We are like a street-corner prostitute – if you want something you can get it, if the price is right.'

A secretary for a firm of company managers, she wishes the islands had never become a tax haven. 'If it hadn't, we could have developed much more slowly, with tourism, and we probably would have been better all round.' But she accepts that few Caymanians would agree with her. 'It was a hard life and people don't want to go back.'

On the contrary, young Caymanians, when they return from trips to Miami, complain there is nothing to do and nowhere to spend their money. 'Frankly, it's boring and monotonous,' said one boy, now studying architecture in the USA. 'There's only one cinema, there's only a few nightclubs and *they* only stay open until a quarter to one.' But he was going to come back. 'There's a huge number of jobs here.'

Caymanians, as the Governor said, are common-sensical. Their children know the value of money. The first room in the small, and humdrum, Caymanian museum is dedicated to a display of its new currency and childish tributes to dosh. 'You can't just go and get things for free,' writes an 11-year-old Caymanian poet. 'My advice to you is to know that using money wisely is the best thing to do.'

January 31, 1992: Dan Atkinson

Depreciation of the currency

Gaffer Hexam, the venal bargee in *Our Mutual Friend*, had the unsentimental attitude to money that would surely win the approval of the Governor of the Bank of England. Justifying his decision to steal a purse from a corpse, Gaffer asks: 'What world does a dead man belong to? T'other world. What world does money belong to? This world.'

Perhaps it was this creation of Charles Dickens that prompted the Bank to hand Florence Nightingale her

P45 and install the author on the new, slimmed-down, inflation-eroded £10 note.

Or perhaps it was Mr Merdle, the financial swindler in *Little Dorrit*, who caught Robin Leigh-Pemberton's eye. Merdle was based on a real-life Victorian Robert Maxwell, John Sadleir, whose bankruptcy in 1856 fascinated Dickens. In the wake of recent collapses and scandals, Dickens the Moral Avenger may have been thought appropriate for British money in these more financially prudent times.

Whatever the reason, the Bank announced yesterday that the Lady of the Lamp, after 17 years' devoted service on the back of the nation's tenners, is to be replaced by the man who, in 1856, wrote an article entitled 'A slight depreciation of the currency'. Since then it has continued to depreciate, though rather less slightly. What cost £1 then would cost £39 today.

In the years since Florence Nightingale made her debut in 1975, the pound's purchasing power has shrunk to the equivalent of 22p. If the tenner reflected this shrinkage, Dickens would find himself squeezed on to a bank note rather smaller than a Tube ticket. As it is, the real reduction is more modest, from 3½in by 6in to 3in by 5½in.

Dickens has been accused of displaying hopeless sentimentality about money and wealth in his novels. As George Orwell said, if rich men really behaved in the kind-hearted way Dickens imagines, they would not stay rich for very long. In his private life, the son of a bankrupt was more hard-headed. He negotiated all his own deals, and had little time for penniless fellow writers on the look-out for subventions.

August 2, 1991: Martyn Halsall

Suck it and see

The flavour of the wind changed suddenly, from fish-dock to menthol. Across the tracks from the Lingfield Road tram stop on the edge of Fleetwood, Lancashire, the world headquarters of Fisherman's Friend was busy producing its internationally-famous throat lozenges at a rate of 20 million a day.

The plant expects to produce some four billion oval brown tablets this year; four out of every five for export. Europe is acquiring an increasing taste for the trawler-decorated packets. It's a case history of how an old-fashioned British company is being turned around to exploit the advantages of the EC market where it faces no established competitor.

Continental Europe offers a pungent consumer profile of maximum sales to the 18-to-35 generation, compared with most UK customers being 50-plus. 'In the UK it's perceived as a very medicinal product for coughs and colds,' the company says. 'On the Continent it's perceived as a confectionery product and people consume it right throughout the year.'

In its modest way Fisherman's Friend is now looking to expand by appointing an additional European area manager (£26,000 plus BMW). The appointment will underline an unusual commercial relationship. The new manager will work for Impex Management, based in Basildon, Essex, which markets and sells the lozenges throughout the world. The company, employing 21, works solely for Fisherman's Friend. There is no financial link between the two but they are mutually and exclusively dependent.

Fisherman's Friend appeared first in 1865, the year that saw the first prototype carpet sweeper and oil pipe line. James Lofthouse, a Fleetwood pharmacist, devised a fluid made with liquorice, capsicum, eucalyptus, and menthol to protect fishermen against the rigours of the North Atlantic fishing grounds. Casualties were high among squat glass bottles on heaving trawlers, so Lofthouse developed lozenges. Fishermen visiting the shop for 'an ounce of Friends' effectively christened the product over the counter.

The Friend was unknown outside Fleetwood until 1963. In 1969 the Lofthouse family gave up an unequal struggle of hand-packing their growing orders and turned an old tram shed into a packing and distribution warehouse. In the early 1970s they mortgaged everything to develop 20,000 sq ft of custom-built facilities.

The company then employed eight. Now it provides work for 300 as the town's second-largest private employer. It has a 300,000 sq ft plant with computer-controlled lines producing lozenges for 21 hours a day.

By 1974 the Friend was being exported to Norway and was beginning to move into the EC. A second flavour, aniseed, was introduced in 1976, a mere 111 years after the first.

The company laid out its 'pan-European policy' in 1983. Ivan Gibson, chairman and managing director of Impex, has six colleagues trawling for shoals of orders. All the distribution agreements were settled by 1987, with plans to double business by 1992. The target was achieved in 1990. Exports now reach more than 50 countries and the company has twice received Queen's Awards.

Doreen Lofthouse, managing director of Fisherman's Friend, is optimistic that the product's 'green' credentials – 'very natural, no colours, no preservatives' – will guarantee sales growth in Europe. The UK will have a new sugar-free brand this autumn, after three years of successful sales in Europe.

But are there enough fishermen to suck them? Ken Valentine, chief executive of the Fleetwood Fish Producers' Organisation, said there were now only 80 vessels employing between 400 and 500 men compared with up to 500 larger trawlers employing up to 5,000 before the cod wars.

March 28, 1992: Victor Keegan

Getting on his Zike

A small British company was unveiling a new product of the kind which could easily have passed untrumpeted in one of those consumer technology supplements that fall out of the Sunday papers. Instead, crowds of journalists and television crews turned up for the launch which generated plenty of column inches in the national press without the company having to pay a penny piece in advertising. Sir Clive Sinclair, Britain's most prolific inventor, was back in town.

Actually, he never left. Over the past few years he has been beavering away in his component-strewn lair on the third floor of a faded building north of Oxford Street, London, on his latest project, a power-assisted bicycle. The Zike, due for delivery in May, is a technological stepping-stone between Sinclair's ill-fated C5 and his long-term ambition to produce an environmentally-friendly electric car.

Sinclair has his detractors, including buyers of some of his less reliable products. But his enduring appeal is based on the potting-shed patriotism of an electronic David taking on the giants of Japan and America and who, with true British grit, survives failure and comes bouncing back.

Industrially, he is much more a symbol of the strengths and weaknesses of Great Britain Inc: brilliant at invention, fallible at follow-through.

Britain is the most innovative country in the world (with

half of the most important post-war innovations to its credit, according to the Japanese), but we can't make a success of them ourselves. Sinclair's inventions list reads like an encyclopaedia of consumer electronics including the world's smallest amplifier (1962), a slimline radio, the first small calculator (sold in large numbers to the Japanese), the world's first pocket television (well, almost), the first low-priced computers (ZX80, ZX81 and the Spectrum), the QL computer (which, for all its later problems, stunned the computer world when first announced), the impressive Z88 laptop and the first (and last) C5, the much-mocked electric tricycle with stalled ambitions to become a car.

In 1981-2, while Britain wallowed in recession, he sold more computers than anyone else in the world and, as recently as 1986, could claim 40 per cent of the UK home-computer market.

Sinclair says British companies pay out too high a proportion of their profits in dividends driven by the fear of takeover. 'What is sad is that we have pioneered things like pocket calculators, but the benefit has been taken up by Japanese companies instead of the GECs of this world.'

What would he do about this? 'I wish I had a slick answer. I apologise for not. I can see the fault, but I am just not expert enough to know the answer. You need a different sort of investment. You probably need banks and investors getting on to the boards and, as Akio Morita of Sony said recently, you need engineers running companies. It's a lack of intelligent investment.'

Ten years ago Britain had a Japanese-style cluster of pioneering micro-computer companies, including Sinclair, Acorn, makers of the BBC computer, Dragon, and Research Machines. Any one of these could have become a world-scale company, but didn't. Sinclair says these young companies lacked the mature entrepreneurial approach of the Americans. And there were no bigger electronics companies coming in on the act. In the US Apple managed to mature into a big computer company, but in England none of them did with the exception of Amstrad, a late arrival which, unlike the fledgling British companies, made its computers compatible with the IBM standard which dominated computer systems in the 1980s.

What of the economic climate? 'I think the macro-economic climate was excellent and it was because the climate was good politically and economically that many companies got so far. If it hadn't been for that, you wouldn't have Amstrad today. I would dread to see us going back to the old days, with governments thinking they can manage these things and screwing them up.'

Why couldn't Sinclair have become a world force? 'The trouble is that the IBM standard came along. Had we been better businessmen we would have said, well, we've got to go along with that. But the trouble was we were inno-vators and that [accepting system standards laid down by IBM] ran contrary to our culture. I don't want to be in the position of making commodity [high volume, standard-ised] products. It's not my job.'

Sinclair would dearly love the Conservatives to win the election, but, apart from raising marginal rates of tax which he regards as bad, but not disastrous, he doesn't see much difference between the main parties. He will go on inventing.

Surely, 30 years on, he must be slowing down? 'No, on the contrary, the opportunities are greater now and I have got the hang of it all, I think. The interesting thing about invention is that, in order to come up with something, you generally need to bring different technologies together. The Zike is exciting to do because it requires solutions to mechanical engineering, electrical and electronic prob-lems.'

Sinclair has two long-term research ambitions. The first is electric cars. 'Electric cars,' he says, 'look attractive and with the greatly increased wealth in the West it might make more sense for people to stop trying to have the one all-purpose car. A family might choose a Volvo because it's a very good car, long-legged and will take everybody. That's fine if they are going on a long journey: but at least 90 per cent of the time they are not doing that at all. What's happening is that one or two people are going around town or going into the village. It's abused for short local journeys for which it is ill suited and inefficient. There might be another solution; for the family to own such a car just for the long journeys and to have another sort of vehicle for local journeys.'

What about solar energy? 'I think that really is very exciting. It's one of those things that ticks away year after year and we tend to forget about it. For electric town cars it's looking as if it will pay within a few years to cover the available roof surface with solar panels. Even in our relatively gloomy climate it would provide a useful proportion of the energy, say, pessimistically, 20 per cent, but it could well be quite a bit more. In California, or Portugal, or somewhere like that, with a lot of sun, it could possibly provide all the energy needed. It's going to be very cheap: the new technologies are coming through, there is nothing to stop them. If you have got fundamentally low-cost raw materials and no fundamentally appalling production problems, you can bet your life you can do solar energy cheaply.'

Sinclair's other long-term ambition is in the application of parallel processing (computers doing lots of functions simultaneously) where he is expecting huge leaps in performance. 'I am interested in a machine that can talk to people. I think we can make a huge improvement in people's lives on average if we can provide them at home with the expertise of a doctor, a solicitor, a teacher, in the form of a computer. We will never be able to provide enough teachers and doctors to meet all the needs one would like fulfilled, so we have got to use machines to supplement the human experts.'

The acquisition of knowledge at home is a fitting

ambition for a man who is celebrated for his lack of formal qualifications. Born in 1940, he left the last of his 13 schools, St George's College, Weybridge, aged 17 in order to apply his formidable problem-solving brain in the real world. At school the shy, insular Sinclair liked only mathematics and English, which remain his true loves to this day. He became bored by the inability of the syllabus to fulfil his fanatical interest in the burgeoning field of electronics which was being revolutionised by the application of the newly discovered transistor.

While in his early teens he designed a calculating machine which he programmed using a numerical language he had dreamed up consisting solely of 1s and 0s. He was later disappointed to learn that the binary system had already been discovered. Before taking his A-levels he designed his first micro-radio in a school exercise book complete with costings and a planned initial production rate of 1,000 a month. He left in 1957 to become a technical journalist on *Practical Wireless*, for whom he had already written. Before a year was out the editor retired and he was running the magazine.

The avuncular Sinclair is as well known for his low boredom threshold in some areas as he is for his voracious ability to absorb facts in subjects which interest him. A few years ago, to fathom Britain's economic problems, he enlisted for an economics degree at Cambridge. He was pleased when his supervisor decided to enter him after only one year, but the university told him that as he was at press conferences and running a business at the same time as taking a degree, it was against the rules. 'They said I could take my exams if I wanted to, but they weren't going to give me a degree, so I didn't bother.'

What he did bother with was his Zike, which displays all the Sinclair brilliance of lateral thinking, risk-taking and miniaturisation. The energy from braking and freewheeling downhill recharges the batteries which are themselves shrunken enough in size to fit inside the central shaft with the motor. The whole thing weighs under 11 kg (less than 25 lbs) and takes only one hour to recharge. It costs £499. And, above all, he is launching it, with his own money, in the middle of a recession.

He sounds indignant when asked whether the Zike will prove, like some of his previous products, to have been brought too quickly to the market and with too many teething faults. 'I think that is going back in history a very long way. We never had the slightest problems with the Z88 computer, with satellite receivers or the C5. The Zike is being made by a company in the Rolls-Royce league which supplies the motor industry, and to supply the motor industry today you have to have a quality that is absolutely superb.'

Some people, I said, were worried because the model displayed at the launch was a prototype and people weren't allowed to ride it on the road.

'We allowed 2,000 people to ride it.'

But that was inside the hall.

'Sure, you don't risk life and limb on prototypes.'

But can you go from hand-made prototypes to production in a couple of months?

'They are prototypes because they were the first ones coming off the line.'

And how are orders?

'Um. Very encouraging, but it's early days. There has been a huge amount of interest.'

December 27, 1991: Roger Cowe

Untying the package

As you crush the fancy wrapping-paper, empty plastic bubble packs and cardboard boxes hopefully into bulging dustbins, spare a thought for the packaging industry, wondering how many more throw-away Christmases there will be.

Talk of taking back every toothpaste tube has abated. But 1992 will be a challenging year for the makers of all forms of packaging, the manufacturers who use them to enhance the appeal of their own products, and the retailers who happily sell twice as much plastic as product.

Consumer waste may be an insignificant molehill compared to the mountainous scale and toxic danger of industrial waste, but its high profile has led most European countries (with Britain lagging behind as usual on environmental affairs) to try to tackle the problem.

The toothpaste-tube scare stories came from Germany, which has been fulfilling its role of leading the way in green developments. In theory, like all the best scare stories, it is true. By January 1, 1993, every toothpaste tube, and all other consumer packaging, may have to be taken back by manufacturers for recycling.

Also on that date, a mandatory deposit may be introduced on non-reusable drink containers, paint cans, detergent and cleaning fluid bottles.

This is the final stage of a comprehensive recycling law, the first part of which is already in operation. For the past month, the law has required manufacturers and distributors to take back all transit packaging. From the beginning of April, the same will apply to outer packaging, leading up to consumer packaging by the end of the year.

This conjures up a vision of Colgate collecting its rubbish in one corner of the supermarket car park, Proctor & Gamble in another, and still other collections leaving no room for shoppers' cars. That is not what is intended.

The purpose is to nudge manufacturers into financing recycling schemes. The ultimate requirements will be waived if industry has established an acceptable collection system before the January 1 deadline. And this is what is happening.

A scheme began in two German cities in July and has spread to create a collection infrastructure aimed at meeting government targets of collecting half of all packaging by the beginning of 1993, rising to 80 per cent in three years.

Elsewhere in Europe, the usual howls of anguish have been heard about unfair competition, unbearable costs and the like. INCPEN, the industry pressure group supposedly *for* packaging *and* the environment, has complained to the European Commission. But the Commission is busy trying to develop a similar scheme for the whole Community, and countries such as France and the Netherlands are working on their own recycling projects.

And why not? As the Germans have pointed out, the developed world is in danger of being buried under mountains of paper, PVC and polystyrene. Over a third of all plastic is estimated to be used in packaging – and most of it is thrown away as soon as the consumer gets home (just look at the kitchen rubbish-bin after a trip to the supermarket).

The traditional response has been to dump everything in landfill sites, with a belated move to try to make the rubbish biodegradable even if the dump conditions meant that nothing could degrade. In many countries, space for such sites is running out. The obvious alternative is incineration, but it is far from obvious to people living in the vicinity of the incinerators. In any case, throwing rubbish away (by whatever method) is hardly in keeping with the new spirit of conserving raw materials. Hence, the new emphasis on recycling.

Attacking the waste problem by re-using it is one thing, and bad enough as far as the companies that have to do it are concerned. But the real nightmare for the packaging industry may just be beginning, if green concerns follow their usual progression.

Take the issue of industrial waste. Initially, action was

aimed at containing waste within the factory, and especially preventing leaks into the atmosphere, land and rivers – so-called 'end of pipe' solutions. Companies soon realised it made more sense to avoid producing waste in the first place. That way, the problem of what to do with the waste material disappeared, and even without that saving, the process became more efficient as more of the inputs went into the final product.

Following the same logic on a larger scale, it surely makes more sense not to produce huge quantities of consumer packaging than to put enormous effort into recycling it. The consequences of that logic are, however, profoundly disturbing for manufacturers and retailers alike.

Could we be incited to buy a Were Bear without the gaudy box it is almost enclosed in? Probably, thanks to children's demands. But children are some of the greenest consumers. How long before they refuse to countenance even a Game Boy machine if it is embedded in unnecessary plastic and card?

As for the adults, where would the presentation bottle of port, brandy or malt whisky be without its presentation box? Left on the shelf, perhaps.

A fundamental attack on packaging threatens to undermine one of the keys to consumerism, and especially that sector of consumer goods which has moved closer to the packager's dream represented by the perfume business, where the product virtually is the package.

Retailers also face a nightmare return to labour-intensive handling, if environmental pressures manage to strip away some of the plastic and card that even enclose much of our supposedly fresh food.

Managers at Marks & Spencer (surely the worst culprit in 'protecting' food this way) began looking at the problem years ago, when business first began to take green pressures seriously. It was supposedly a six-month project, but two years later, the team had still failed to find a solution.

Their dilemma is clear – how to cut down packaging without pushing up labour costs. But it must be faced, and as German industrialists have found, cost is not a sufficiently strong objection.

Sporting types

August 26, 1991: Matthew Engel

The fastest show on earth

As Carl Lewis and his two closest rivals in the 100 metres stood on the victory rostrum at the World Championships last night, a full moon of improbable clarity and beauty rose above the line of the stadium and the smog into the Tokyo sky.

The night was like that. Carl Lewis, aged 30, beat Leroy Burrell and all the odds to win yet another gold medal and break the world record. Lewis called it the most incredible race of all time and no one could argue.

Actually the race that was really incredible was the one Lewis originally lost to Ben Johnson at the Seoul Olympics three years ago. This time Johnson rose in the stands to cheer; he had predicted that Lewis would win, one of the few things the poor sap has ever got right – not that anyone cares much now what he thinks.

This – subject to final confirmation in the laboratories – was for real. Lewis won in 9.86sec, two-hundredths of a second ahead of his friend and training partner (or, as Burrell put it, about eight inches), four-hundredths of a second ahead of the world record Burrell set in New York in June.

Only eight undrugged men had previously ever run 100 metres inside 10 seconds; only three had done it in 9.96 or better unassisted by drugs, wind or altitude. Last night Ray Steward did 9.96 and he came sixth.

Eight black men from six countries and four continents left the blocks. And the first three home were not merely all Americans but all grew up within 20 miles of each other in Philadelphia. The first two were mates and so delighted for each other's achievement that the detail of which one won and which lost seemed almost irrelevant.

The literalists will insist that the new-technology track was every bit as responsible for the fast times as Johnson's medicine chest was for his now-expunged record in Seoul. The romantics will remember this as the night sprinting – and maybe all athletics – regained its soul and forgot about Seoul.

Everything else this weekend was merely a prelude to these few seconds. Across the stadium men were throwing hammers and hop-step-and-jumping and hardly anyone was taking any notice. Even the arrival of the Emperor of Japan attracted little attention (though the appearance of three famous sumos did).

The weather was perfect – no unbearable heat or humidity, no more Typhoon Gladys – but there was something unmistakably crackly in the air. A visitor from outer space would have sensed that the earthlings were about to do something spectacular.

It all happened very suddenly. The first start was a clean one. But it seemed as though Lewis was not away suddenly at all: there were five, six men in front of him even at halfway. But, as he said later, he did have a fast start. The men ahead were simply faster, phenomenally so – they probably all went under the 60 metres record.

'I felt great at 60 metres,' Lewis said afterwards, 'and I was still about fifth. At 60 metres I said, "Hey, I have a shot." At 80 metres I felt very good, I said, "Hey, I have a great shot." And then at 90, when I'd cleared everyone except Leroy, I thought, "Hey, I can win this." I felt I was really rolling.'

Does anyone have time to think all that and run so fast? By heaven, he was rolling. His closing strides were those of a lioness closing on an antelope. Before crossing the line, Lewis turned to his left to make sure where Burrell was. The answer was behind him, by about one body's width.

Burrell wanted to see where Lewis was. In this he had one huge disadvantage; he is blind in his right eye and he was drawn in lane three, two to Lewis's left, which meant he could not pick up what was happening. It was in keeping with the extraordinary spirit of the occasion that he mentioned this only very casually.

Lewis raised his right arm as he crossed the line, glanced at the clock, realised the extent of his triumph, raised the other arm, leaped upwards and then put his head in his hands. Then he saw Burrell and they embraced like warriors who had come through terrible danger together.

This was not the perfunctory courtesy that used to pass between Lewis and Johnson, nor in Burrell's case the graciousness that prudent losers maintain for the television cameras before going away to kick their wives or cats.

It sounds daft to say there were no losers, but no one looked as though he had lost. I do believe they were genuinely thrilled to have been part of it.

'I feel like I won, you know,' said Dennis Mitchell, who was third. Even Linford Christie, who is not famous for being Cheerful Charlie at the best of times, was grinning ear to ear and he had missed out on a medal by one-hundredth of a second, a timespan only a top sprinter can ever truly comprehend. 'Great night for racing, eh?' he said.

Burrell was simply awe-struck. 'I'm just proud to be part of the greatest race of all time. I did break the world record, it's just that somebody broke it a little better than I did. He passed us like we were standing still.'

The emotions were never far away. Lewis cried several times, especially when he talked about his dead father; Burrell's father has just had open-heart surgery and came out of intensive care a few hours before the race. The two men had spent much of the day talking together in Burrell's room.

Lewis's tribute to Burrell was warm and heartfelt: 'Leroy set the tone for this entire competition. I had to run the best race of my life, technically and timewise. If I'd have been one per cent below the best I've ever been I would have lost, and that's all to do with the standards Leroy set.'

There had been omens that the old man (beaten five times out of six by the 24-year-old Burrell) might just make this race different. Lewis's wind-assisted 9.80 in the heats, of course, was one, but there was also the fact that gold medals had been won earlier by a balding 36-year-old hammer-thrower and a 34-year-old walker.

'It gets you,' said Lewis, 'when they say: "OK, all of sudden, Carl's dead." I didn't think, at 24, 26 or 28, I'd run the best race I'd ever run at 30. I'm still having a tough time with being 30, forget the race.'

How does Lewis do it? 'Those knees,' said Burrell. 'Those knees can get up so high it's ridiculous.'

'Legs,' said Lewis when a Japanese journalist tried to push him to say that the track should get the credit.

The bonhomie was almost overwhelming. Someone thought Lewis's post-race performance was comparable with Ali at his best, though, if so, it was Ali with just a touch of camp.

Undoubtedly, three highly articulate, likeable men who like one another won the medals last night. Burrell was the man who said what the others left unsaid: 'We needed to wipe out everything Ben Johnson ever did. That was aided; this was real. This was hard work, dedication and competitiveness, what sport is all about.'

Johnson, without his magic potions, failed even to qualify for the 100 metres. His only roles here are to run in the relay and to wander round like Banquo's Ghost – not quite forgotten, not quite gone – a reminder to every competitor of the dangers of drugs, or at any rate of being caught.

It is an important job. But last night Lewis and his cohorts went a long way towards completing the process of exorcism. Everything in athletics is subject to ratification, and honesty is a slippery commodity. But one has to believe this race was the honest truth.

They ran with a hi-tech track, newfangled spikes and ultra-light costumes, but also with class, bravado and respect both for one another and themselves. In the process, they did something bell, book and candle never could.

February 29, 1992: Matthew Engel

Thunder and brightening on the veld

On a summer afternoon on the Transvaal high veld the rain clouds build up along with the heat. Then at four o'clock there is a short, cleansing thunderstorm before the sun comes out again. It is a marvellous way to organise a climate.

This summer the heat has built more intensely day by day, but the rain has refused to come. In South Africa nowadays it is impossible to trust any of the old certainties.

There has been nothing like it since the 1930s. But as they pray that the drought will break before the crops completely wither, South Africans have this week been diverted and bewitched by something almost as long-forgotten: international sport.

As the celebrations started for the victory over Australia in the cricket World Cup, the drivers began to arrive in Johannesburg for the South African Grand Prix, the first major sporting event of the post-apartheid era to be held within the country.

People have long dreamed what symbolically non-racial form this moment might take: a grand reconciliation soccer match between South Africa and the rest of Africa, perhaps? Instead, in the haphazard way that history has, the honour goes to motor racing, which was even slower than rugby to recognise that there might be a tiny problem with South Africa – the last grand prix here was only seven years ago – and is the most perfect representative imaginable of the old, unreconstructed country.

Formula One typifies the spurious international glamour which white South Africans have always admired but have lately been denied by sanctions and – far more effective – the collapse of the rand. At the Kyalami circuit Blacks are largely confined, as ever, to erecting stands and selling ice cream.

It is not apartheid; it is just the way things are. The sports that most truly reflect the interests of the nation as a whole have proved, almost inevitably, hardest to unite and bring back to the global community. Soccer, the game of the urban blacks, has always been particularly rumbustious; the game's former leading executive is in jail for fraud and an official from a club known as Dangerous Darkies has been accused of attempted murder after a gun was fired at the league's weekly press conference.

At this precise moment, however, the Blacks are not the most urgent priority. With every ball that South Africa bowl or face in the World Cup, with every revving engine

at Kyalami, there is a subtext that the most doltish tele-
vision-watcher can read.

On March 17 the Whites vote in the referendum on
continuing negotiations with black leaders. If the answer
is No, President de Klerk will resign and sanctions will be
reimposed far more unanimously and vigorously than
ever before. The sporting boycott is liable to be resumed.

The referendum was precipitated by the government's
defeat at a by-election in the Western Transvaal town of
Potchefstroom ('Potch') by the right-wing Conservative
Party this month. On Thursday night, amid a deafening
clash of symbols, there was an athletics meeting in Potch at
which the star attraction was a Mrs Pieterse.

If Mrs Pieterse's first name had been something common like Jane or Mary, then the casual observer might
never have recognised her. Her glasses have gone and her
hair is longer; she is not so waif-like either and indeed
now looks almost housewifely, with the suspicion of a
matronly future. She is running in shoes too – reluctantly,
because of a hamstring injury. But since her name is Zola,
no further identification is necessary.

She is no longer Zola Budd, the little Miss Magoo who
blundered innocently through the thickets of world politics and, far thornier, the Fleet Street circulation war when
the *Daily Mail* arranged a British passport for her before
the 1984 Olympics. She has learned a lot about life the
hard way.

Here she was among her own folk: Afrikaans girls in
uncompromisingly feminine dresses, their fair-haired
brothers in crisp, white school shirts, heavy-forearmed
fathers and mums with earrings brushing their shoulders.
The crowd cheered when Gerhard Barnard beat Tshakile
Nzimande in the 100 metres but there was no hint of racial
malice in it. Even Potchefstroom has gone beyond that.
And though athletics has not been easy to integrate, the
black-white problem has always been secondary to the

sport's long-standing bitterness between English-speakers and Afrikaners.

The climax of the evening consisted of Zola, who was being paid good appearance money, running the 1500 metres. After the first bend she was more or less alone except for a TV cameraman on a motorcycle. Her time was indifferent but she did her job. And every time she rounded the home turn she passed a banner saying 'Yes for Barcelona'.

The banner was put there by a group of local business-men with the full approval of the meeting's organiser, a formidable woman called Daleen Snyman. Miss Snyman is convinced that the voters of Potch have had their emo-tional spasm and will now come into line behind Presid-ent de Klerk. 'There won't be any nonsense like that this time,' she insisted. 'It was ridiculous.' When the banner was mentioned to Mrs Pieterse she almost cowered: 'I want to stay out of politics as far as possible.'

But in South Africa this week sport and politics are intertwined more closely than ever before. At Potch Elana Meyer, the country's new middle-distance star, was run-ning with (US) after her name in the programme. Hea-vens, had she done a Zola and defected? It turned out that US stood for the University of Stellenbosch. But if the Whites vote No, this might not be a joke.

Over at the World Cup the director of the cricket board, Ali Bacher, left off negotiating South Africa's future Test programme and all but cast his players' ballots for them. Other sporting administrators have followed. At South Africa's Olympic headquarters the president of the com-mittee was feigning indifference. That, however, was solely on the grounds that a Yes vote was a foregone conclusion. No one ever accused Sam Ramsamy of being apolitical.

It is still a shock to find Ramsamy here. He spent years of exile speaking to left-wingers in dingy London meeting-rooms or arguing – more and more bleatingly – the case for some obscure cricketer to be blacklisted because he had once spent a fortnight in Bloemfontein. And the cricketer would be barred from Zambia and Zaire and get on with his life.

Now Ramsamy is installed in an office in the suburbs of Johannesburg, receiving delegations from roller hockey and volleyball and deciding whether they meet the criteria for admission to the brave new world of South African sport.

The government is no happier about Ramsamy's position than it was before. 'The furniture we are sitting on now is a gift from the Australian government,' Ramsamy said. 'We have not had any money at all from the South African government and they are going out of their way to sabotage us.

'Government wrath came upon us when we decided we would march in Barcelona under our own flag and emblem. Not only are they not funding us but we believe that certain companies are refusing to support us because of ministers' attitudes. I think it's pique. They are upset because someone who's been fighting them for so long is in charge and because sport has become an area in which they are impotent.'

A government spokesman said the Olympic Committee was not a democratically elected body. 'I don't know what the South African government knows about democracy,' said Ramsamy.

It will be particularly bitter-sweet for the government if Budd or Meyer or – more likely – a yachtsman does manage to win a gold medal in Barcelona and the band strikes up, not their anthem, but the Olympic hymn, putting their athletes in the same category as the Russians.

There are also acts of sabotage that can hardly be laid directly on the government. Dan Moyo, Ramsamy's assistant, says he had the wheelnuts of his car loosened while it was parked at the Wanderers' Club, the bastion of Johannesburg's sporting establishment. Moyo never lets Ramsamy drive anywhere without an escort.

For the moment South African politics may have become unusually simple: Yes or No. But the sporting politics are likely to remain confused and bitter long after Zola, Elana and the rest have marched into the Olympic stadium.

Everything is still so novel. The win over Australia on Wednesday was greeted with something close to hysteria; proof that, even after two decades of boycott, South African really was best. 'South Africa World Champions 1970–1992 (unbeaten)', as a banner in Sydney put it.

The Johannesburg papers have given the cricket far more prominence than the referendum. A normally mature country would be aware that, on the day, any competent one-day cricketing side can beat any other and that one win, however comprehensive, proves nothing. But then, even before the 22 years of exile, South Africa never showed any signs of normal maturity.

In reality, though, the sporting boycott has played a crucial role in bringing white South Africans this far and its well-timed end is likely to play just as important a role in keeping them there. South African sport now has the potential to restore the country's good name.

Slowly, painfully slowly, white South Africans have been made to face the necessity for the political thunderstorm that is inevitable when majority rule comes. It will be drenching. But it may just leave them cleansed and invigorated. .

November 18, 1991: Dave Hill

Ducking and diving

For a man who knows how to take care of himself, Frank Bruno receives incomparable protection from others. And it is a measure of its effectiveness that this defensive cordon rarely assumes palpable form.

Everyone knows that the public personae of celebrities serve both to project them to their audiences and to conceal the private individual from a prying outside world. But, when it comes to the personality market, the package of affable self-deprecation Bruno comes wrapped in outscores all-comers with the subtlety of its positioning and the completeness of its presentation.

Drawing: Peter Clarke

Consider the components: an Englishman and a gentle-man, a heavyweight with humility, a down-to-earth dia-

mond geezer whose most heroic moments have come in
defeat, Big Frank embodies every romantic fancy the
island people have cherished about themselves since
Dunkirk. Result? Lager drinkers, little children, and cru-
cially, all the popular papers are united in their affection.
To them, it seems, it doesn't even matter that he's black.
No one cares to see this product of the hardest game there
is as anything other than pristine.

So, it is easy to be cynical; easy, too, to react with
patronising disapproval as the Bruno bandwagon rolls
again with his comeback fight against the Dutchman John
Emmen just two days away. There's Big Frank on the back
pages of Saturday's tabloids, cutting his giant 30th-birth-
day cake for the paparazzi's gratification. Next to the
pictures, the blurb does Bruno's talking for him: It'll Be A
Piece Of Cake! Know Wha' I Mean, 'Arry? And so on:
another photo opportunity negotiated; another season of
pantomime guaranteed to please as soon as the business
in the ring is done.

But there is more to all this than just a fatuous cycle of
hyperbole. And it is only when you become a part of the
process yourself that you begin to detect that the reasons
for its existence are not uniformly crass.

Frank Bruno, it is clear, is a very sensitive man. This
becomes apparent not simply because a mutual friend
insists that it is so, not simply because his wife Laura – who
politely vets me before an interview is granted, and who
would be happier if she could vet my copy too – advises
very strongly against taking the line of a hack from another
broadsheet who had 'really upset' Big Frank by, she says,
asking if it was true that Terry Lawless, Bruno's erstwhile
manager, had taught him how to use a knife and fork, but
also because when I finally find myself in a small, bright
room at the Leicestershire health farm where the boxer
has been gearing up, sensitivity seeps from behind his
fortified exterior like juice from a Kiwi fruit.

We begin with some talk about boxing. Now that he is

rich and familial, is it harder for the father of two darling daughters to get in touch with the fighter in his soul? 'Not really,' he says, 'because I like what I do. Sometimes you get a busted nose, sometimes you get a bruised rib, but it's the trade. Like, in your trade you might get a sore finger here and there. Your expenses might be cut. But it's the hassles of the trade.'

This wind-up is delivered with practised deadpan in a voice whose deepness is all the more uncanny emerging directly from the flesh. As the exchange develops, it becomes clear that Bruno was also laying the foundations of a defence of his sport.

Quite unprompted, he goes on to profess his affection for both Chris Eubank and Michael Watson, the latter still stricken from his shattering encounter with the former earlier this year. 'I didn't want nothing to happen to neither of them. Look at the rugby,' he continues, invoking comparisons he has already used in other interviews since the Watson nightmare began. 'They've been kicking and punching each other. And, like, in the olden days people used to offer each other up for a duel. They used to slap 'em in the face and say, "I'll meet you outside at eight o'clock," and they used to have a gun, back to back, turn round and fire, then go to the pub and have another drink.'

But what about boxing's spectators? What do they get out of watching two guys from nowhere damaging each other for cash? 'It's showbusiness with blood, yes. But I couldn't really answer that question to the full, you know.' Big Frank stops shadowing and advances an exploratory jab: 'I'm not sure if you're trying to knock boxing or what. I'm not sure what you're trying to get to.'

My rooting for a handhold on the psychology of the game had been misinterpreted as a set-up for a dig. There are other moments of tension. For example when Bruno is quizzed about his faith. 'I am a Roman Catholic, yeah. I put my faith in the man above, you know, 'cos he is the greater. Is there anything wrong in that?'

And again, when asked about the contrast between his impeccable off-duty manners and the mean streak so necessary to success in his job: 'So am I wrong in being polite to you and easy to get on with?'

It wasn't that Big Frank was being nasty. But these tremors of testiness – the quick resistance to lines of inquiry about matters close to his heart, the hint of a hard look from a momentarily hooded eye – betray the part of his personality the media massage launders from view. Bruno is streetwise. He is fully acquainted with a school of wisdom which dictates that slights must be resisted and outsiders warily appraised. He implicitly acknowledges this in a catchphrase routinely uttered for anyone holding a notebook: 'I'm just a ducker and diver, you know.'

These are skills which have served him well on his long, tough road to fortune and fame. A repertoire which for black radicals and white lefties is seen as a hopeless sell-out, for Bruno appears to be more like making a deal, a strategic trade-off, perhaps, in a sport where black boxers have generally failed to maximise their incomes amid a surrounding chauvinism which has habitually insisted that true Englishness can only be white. 'Some people take kindness for weakness, you know,' Bruno observes of the press, which, none the less, has served as his shop window from day one. 'But if they wanna take liberties with you, you don't give 'em what they want.'

Bruno will have grasped early in his career that the British could be persuaded that they wanted him: that is, that they were prepared to buy what he had for sale. Since the retirement of Henry Cooper, there had been an unfilled vacancy for a charismatic heavyweight. Joe Bugner never got to filling it, perceived as being too cissy for a man of his size, and never forgiven for taking the British title of 'Our 'Enry' on a controversial points decision. But Bruno had most of the right credentials: a sense of humour, a London accent, a humble demeanour. Meanwhile, an otherwise xenophobic press has negotiated the 'problem' of his blackness thanks to an ideological mechanism which decrees that he may be a Black but he's *our* Black.

Much of this marketability has been attributed to Terry Lawless, whose long managerial experience put him at the centre of the British boxing network, not least its coterie of journalists. It was in 1980, shortly after becoming British amateur champion, that Bruno joined the Lawless camp, to the chagrin of businessman Burt McCarthy, whose previous arrangement with Bruno was deemed not binding by the British Boxing Board of Control. McCarthy issued a writ and eventually received substantial out-of-court compensation.

Lawless's initial investment did not stop there. In October 1980, the Board turned down Bruno's application for a professional licence on the grounds that he suffered from a complex form of short-sightedness in his right eye. The right surgery could only be obtained from clinics in Moscow or Bogota. So £5,000 bought a flight to Colombia, a fortnight's bed and board and the attentions of Professor José Ignacio Barraquer.

After deferring judgment for a year, the Board finally gave Bruno what he wanted. His first pro bout took place on March 17, 1982. He knocked out Lupe Guerra of Mexico in the first round. By the end of the following month, two more opponents had met similar fates. Before the year was out, Bruno's profile was already taking shape. 'He's Big, He's Brave, He's British,' read the headline of one colour supplement profile, proclaiming Bruno to be 'the first Briton since Henry Cooper to aim a serious blow at the world heavyweight crown'. Lawless was quoted: apart from his future boxing achievements, the manager declared, Bruno was going to be 'an ambassador for the human race'.

Quite a prospectus for a man who'd been working on a building site and who had been educated at a corrective school in Sussex from the age of 11. 'I used to fight a lot on the streets. I had a lot of aggression in my system. I tried to get a decent education, O-levels, A-levels and so forth, to get into an accountant's job or a solicitor's job, but I couldn't really get into that. So I decided to get into something that could use my strength and energy up.'

There is little doubt in Bruno's mind that his pugilist's instinct is more the product of nature than culture. Born in Hammersmith and raised in Wandsworth, he moves swiftly to pre-empt any potential implication that his family background was the cause of his youthful delinquency. His mother, who came from Jamaica (and who still refers to her son by his full forename of Franklyn), is a devout Pentecostalist and worked as a district nurse. Bruno speaks equally fondly of his Dominica-born father, who died when his son was 15. 'He was a big inspiration. His death had a very, very big effect, because I loved my dad . . . it was one of those things. Very hard to get through. Still hard now, to be quite honest.

'My mum and dad were down-to-earth people. Not saying they were poor, not saying they were rich. They done very, very good for themselves, you know? They had a nice house and there was food on the table. But it was hard. If I had a daddy who was a stockbroker or a mummy who was a stockbroker, then I could cry back to mummy or daddy.'

A childhood visit to Jamaica left a big impression: 'I remember seeing my grandma and I bawled my eyes out, you know, because she looked like my mum. She was 85 and in a wheelchair. I just cried my eyes out, seeing her there and how people lived.' Surveying that heritage and considering his own life options, there was only really one way forward: 'I just had to take to boxing, you know?'

Bruno first tried his hand at ring technique with the help of a Guyanese neighbour. The idea was to manoeuvre inside a circle set out on the floor. 'We used to spar together. He used to beat me up, take me running and that. He was the same size as me but he was a man and I was a boy.'

Make no mistake – and it is sometimes forgotten – Bruno has gone on to be good. Not quite good enough, in the final reckoning, to resist the attentions of top Americans like James 'Bonecrusher' Smith or Tim Witherspoon, who beat him in his first bid for a world crown at Wembley in 1986. Not good enough, either, to survive the terror of Mike Tyson nearly three years ago, another world title contest which the experts who attended Bruno afterwards believe caused the detached retina which forced his temporary retirement. But good enough to hurt Tyson. Just once, true, but hurt him good. Enough, perhaps, for Bruno to decide that, millionaire or not, boxing was still in his blood.

'When you lose,' he reflects, 'it doesn't really get out of your system because it's like being in love with someone and they've run out and left you. It's still in your mind all the time. It still flashes back. It doesn't really leave you.'

Through all the knockabout, was this a fleeting glimpse into the heart of this deep and dangerous game whose rituals of fear and confrontation invariably conclude with its participants locked in an exhausted embrace?

'My dad always taught me,' Bruno says, 'that a man is a man. Just respect people. If they've got respect for you, you respect them.'

But does Bruno command respect? Does all the self-parody and pump-primed public relations really instil in his public the proper appreciation (and we should note that he is now self-managed, his own man) his accomplishments deserve? Big Frank handles that one with care: 'It's beautiful to be respected, from not having no O-levels, or not being qualified in this or that. It's well appreciated by me, anyway. But it's here today, gone tomorrow, maybe.

'I don't wanna get too carried away. People think that because you meet this one and meet that one, and you go on television, that you're entitled to do this and that. You ain't entitled to do nothing. All you can do is, like, be yourself. The sooner people accept people for what they are, it would be a much more better world. People are saying that one's gay, that one's a Catholic, that one's a Protestant, that one's a Jew. That one's black, that one's white, that one's got green eyes. You know what I mean? You've just gotta be natural and get on with life.'

And when the party's over, and the gloves are finally mounted in a glass case on the sideboard, what will Big Frank be doing then?

'Being your apprentice, mate.'

Touché.

May 8, 1992: Stephen Bierley

Changing the locks at Anfield

Before Bill Shankly was appointed manager at Anfield on December 1, 1959, the newspapers of the day played the usual game of name the successor. Harry Catterick, Jimmy Murphy and Jimmy Hagan were all in the frame, as was a little-known back-room boy – one Robert Paisley. And in the back room, or perhaps more properly the boot room, Paisley remained for another 15 years.

There is a lovely photograph of Shankly, not quite able to bring himself to smile for the camera, standing somewhat gauchely alongside his Anfield henchmen: Paisley, Ronnie Moran, Joe Fagan and Reuben Bennett. This simple black-and-white snap, much more than a thousand words, brings into startling clarity the red thread of continuity that has run through the club since that momentous winter's day when Shanks said 'I will'.

On his first morning he told the staff he would be introducing no new assistants. 'I'll give you loyalty if you give it me.' There was never any question.

Paisley, who had joined Liverpool from Bishop Auckland in 1939, described the pre-Shankly Liverpool days as 'easygoing'. A born winner, he collected a League championship medal in his first full season at Anfield, 1947, yet remarked: 'We were not a team of real winners in those days. There was a feeling we belonged in the middle of the table. But Bill changed all that.'

Nearly 33 years and 27 major trophies later, the feelings of uncertainty, both inside and outside the club, are perhaps greater than they have ever been during the last three staggeringly successful decades.

Such doubts may be no more than the pulses of underlying unease caused by 15 months of, in Liverpool terms, quite astonishing flux, set off by the enigmatic departure of Kenny Dalglish.

Paisley and Fagan had been promoted from the ranks, in seamless succession to Shankly. Dalglish, with Paisley still very much at his elbow, had jumped over Moran and Roy Evans in being appointed in 1985, but his promotion was nevertheless within the delineated requirements of internal accession to the crown.

The arrival in April last year of Graeme Souness, albeit the club's former player and captain, was an 'outside job'. And, unlike Shankly, Souness brought an assistant, Phil Boersma, who thus gained automatic entrance to the mystical boot room. Noses were immediately and obviously put out of joint.

On the day Souness was paraded Moran made a short speech of welcome, publicly stating he would do everything to help. But there was little conviction in his voice or joy in his eyes. Whatever disappointment he had felt when Dalglish took over from Fagan had been well hidden. Not so now.

Souness changed the locks on the manager's door, and Moran has not bothered to learn the combination. Telephone calls by him to the Cheadle hospital where Souness has been recuperating from heart surgery have, for reasons unexplained, frequently not been returned. Outwardly Moran remains loyal but the deep, organic trust of the boot room is being severely tested.

This poky little cubbyhole under the main stand where the boots of the first-team players are stored has, since Shankly's days, become a potent symbol of the club's tight-knit homogeneity. It is, perhaps, the equivalent of a church vestry where, in strict privacy, the vicar can discuss everything from the thinness of the communion wine to why Mrs Smith's husband has been missing for three of the last four evensongs.

Shankly nor Paisley were not pulpit or manager's office men. They both knew when to be formal but the socialist gatherings (cabinet by consultation, if you prefer) in this cramped room were where policy, style and the way forward were thrashed out. All for one, one for all.

Trust was and is paramount. Those upstairs – Peter Robinson, the chief executive, and the board – could sort out wages, contracts and sundry other fiscal matters but, down in the boot room, little other than the game itself was talked about.

Thus it was, whenever Dalglish faced potentially awkward questioning about team or tactics, he would say quite simply, and ad infinitum, that 'such matters would be dealt with internally'. It is now possible to argue that he used the 'secret' fabric of the Anfield set-up to hide or mask his own inadequacies as a manager in the final year and a half when the team were showing sharp signs of decline, his tactics became increasingly curious and his purchases often bizarre.

What may have been forgotten amid the shock of Dalglish's resignation – because of 'pressure' – was the decline in the quality and influence of the boot room itself. Fagan, deeply scarred by the Heysel tragedy, had gone, and Paisley's gathering illness further isolated Dalglish from the wealth of the past. Not that he was a great one for advice in any case.

Souness, via a French magazine interview last October, spoke of complacency and the need to regenerate the spirit of old. It was assumed he was talking only of the players. It may not have been so.

And so the rumours have strengthened of Souness wanting a clear-out from top to bottom. A number of players – McMahon, Ablett, Speedie, Carter, Staunton and Beardsley – have gone. Others will follow this summer. But what of the boot room? What of Moran?

Here the true power-play will be decided. There is every reason to suppose that the leaking of the manager's alleged wish to get rid of the long-serving Moran, and the resultant anger in certain areas of the board, was carefully orchestrated from within.

Such is the pervading uncertainty that when Souness briefly left hospital on Thursday and was driven to Anfield by his solicitor, the knee-jerk conclusion was that he was about to resign. And this two days before an FA Cup final.

Souness is a man with scant regard for tradition when tradition stifles progress, as his signing of the Catholic Mo Johnston at Rangers testifies. He can also be a man of instant decisions, not all of them right. His selling of the story of his heart operation to the *Sun* was a clear case in point, an awful misjudgment.

Tommy Smith, talking of Liverpool's so-called magic formula, once said: 'When you play professional football there are one or two basics and if you stick to them you don't go far wrong. The system only breaks down with individuals.'

There is no mistaking Souness's individuality, but that may not be enough. Much of Liverpool's future will depend on his future health. His operation has merely added to what has been, since Dalglish's departure, a continuity of uncertainty. But it was always possible, given Paisley's quite outstanding gifts, that once he went nothing would ever be quite the same again.

August 5, 1991: Stephen Bierley

All of them awesome

They appear over the horizon like multicoloured flies hanging in the heat. For a split second there is no sensation of speed. Then suddenly they are at your feet, the distant snarl bulging to a full-throated roar.

Television sanitises motorcycle racing, as it does so many sports. No amount of cameras mounted on bikes, or remote-control lenses lurking at the tightest of bends, can do the men in leather justice.

The thousands who clustered in and around Donington Park yesterday, Britain's mighty brigade of bikers, would no more have watched from their armchairs than be seen dead in a car. The British Grand Prix, and the 500cc battle in particular, is their day of days.

At Redgate corner, a right-hander at the end of the finishing straight, a long man-made bank of Hickstead proportions was crammed with transfixed spectators, perched like auks on a cliff face. It was here that Kevin Schwantz hurled his gloves and helmet over the safety fence to the crowd – a grand winner's gesture of delight and empathy with those who would later don their own leathers and hurtle home (within this country's speed limits, of course).

The donned impersonality of grand prix motor-racing drivers, squished into their micro-cockpits, is far removed. The last 30 years have seen enormous advances in the speed and sophistication of motorbikes, but the thrilling spectacle has changed little.

As the bikes blast at colossal velocity down the straights, the riders remain in full view, suddenly rising like startled rabbits as the corners approach, legs yawned to right or left as the mean machines complain and shudder before the throttles are once more yanked, twitching the back wheels.

As their bikes and bodies lurch over at ridiculous angles, defying both gravity and commonsense, it is impossible not to feel a surge of admiration for these unassuming sportsmen who spend large chunks of their lives risking their lives. This is the world of the quick and, please God, the fewest of few dead.

A disembodied voice on the Tannoy system informed all and sundry during a practice session that 'Eddie Lawson's bike had somersaulted several times . . . but Eddie is OK'. All in a day's business. But there are times, many times, when you want to close your eyes.

The admen and the image-men desperately want everybody to believe that motorbikes are the upmarket market of the future. Those with the loot to shoot are not buying a second car but two wheels and a set of leathers. Hasn't Simon Le Bon recently bought himself a £20,000 Ducati, while isn't anybody who is anybody in the United States wearing a biker jacket this summer?

There remains precious little glitz or vacuity on the pro circuit. As *Motor Cycle News* so graphically previewed this race: 'You'll be a prat if you miss it.' Not for them or their readers the language of the soft-sell merchants.

The atmosphere in the paddocks and pits yesterday morning was, if not exactly hushed, one of intense and immense concentration. The huge mobile homes, with their diverse European and American number plates, stood empty, save for a sleeping rider or two. Everyone else was huddled around a myriad of machines.

A little tinker here, a little touch there. The precise setting up of the bikes is what separates grand-prix racing from domestic competitions. Yet even after such exhausting and exhaustive checks, the heat of competition can blow the best-laid plans apart in seconds.

To err is human, but if you really want to foul things up employ computers. They are being used more and more, saving precious time for the technicians and tuners.

Yet in the end it is all down to the riders, their skill and their nerve, or rather lack of it, and yesterday's joust between Schwantz and Wayne Rainey was as exciting as anything you could wish for.

'Kevin was pretty awesome today,' said Rainey. He was. But then so was everybody else.

April 4, 1992: Chris Hawkins

The other Scudamore

There is no obvious physical similarity between the father and the son, but conversation reveals the same earnest, ingenuous attitude and the same pride in a job well done.

Michael Scudamore still cannot quite believe just what a good job he did when he met a local girl called Mary in the queue for the pictures at Hereford one evening, married her in 1957 and produced a boy named Peter.

'When I was a young jockey I had my heroes like Bryan Marshall, Tim Molony and Jack Dowdeswell,' explained Scudamore senior. 'They were like gods to me. There they were riding their 70 to 80 winners in a season and then I breed this boy who rides 200 and keeps on doing it. I never dreamt such a thing would be possible.'

The possibility was turned into reality in Michael's view by the boy's possession of three key qualities, not forgetting, of course, the Pipe factor.

'First, I think he's got very good hands, which enables him to relax and settle horses,' said Michael Scudamore. 'He can give horses a bit of rein and allow them to jump. If you've got too tight a hold of a horse's head he can't help himself – he wants freedom to jump, but Peter does slip a bit of rein and give them a chance.

'Secondly, he's got this desperate determination. When I was riding I thought I was determined, but when I see him I'm not so sure. I've seen some tough, hard men like Fred Winter, Stan Mellor and Jeff King. I think anybody who gets near the top must be determined, but I've never seen anyone quite like him.

'The other thing is he's also a very good horseman. He can see a stride and get horses jumping and, of course, he does a lot of schooling – an awful lot more than jockeys did in my day.'

Not that the young Scudamore was quite such a sensation the first time his father watched him, getting over-excited and unbalanced on jumping the last in a point-to-point under the gaze of his headmaster at Belmont Abbey.

'I knew he'd been practising pulling his whip through and riding a finish, but when he came to do it he fell off right in front of us,' said Michael.

'But shortly after that he rode in a point-to-point on a horse of Herbie Sharpe's and he was in the right place on the winner all the time. I thought then coming home that perhaps he could ride a bit.'

Despite his subsequent record, Peter has never won the Grand National nor the Cheltenham Gold Cup – races his father won on Oxo in 1959 and Linwell in 1957.

Michael was just about the most experienced jockey around Aintree and had 16 successive National rides, which he thinks is a record, but got round 'only about five times', quickly getting a taste of what was in store when falling at the first with ten others in 1951.

The following year he finished second on Dorothy Paget's Legal Joy and in 1954 was third on Irish Lizard.

Victory on Oxo was a vital affair for Willie Stephenson, the trainer who had incurred heavy financial losses on the first day of the meeting and backed his National runner to get him out of trouble.

'Willie was a good man to ride for and on the morning of the race he told me to come up to his hotel room and he got out a bottle of champagne and a Guinness and we had a black velvet before we went to the races,' remembers Michael. 'This was most unusual for Willie because normally if he saw you have a drink the night before he'd go berserk. But the previous day he'd backed a two-year-old heavily which got beat and a horse called Farmers Boy, ridden by Arthur Freeman round the Mildmay, and that fell. So he seemed to throw caution to the winds and after he led me out on Oxo he went and doubled his bet, a brave thing to do in the National.

'In the race itself he told me to hold him up because he was afraid he wouldn't get the trip. I went up over the first six on the middle to the outside and I was about 15th when we got to Becher's, where there was a right old shemozzle. Six or seven came down and I came out of the fence third or fourth.

'Going into the country for the second time, Tim Brookshaw on Wyndburgh and I had it between us and I remember he shouted over to me, "At least we shall be on the pictures." We jumped the last five up-sides, but at one of them Tim's stirrup iron broke. Knowing this, I kicked on going to the last and went clear, but then he started to catch me and I was probably lucky in the end to win by a length and a half.

'I was thrilled to bits, but Willie came across to me and all he said in his high-pitched, North Country stutter was: "You c-c-came too soon." I said "Do you really mean that?" and he said, "C-C-Course I do." '

The National in those days was a fearsome race according to Michael, the fences being so big that you could not see over the other side as you approached, so that there was a constant hazard of being brought down.

Modifications over the years have made it easier and he

is generally in favour, saying that anything which stops animals being hurt must be good.

He is a great horse lover and still trains a small string at Hoarwithy up a little winding lane in the depths of the Herefordshire countryside. He has lived here since 1957 and this is where Peter was born and brought up. The Scudamores are a strong, close family and Michael is not averse to telling the boy when he makes mistakes: 'Sometimes when we're driving home from somewhere I can't help telling him if he's made a mistake. It's silly really because he knows and it annoys him. There's nothing worse than somebody telling you you've gone wrong when you know it. Mind you it doesn't happen often.'

He can say that again.

September 7, 1991: Andrew Moncur

A glance on the leg side

I may have imagined the tinkle of breaking glass. There was no doubt, though, about the obscene chants effing and blinding down an otherwise peaceful train carriage on a London suburban line. I could swear to it.

Oh well. Another football season begins. Here we go, here we . . . Just then the truth dawned. These were *cricket* fans. You could tell because they were grown men dressed like 11-year-olds: meaty legs sprouting out of little shorts; T-shirts, including one showing field placings (stretched horribly between mid-off and mid-on), and ridiculous hats. To hand, the statutory picnic cooler-box, now presumed devoid of extra-strong lager in cans. They were coming home from Lord's and the Sri Lanka Test.

Now, just as I couldn't be positive about the shattering glass, I can't be completely sure that every England cricket supporter used to wear, or carry, a gabardine mackintosh, with belt. They certainly gave the *impression* of doing so. I am certain that they would have thought that lightweight summer trousers were somehow foreign and suspect. They definitely didn't take them off, possibly not even in private.

It seems only yesterday that international cricket was played to an audience dressed by Dunn and Co. I can remember members at Edgbaston – they may survive there, for all I know – who would have been scandalised if asked to remove their jackets and ties. Their teak-like weathering must have ended, abruptly, below the Adam's apple and above the wrist.

One of them was, to my certain knowledge, a woman. She had played for England in her time and retained the sort of cool, distant eye and whippy frame otherwise found among retired cavalry officers. She was the only grandmother I ever met who kept a metal bar slung across her kitchen door. She used it for doing pull-ups. You don't mess with women like that. You wouldn't invite her to take part in a Mexican wave.

She would have been far more tolerant of the two gents who were sitting just below me at last month's Oval Test. During a peculiarly tense spell, when England were straining to winkle out an immovable Richie Richardson, one of them was fast asleep. The other, yet more bewilder- ingly, was reading the comment pages of the *Independent on Sunday*. Well, they weren't distracting anybody, were they?

All around was New Cricket Man. The first thing about going to a match now is to look as though you are *taking part* in the game. So NCM carries a sports holdall and dresses in trainers and a shell-suit. In the event of sun- shine, the trousers can be whipped off to reveal the shorts and meaty knees. The bag is for drinks. But, please, no glasses. Real men drink lager from the can.

This sports outfit gives greater freedom of movement when, in moments of high excitement, NCM springs to his feet and does a Cameroon wiggle with arm-pumping action. NCM can then start to sing in that curiously monotonous way reserved for Englishmen in crowds. 'You'll Nev-er Walk A-lone', cracking painfully on the high notes, always seems suitably inappropriate as another English batsman makes the solitary trudge back to the pavilion.

Sportswear also helps NCM to spin more freely on his axis to abuse those responsible for delaying play by moving behind the bowler's arm. This is particularly gratifying when the suspect turns out to be a fatcat in a sponsor's box; or, better still, a waiter serving his drinks. At the Oval there was ample opportunity for baying of this sort. One waiter, in response, raised a single finger to the crowd. It was not the one used by umpires.

The meaty feet can also be draped over the backs of the next row of seats. This levers the belly into a position where it acts as a table for NCM's can of lager. At Lord's during last summer's India Test, I watched a gent (possibly dressed by Dunn and Co, Bombay) having to call a policeman. Four Englishmen, reclining in this manner, had refused to shift their feet to allow him to shuffle back to his seat.

The sports bag also contains the Walkman. This is necessary in order to listen to Radio 3's *Test Match Special* and to abuse its commentator Christopher Martin-Jenkins. NCM thinks CMJ is an upper-class twit. He doesn't allow this to spoil his lunch: a pile of sandwiches whose sheer scale reinforces the suspicion that everybody present is aged 11. There must be a lot of mothers at home with firm views about feeding growing boys.

A neighbour at the Oval, clearly motherless, had brought along a Thermos of gin and tonic, and two of Mr Kipling's exceedingly small cup-cakes. That was his breakfast. He declined to listen to *Test Match Special* at that stage, explaining: 'I can't stand the sound of upper-crust accents before lunch.'

The Englishman may have lost his inhibitions about

removing his trousers but, by God, nobody's going to catch him dropping his attitudes.

March 3, 1992: Mike Selvey in Australia for the cricket World Cup

White balls are something else

This is about balls. Two of them, and white ones at that. As we are constantly being reminded, this is a World Cup of firsts: South Africa, southern hemisphere, round-robin, day-night, coloured clothing, Australia getting beaten and, of course, black sightscreens and white balls. It is the last item which is having a marked effect on the progress of the tournament.

White balls are an integral part of day-night games, research long ago having shown that they stand out like a beacon even in daylight whereas the traditional red article is hard for batsmen and fielders to pick up in artificial light and, equally important, is almost impossible for the spectator to follow. Indeed, one Test umpire has even said that he has never had to suspend play for bad light with a white ball. So their adoption for this tournament might be seen as not only innovatory in the short term but also, perhaps, a pointer to the future.

Apart, that is, from one thing. The Kookaburra white ball appears to have properties of movement over and above those of its red counterpart. This is causing all sorts of havoc, as on Sunday when the bowlers of England and briefly Pakistan made the thing not so much talk as recite the complete works of Shakespeare.

Professionals maintain that they can always – or, more

correctly, think they can always – pick from a box of brand-new red balls the one that will swing. They will inspect the seam to see how proud it stands, all the better to act as a rudder. Next they will look at the ball's shape, on the basis that a slight distortion from round towards a discus shape will further improve its swing.

Then there is the colour. The bright-scarlet types will be discarded, as the bowler is looking for the deep colour, heading towards maroon. The colour probably has something to do with the leather's capacity to take dye, since all balls are manufactured to a standard. Certainly the darker ones seem to polish better.

Of course there is nothing rigid in this, and some dark-red balls will go depressingly straight while some scarlet ones can loop the loop. Sometimes a ball will have an inner weight bias which helps it swing.

All that said, the white ones are something else. The weather can be sunny or cloudy, the atmosphere humid or dry, there can be grass on the pitch or it can be as bare as the Nullarbor, but the damn thing always swings.

Why? It can only be a function of the seam and the properties of the white dye used on it. A traditional ball's seam is not dyed.

All this has been in evidence since white balls were first used for Kerry Packer's World Series 15 years ago.

But there is a problem which, until it is adequately tackled, could prevent the white ball being used in long matches. It gets dirty. From Persil-white it rapidly deteriorates to a wash-day grey that prevents it being seen so clearly. That is why in this tournament they are using two balls an innings, alternately from either end.

So in terms of the wear on the ball, the games are being played not over 50 overs but 25. This means there can be little deterioration in the hardness of either ball or seam, or in its ability to swing. It is causing mayhem in some instances, reducing what should – let us be honest – be an exhibition of batsmanship to a bonanza for the medium-pace swing bowler.

Worthy players they may be, but there is something wrong when an international tournament can be dominated not by Curtly Ambrose, Wasim Akram, Bruce Reid, Allan Donald or any of the class fast bowlers, but by Gavin Larsen and Rod Latham, Derek Pringle and Ian Botham, Maṇoj Prabhakar and any other dribbly bowler who cares to turn his arm over.

There is nothing wrong with medium-pacers, but they are not really what this event should be all about. The fact is that in seeking to be innovative, the organisers have succeeded in finding a method of destroying the game as a spectacle. They might well need to reflect on that come the end of the tournament.

May 16, 1992: Frank Keating

Ian Botham at home

With a proprietorial attention to detail, the squire with the raffish moustache inspects his estate. He is wearing a multi-pocketed, yew-green poacher's jacket and battered grey-kneed jeans tucked into tall leather boots. He looks very much the part: he could be a young Tory knight of the shires just biding his time organising the family acres before the inevitable call comes from the local constituency for him to take his rightful place as the voice of his people at Westminster.

This could yet come about. If Seb Coe can charm votes out of faraway Cornwall, could not Ian Botham do the same in his very own rustic neck of the north Yorkshire woods.

It is a sparkling springtime morning of timeless renewal and contentment: buds and blossom and birds on the bough. There is no cricketing today but, with Tigger the busily-snuffling boxer at his heel, the young landowner could not tarry on his rounds.

There is another sport to play after a check on the lake, well stocked with brown and rainbow trout, a threatening glance upwards at the circling jackdaws as they beady-eye from on high the chirruping clusters of newly hatched goslings at the lakeside, a thwacking morning pat and fond nuzzle for the horses and, in one of the evocative old stone barns, a brief surveillance as father-in-law supervises the preparation of the great iron salmon-smoker.

Then, all creatures great and small present and correct, his sometime foe and good friend, the Australian bat and equally new Durham debutant Dean Jones arrives – and off go the two dauntless, bold Lochinvars for a round of golf on top of a Yorkshire moor.

In 19 summers this with Durham is to all intents only Botham's third as a 'home' player. After his very first championship curtsey (May 8, 1974, v Lancashire, c D. Lloyd b Hughes 13, and 0 for 15 in three overs), he played only two seasons for Somerset before he and Kathy, a Yorkshire girl, married and set up house in her home county.

With Somerset and Worcestershire Botham rented cottages and lived out of (very large) suitcases. 'Now, at last, home games really feel like home,' he says with relish. 'It's wonderful having him home with us all at the start of a summer,' says Kath, adding with a giggle, 'although ask me again in six or seven weeks and I might give you a different answer.'

Botham has already given some ravishing appetisers to Durham folk. Irrespective of the sabbath slog, a high-calibre championship century, two boundary-peppered 70s and some pin-sharp defensive bowling in the Benson & Hedges games, plus, it goes without saying, a handful of spectacular catches, have made sure he kept his World Cup place for England.

And it is devoutly to be wished that his form in next week's one-dayers ensures his place in the Test side when the rubber against Pakistan begins at Birmingham on June 4. Then a summer already to the brim with opulent promise will be colourfully overflowing.

Hotfoot from the beanstalk and Bournemouth's panto-mime boards, Botham played his 100th Test at Wellington in February. In the World Cup he was, after Wasim Akram (18 wickets at 18 apiece), the competition's most success-ful bowler (16 at 19). His Test tally is now 5,192 runs, 383 wickets and 118 catches. Three more catches and he will overtake Sir Colin Cowdrey's England record of 120 (in 114 Tests), an astonishing figure, for the new knight of Lord's was able to pouch his from both ends, not being required to bowl the 21,561 Test deliveries which Botham has – more than any other Englishman except Derek Underwood's 21,862, another record certain to fall to Botham if he plays this summer.

So are there one or two challenges left? 'Oh, sure. Well, to play for England is challenge enough, and always has been. I love it, and will always keep trying to get selected for as long as I'm physically able. Blimey, I'm only 36, why do you always keep writing me off? It's up to the selectors, of course, but if I make it my priority to do really well for Durham, well that goes hand in hand with my chances of playing for England, doesn't it?'

After beating Australia almost single-handedly in the World Cup, the final itself was an anti-climax. Launching England's innings, he was given caught behind at once, though even a fuzzy satellite picture still showed a wide shaft of floodlight between his bat and the ball. His immediate, but obviously seething, departure from the crease was accompanied by the strident suggestion from Pakistan's impudent and long-memoried little Sohail, at short-leg, that Botham should 'next time send out your mother-in-law to bat'.

Touché – and now the seen-it-all old warrior can laugh

merrily at the cheek of Pakistan's young blood. The mother-in-law in question, by the way, was in the kitchen helping Kathy make cakes. The two girls, Sarah and Becky, are whizzing around outside, pretending to help the gardener mow the lawns.

The eldest child at 14, son-and-heir Liam, is in from his early shotgun patrol round the estate and now preparing to return to school at Rossall. The tall, tousled, engaging teenager is a chip off the old block; Liam is looking forward to the new season, too – last year he became the youngest ever to play for Rossall's first XI – after a brilliant winter for the school at rugby (full-back or fly-half).

Not far away the glorious, babbling, deep-gullied Greta flows into the Tees – small fry for Botham the angler, who has just bought a £50,000 timeshare for a stretch of the real McKay on the Tay. There Turner painted the *Meeting of the Waters* and, for good measure, Scott wrote *Rokeby*.

In the inn at Greta Bridge, Dickens stayed when he was researching *Nicholas Nickleby* and the horrendous Yorkshire board schools. As we strolled through his own acres, the young squire of cricket was surprised to be reminded of his own education at 'Dotheboys Hall'.

Twenty years ago this month Botham set off with gangling bravura from Yeovil to be a groundstaff lad at Lord's. He sold scorecards, cleaned the Long Room windows, worked the scoreboard, bowled interminably to snooty MCC members in the nets and wheeled the covers on, and off, and on again.

The two grizzled old coaches, Harry Sharp and Len Muncer, winced fondly enough at the boy's lusty confidence, but not much else, and they thought at very best the kid might make a fair-to-middling, lower-order county professional for a season or three. Then what? A carpet layer perhaps or a corner shop?

The two, sage metropolitan coaches could not have remotely thought their rustic and rumbustious pupil would first break every all-rounders' Test record that was going; resurrect the game as a sport of, and for, the people; and end up ushering in a brand-new county championship team as an estate-owning squire with columns framing the front-door steps, trout in the lake, horses in the stables, farm workers in the yard and a Mercedes on the gravel.

And still, he insists, there is a lot of cricket in him. 'I didn't think I could enjoy it more than my time with Worcester, which was great, and I thank them for it. But, who knows, why can't I still be playing for Durham when Liam makes his county debut? That's something to aim at, isn't it?'

And he laughs that relishable and wolfish laugh that has never been far away through the two decades in which he has played his game with the whole man of him, body and soul, spirit and skill, and especially that bold courage which Chesterton defined as almost a contradiction in terms – 'courage displaying a strong desire to live, taking the form of a carefree readiness to die'.

The much-travelled young squire sniffs a new summer with satisfaction. He has come home at last.

May 30, 1992: Matthew Engel

First-class act

The Mousetrap is the play in which the cast changes all the time but the plot, set and props remain unchanging forever. English county cricket is the exact reverse. Quite regularly, everything turns upside down – three days, four days, cover the wickets, uncover the wickets, dozy-doh, change your partners and do it all again – but the cast remains exactly the same.

Until now. This year Durham became the first new actors in the county championship for 71 years. Since 1921 no one had got on and no one had got off, a period of stasis that may be unprecedented in world sport. The new entrants might have been expected to tiptoe in quietly, make everyone feel sorry for them, win their first game around July and shut up in committee for about 30 years or so.

Durham won their opening competitive match and have made it clear since that they will be a force on the field; meanwhile, the second team are walking away with their own championship. Some county chairmen were willing to let Durham have three overseas players in their first year, a concession that now sounds more than a little preposterous.

Off the field, the club have reached a membership of 6,500 – a figure beaten only by Lancashire, Yorkshire, Middlesex and Essex – and are believed to be considering the possibility of closing the books as if this were the MCC or the Garrick Club.

The workmen have just moved in to begin levelling the land for the new £6 million stadium on the banks of the Wear at Chester-le-Street, perhaps the most ambitious cricketing project undertaken from scratch in this country. Some of their organisation – though they have struggled to keep up with the pressure of demand – is superb.

The crowds at all their games have been enormous by normal standards – and enthusiastic too – yet when Ian Botham came out to bat at Stockton this week he received no more applause than anyone else. Botham? Big deal. You could say that Durham look as though they have been putting on first-class cricket matches for years, except that the ones who have been doing it for years are far less good at it. Other county officials are now ringing Durham for advice.

The question now is why on earth this never happened before and why counties such as Staffordshire and Devon cannot follow the Durham road into the first-class game.

The answer lies in the peculiar nature of the Minor Counties Championship, a competition which has never functioned as a genuine second division or even as much of a breeding-ground for young talent. At best, it is an unambitious place. At worst, it is downright cliquey, a haven for mid-30s professional types who have organised their offices so they can take extra days off.

Durham moved up because, in effect, the old club ceased to exist. It was taken over by more dynamic figures, chief among them Don Robson, a former Gateshead and Doncaster footballer ('when boots were boots'), construction company and sports-shop owner, Labour politician, leader of Durham County Council and an altogether higher roller than is usually seen round any cricket ground, never mind a Minor Counties one.

Under Robson, Durham have become the first county to organise themselves as a limited company – one member, one share. They hired an agent, Brendan Foster, who is not unknown in the North-east, to fix the sponsorship deals. There appears to be hardly a widget-maker north of the Tees who has not contributed something.

However, we have all lived through the 1980s. Traditionally county treasurers have taken a deep breath before investing in so much as a new toilet block. The worrying thing about Durham is that at Chester-le-Street they might be building not a new cricketing Jerusalem but Canary Wharf. At the moment they are being borne aloft on a thermal of novelty and enthusiasm but they might find themselves bumping their heads very painfully on the ceiling. No one, including Robson, yet knows who is going to pay for the stadium.

Not a problem, he says. The answer is 'block module relativity'. In plain English, they will build the stadium in stages within the resources available at the time and if they have to play on an open field, they will. 'Newcastle United have debt repayment of £680,000 a year for their new

stand,' said Robson. 'It's crazy. We won't be big borrowers.'

And it really does seem as though people will want to
go on watching Durham. Their attractiveness derives from
hiring the right men, Geoff Cook and David Graveney, as
director of cricket and captain. They are old friends and
easygoing men, at ease with themselves and their cricketing beliefs. Any team with a high proportion of old sweats
is going to have the odd argument and, once the intitial
enthusiasm wears off, Durham are bound to have their
share.

But there is a nicely humorous spirit about all their
games: even Ross and Judy, the alsatians employed to
maintain order, spend most of their time being stroked by
children, though Judy did glare on cue to empty the bar
after the first Sunday match.

Graveney's team have yet to find a need for the currently fashionable Stakhanovite approach to practice,
partly because it is so hard to get everyone together: most
of the older players have not managed to sell their houses
in the south yet. The first team have not had half-a-dozen
proper net sessions. It does not seem to be doing them
much harm.

Where on earth have they been the past half-century or
so? And if Durham can do it so spectacularly, is there not a
faint stirring in a few Minor County hearts in Norwich or
Plymouth or Stoke-on-Trent?

June 30, 1992: Matthew Engel

Point of no return

Jeremy Bates walked into Wimbledon yesterday morning
surrounded by a posse of security guards. On the way in
he passed Stefan Edberg, who was accompanied only by
his coach.

Just before four in the afternoon Bates was serving at match point for victory over the No. 9 seed, Guy Forget of France, and a place in the Wimbledon quarter-finals.

He had dipped a toe in that tide in the affairs of men that leads on to fortune, and promptly stubbed it on a rock.

Less than an hour later he was beaten. There were many rational explanations: a weak second serve at the crucial moment, a few critical net cords that fell lucky for the Frenchman, the sheer difficulty of coping with a serve that comes at you as if propelled by catapult from a second-floor window.

But if years of sports writing teaches one anything, other than how to wheedle one's way past gatemen and hall porters, it is that at the highest level sport is only marginally about ability and primarily about desire.

Bates talked yesterday about how he had enjoyed his week of glory and how disappointed he was in defeat. Neither he nor even his psychologist will ever really know if in the end he shrunk away from the consequences of glory.

Forget won 6-7, 6-4, 3-6, 7-6, 6-3. The historical analogy everyone had been reaching for was 1970, when Roger Taylor beat Rod Laver and momentarily raised British tennis somewhere close to the pinnacle. It was the right summer, but the wrong event: this was a rerun of Leon, where England's footballers stole defeat from the jaws of victory against the Germans.

Bates played some superb tennis. All week he has served better than at any time in his life; his volleying was magnificent; he matched Forget touch for touch. But once his moment had passed he succumbed rapidly. For an instant an entire division of the national joke industry was in danger: it was possible that tennis would cease to be a source of constant derision. Normality has now been restored.

The *Sun* said yesterday that Bates could not possibly

lose to a Frog. In the end, everyone was reminded that British tennis players can lose to anyone.

All along, Forget's aces were his aces. In the first set, neither man could break service and they fought out a tie-break amid enormous tension with Bates escaping set point against him with a brilliant forehand down the line and then clinching his own.

Forget broke him early in the second set and held on. In the third, Bates did the same. There were times when Forget only had to put the ball less than six inches from the line for the crowd to insist that it was out; once or twice Bates believed them and began to pout and double-teapot.

Forget, in difficult situations, was muttering Gallic imprecations as if he were Jean-Paul on a bad night in the Grey Gables kitchen. When Bates took the set, half a dozen people started waving Union Flags. And by the time he came to serve for the match, Centre Court was utterly still but intensely alive in a way it had not been for years; even the Royal Box was full, though it was definitely tea-time.

At 30-0, Forget had the first of his net cords. As Bates tried to deliver his first service at 40-30, somebody sneezed and he had to stop. The real first serve was just out. The second was drilled straight back past him.

After a couple of deuces Forget won the game with another net cord. The set went to a tie-break: from 2-2 Forget won five successive points. The rest was straight-forward. The Union Flags fluttered again, but this time rather sadly. Bates waved goodbye with a hint of finality.

No, he said, he did not feel he had chickened out. He had had the best eight days of his life. Was he unlucky?

'No, not particularly, I was playing well enough to win the match. I mean, I got to match point. I didn't do that with luck particularly, I did it with good tennis. I think the example I've set is that the whole thing is mental. Everybody has the ability and it's when you have the self-belief and stuff to go out and do it. We are all capable of doing it.'

Did he wish for anything else? 'A huge serve.'

Forget served 31 aces to Bates's nine, but on every other count the Briton equalled and often surpassed him. When he took the initiative in a rally he regularly mixed power, delicacy and cunning in a manner of which he has every right to be proud.

But all week Bates has been unable to disguise his unease at it all. He seemed out of place amid the security guards. And when he looked out of his window last Wednesday and saw four journalists in his garden he was angry and astonished.

Of course he was right to be angry: he should have got out the shotgun. But how could anyone who has been the British No. 1 for five years in a major sport be so astonished? Has his uneventful life in the middling reaches of the circuit really left him so immune to the consequences of a little success – 15 years after Virginia Wade – during this manic fortnight?

Oh well. At least a British player has looked on the Promised Land. On the outside courts yesterday, the boys' singles was starting. Somewhere there may be a British lad who will get there one day.

December 27, 1991: Peter Lennon

Guys and dogs

I am at the dog track considering the merits of Danny's Rose over Rozensky's Bunny while listening to Mr Archie Newhouse, a prominent party in the British Greyhound Racing Board. I am somewhat discouraged by what he tells me for Archie is such a guy as is not easily pessimistic. But now he is saying to me that the dog-track business is about to go kaput. This is because the Home Office politicos will decide that off-course evening betting is jake with them.

Later I sit with Mr John Carns who has spent 55 of his rosy years majordomoing this very Wimbledon Stadium and he is playing the same tune in spades, in addition to which Mr John Dawkins, the company bag man, leans on my shoulder and sheds a 10-dollar tear telling me what happened in 1961 when off-course afternoon betting was introduced and the punting citizens ceased to make the journey in the afternoons.

Further, says Mr Dawkins, the beneficiary of this repulsive move would be none other than the heavy guys such as the likes of Ladbrokes, William Hill and Corals. Their own tracks would be linked by television to their off-course night shops. So they would continue to get the moolah while such as Wimbledon, relying only on the gate, might have box-office takings not exceeding that which greeted Mr Ambrose Hammer's play about Miss Florentien Fayette, which was an affair very low on scratch indeed.

While I think some of what I hear may be strictly counterfeit I see this could lead to very great hardship indeed with 35,000 greyhounds being sold off as guard dogs which is not a great future for them because any citizen will tell you a greyhound will only guard you if you are attacked by a hare.

I fork a plate of smoked salmon and sip my Chatoo Latoo while a lady, who is every inch a lady, named Pauline Burn, stands by my table on the terrace ready to take my sawbuck if I should wish to risk it on, say, Our Maddie Moon and pass it through her cash register. You may look in wonder at a citizen who seems to believe he is, so to speak, on the track at Saratoga while simultaneously harpooning smoked salmon at Mindy's and assume I am fit for the house with the very high walls. But this is by no means the case. We are now on the bend towards '92 far from the hugger-mugger of the old days. Not alone are equalisers and knuckle dusters and such instruments of impoliteness no longer on the menu, neither are chilled footsies. Our feeding terrace is wrapped around with glass through which we view the doggies going past and we rejoice at neon blazing *Happy Xmas* when it does not inconvenience the canines.

I see several influential citizens, such as the like of Mr Jimmy Young on these feeding terraces. Unwrapped from his background he looks a little faded as many a celebrity does while, however, Mr Frankie Howerd, beaming like a boiled lobster, makes the joint look like his own personal wrap around. Such is the mystery of poisonality. To all intents and purposes we are not Guys and Dolls any more but gents and ladies, but for the moment when the doggies skittle past and then one and all put down their forks to produce a thick roar not unlike that of 222 bisons attempting to break out of Madison Square Garden and then go back to being dainty with the turkey.

Now many citizens consider this glass overcoat to be a very great shame, just as they do the disappearance of the Hare Driver from the centre of the track into a little box because it becomes by no means easy to lob a beer bottle at a disloyal dog or better still at the Hare Driver.

But the Hare Driver Mr Parsons, who has been driving hares for 21 years, tells me he is by no means hostile to such an arrangement. He does not cherish the citizens who believe that a dog does not deliver not because it is a cement paw or a wide runner but because Mr Parsons did not drive his hare at the requisite tantalising distance. Although a very rapid little man, Mr Parsons prefers not to be within reach of such mentalities. I now discover that there are indeed places where citizens do stand in the rain and to my surprise this also includes the on-track bookies. The on-track bookies do not have to pay a percentage to the track men, as does the Tote, but the politicos decided long ago that a certain number of on-track bookies must be let in. So the track men gave them the opportunity to have plenty of fresh air. 'Do they like this?' I enquire in some amazement and am assured by Mr Carns that bookies are addicted to nippy and inclement weather.

I congratulate Mr Carns for agreeing to allow the bookies in for a fee only five times the gate entrance which, at £20, is very small potatoes indeed. But this observation is followed by a long pause such as I have noted in the case of the District Attorney versus Harry the Horse. Finally he speaks as follows: 'The bookies also make a voluntary contribution.'

Then I enquire what would happen if a bookie did not come across. But Mr Carns on my right only smiles and Mr Dawkins on my left also gives a smile which suggests to me that I may be the ham in this sandwich so I decide not to pursue this little matter.

Then Mr Newhouse tells me he is worried that the Church might not approve of evening shops which may incite bread-winners into evil late night habits and deprive them of the exercise of going to the track.

Now this is a very great surprise to me since speaking of Church matters is considered to be very bad luck indeed, worse than wearing green or having your floozie come to the track decked in pearls.

All of these parties point with great sorrow to another repulsive injustice. While the bookie shops are obliged by the politicos to take a levy from the punters for bets on horse racing which is passed on to the horse tracks, they are by no means obliged to extract such a tax from the doggie punters. But they do and put it in their own pockets. The doggie track men say the levy should go to keep the noble sport running.

About to burst into tears for the doggie track men, I come across a certain Mr Tom Kelly, a prominent citizen at the Betting Office Licensees Association, and find he is very scornful indeed about the track men and he speaks of Bags (Bookmakers' Afternoon Greyhound Service), a sweet deal for the dog track men which provides the dollars for 12 tracks to operate in the afternoon.

I am finding that it is indeed very difficult for a citizen to keep cases on who is doing the dirt on whom in this crap game, particularly when I now discover a punter crying murder because the influential citizens with whom I had just dined had that day jacked up their pay-off from the Tote from 17½ per cent to 20 per cent.

I begin to think all this is none of my business and seek out the lady Ms Pauline Burn, who is every inch a lady, and hope to chew the fat with her about her 31 years at the track and the great dogs such as Mick the Miller who have skidded there. But Ms Burn tells me that she only works at the track to help bring up her family and then gets the habit and stays on and she lets me know that a dog, skimming or stationary, means less to her than a granny's apple.

I am much cast down by all this and decide I had better go and see Queen Mary or whoever it is who nowadays has the franchise between London and Little Ole New York so I can get out of this town.

Moving pictures

July 11, 1991: Catherine Bennett

Beyond our Ken

Journalists make things up. So Ken Russell says. They don't just misquote him. 'They make up their own quotes.' How profligate, when Russell's own words are, like his films, so calculated to shock and offend, so sure to arouse feelings of embarrassment, pity, rage.

Which journalist, having seen Russell's latest film, *Whore*, in which the Whore discourses to camera on the dangers and difficulties of whoring, could imagine that Ken Russell would sit back and say that prostitution is 'easy money'? Who would have invented that? Or this? 'Well, yeah. I think prostitutes generally are happy about being prostitutes. It's not a bad way to earn a living.'

No worse, he implies, than being a film director. Because being a film director not only means being misquoted, it means being an artist. Which means being a mighty albatross, fallen among mocking fatheads. Misunderstood. Accursed. 'Artists are about 50 years ahead of the general public,' Russell said, pushing off his shoes to reveal bare feet, and toenails painted red to match the varnish on his fingers. He had been appearing on television, and had dressed up artistically, with blue eyeshadow, an odd sight on his round, brick-red face, which looked, as he chomped nuts out of a packet, as if it might burst. 'I mean,' he said. 'That's why they are *artists*, they have visions of the future. I mean, being an artist is to be a visionary. Not to see what is here –' he gestured disparagingly at the furnishings of the Groucho Club – 'but to see them in the context of history. So artists see that, and people say "it's just a television, a lamp and a chair, don't hassle me. It's just what it is". And it's *not* what it is, it's a *statement*.' He screwed up the empty nut packet and tossed it over his shoulder, onto the floor. What was the *point* of talking about his new film, he demanded, ungraciously? 'I mean, what can come out of it? I mean, the statement is the work. The work is the statement.'

But *Whore* is rather a confusing statement. It's adapted from a play called *Bondage* written by David Hines, a London taxi driver and playwright. Hines had often had King's Cross prostitutes in the back of his cab. 'I was moved to anger and pity at the sad brutality of their lives,' he told the *Guardian*. 'It's something out of Hieronymus Bosch out there at three in the morning.'

Ken Russell wanted to film *Bondage*. He told Hines he wouldn't alter a thing. But the title, meant to suggest slavery, was immediately changed to the simpler, more stirring, Whore. When Russell could not get British funds, the scene moved from stinky King's Cross to spanking Hollywood Boulevard, LA, and big, bouncing Theresa Russell was cast as the golden-hearted tart, looking none the worse for her years on the game. Bosch became bosh. Everything Theresa Russell says in the film, about the trials of prostitution, is immediately undermined by her own luxuriant glamour, and the question of why a nice girl like this, who doesn't even have a drug habit, can't find a better, safer job. Maybe it's because – like Russell's previous, ridiculous whore, China Blue, in *Crimes of Passion*

– she really *likes* it? Or are we misunderstanding the Artist again?

We are. *Whore*, it turns out, is not just about prostitutes, but about *people*. About *us*. 'It said a lot about just straight-forward situations with men and women and sex,' Russell elaborated. For example: 'There's this myth that if you've got a big cock, that's what women want. But it's obviously not.' No? No. In *Whore*, Theresa Russell is made to observe that size is not important. 'I think that's the most revolutionary statement that's ever been made in the history of the world,' said Russell, laughing, but possibly serious. 'I think it will give a lot of males tremendous hope, because how many men have got a 16-inch cock?' It's a rhetorical question. But probably not that many, eh? In this way, *Whore* is 'a helpful film about sex'.

There are sex lessons for women, too. Even women who aren't prostitutes. 'Because prostitutes are really women,' Russell declared innovatively. 'They are not prostitutes. They are basically the honest part, they don't have to pretend to themselves.' If his audience realises this, it will help them. They might like to act out an honest, whore–client fantasy. 'I think most women – some women', he amended, 'would love to play being a prostitute. In fact I *know* some women who love it. I know various couples who pretend not to know each other, to be a client and a prostitute, because then they don't have to be ashamed . . . We don't know each other, but if we did, and I went out of that door and I came back and pretended to be somebody totally different, and asked you to do this or that or the other, because you were acting being a prostitute, you would do *anything*, because prostitutes do *anything* . . . That is a tremendously liberating thing.' Though not, perhaps, for the woman acting the prostitute. But the experiment was not tried. *Whore*, it turns out, is another of Russell's attempts to shock the brain-washed masses from their 'cocoa drinking' torpor, by rinsing them in his own, corrective fantasies. 'I mean there was a time when I did put mine in,' he says, of his earlier films. 'I had this fantasy, I've always had this thing about nuns. I mean, you know, everyone wants to rape – well, wants to *screw* a nun, don't they? Because they're holy people, they're virgins and all that. And I think most men would be liars if they said they didn't want to screw an air hostess . . . I put that fantasy into *Crimes of Passion*.'

Then there were the liberating castration fantasies in *Lisztomania*. 'Oh, yeah, well, I was having problems with my wife then,' Russell explained.

So it was a rather strange sort of mass therapy? 'Well, that's tough,' Russell said, 'nothing's perfect in life.' If you don't share his fantasies, that's tough, too. 'I'm not saying I do the perfect thing. I just say I do the thing which excites me. All my films are a thing about self-discovery, of myself. They are not so much about Mahler – they *are* about composers, but on the journey to finding out about them, you also find out about yourself. So I make my films for myself, I want to find out about myself. I want to explore the why, the wherefore, and the fact that someone's given me a million dollars to do it, that's fine.'

Which confirms what many have long suspected about Ken Russell. His films *don't* mean anything, unless you're him. He *did* sensationalise the lives of composers in order to promote his own, malodorous fantasies about sex, corruption and death. He thinks it's artistic expression. But being Russell simply means being paid to bore whole cinemas with last night's dream, to use the director's chair as a psychiatrist's couch. As a result, we know he has difficulties with squirmy things and spiky bits. With worms, snakes, vomit, suspenders, Catholicism, rape, women, death, and prostitution. And sadism. Russell's still very interested in that. For his next trick, he hopes to alert audiences to their suppressed masochism. He's going through a period of sexual liberation, he's heard some interesting things about 'subjugation galas'. He wants to film *Venus in Furs*. 'I'm beginning to feel that most people, although they don't make a song and dance about it, have these feelings. I think that expressing it in a film is something people would go with.'

The extraordinary thing is, that someone may well give this amateur sex therapist the money to do it. Why not? They gave him money to film *The Lair of the White Worm*, two hours of sticky self-indulgence which made a clown out of every participant actor. 'This was the first horror film that had something to do with English mythology and all that,' Russell averred, importantly.

Lair notwithstanding, Russell was invited to film his life story for the *South Bank Show*. He cast his two-year-old son as himself, waggishly confirming his status as 'the oldest *enfant terrible* in the film business', one popular cliché he has never tried to deny, and which, as he gets older and more terrible, will become ever less contestable. The film said very little about his art, but much about being an artist – which in Russell mythology, means starving, shrieking, communing rowdily with nature, and being wronged by pig-headed critics. And the more Russell is wronged, the more it confirms his right to a place at the artists' table, next to Byron, Mahler, Lawrence, and Gaudier Brzeska. Has not he, too, in his horrible way, shocked the public, and paid the price? After *Valentino* flopped, Russell was, for several years, unbankable. 'All the means of expression in this country are governed by the establishment,' he complained. But why should they pick on him? 'It's just that they don't like people who are mavericks, they want people really to conform, they want people that they, the press, can build up to be their nice little guys. And anyone who kicks against this, they try and knock down.'

There was a time when critics loved Russell's sensitive biopics for the BBC's *Monitor*, his *Women in Love* – some of them even liked his *Tommy*. He was a hero. 'Well, I was when it suited them,' he said. 'I made a film on Elgar, ponies galloping across English landscapes, and of course

that was all very pretty, but when I began to get a little
hyper-critical, they just got upset.'

Well, maybe the critics will love *Whore*. It's not critical,
or not so's you'd notice, and Theresa Russell is pretty. And
if they don't, Ken Russell clearly learned a lot of whys and
wherefores. So did David Hines, who had the original
idea. Hines sold his play to Hollywood, but he's still a taxi
driver. He doesn't understand it. The film cost $16 million,
and he can't afford a new cab. He went to the *Whore* pre-
view, and couldn't find a seat. He congratulated Theresa
Russell, who didn't know who he was. Afterwards, the
Hollywood party repaired to the Groucho Club while
Hines picked up his cab, and started looking for fares. 'It
was *unreal*.' A real suffering artist, is David Hines, cast
down among the fatheads. If only nuns took cabs as often
as whores, that Ken Russell could make a film about him.

May 12, 1992: Ken Russell

Back from Sing Sing

I was sitting behind bars in a tiny cell in Sing Sing, the
maximum-security prison situated on the Hudson, in the
State of New York. The zoom lens of a BBC documentary
camera – focused on my worried face – were recording
the moment for posterity.

I was worried on two counts. First, because I was being
sued by Bob Guccione of the *Penthouse* empire, and,
secondly, because I had no idea where I would find the $1
million plus I would have to cough up if I lost the case.
Hell! I had a hard enough job scraping enough money
together to pay the lawyer who was fighting to save me
from losing the roof over my head. In fact, he was the
reason I was behind bars.

Richard Golub is a singing lawyer and as part-payment

of his fee I was directing a pop video of his latest single, 'Dancing for Justice'. The rather unorthodox nature of our deal had aroused the interest of Alan Yentob, Head of Music & Arts on BBC 2 in those days back in 1985. We'd met each other for the first time in NY while attending a season of BBC Classics sponsored by the Museum of Radio. Alan was responsible for a revival on his *Arena* programme of my film about Elgar, which I had made for the pioneering arts programme *Monitor* in the early 1960s.

Over a Budweiser in a Broadway bar after the presentation, he asked me what I was up to. I replied that I was up to my neck in debt if my pending lawsuit with Guccione went his way. Alan asked me to explain. I did so for the next two hours, but to cut a long story short, my tale of woe involved Guccione suing me for breach of contract on *Moll Flanders*, a feature film I was supposed to direct, but which never happened. But what interested Alan Yentob most was the fact that I had hired a smart showbiz mouthpiece who was heavily into hard rock – and I don't mean Alcatraz. He asked me what I'd say to the BBC immortalising the event. I said, 'Yes.' Which brings us back to the start of the story, with a BBC documentary unit filming me filming my lawyer in white tie, top hat and tails, singing his heart out surrounded by a bunch of convicts with such lyrics as:

Now we're gonna celebrate,/Gonna dance right out that prison gate;/'Cause once you're on the outside/You ain't never gonna be retried.

Against appalling odds I finished the video, the trial finished with 'case dismissed' and the BBC finished their documentary. My rehabilitation with the BBC had begun.

It was the BBC who gave me my first big break as a professional film director back in the winter of 1959. Up until then I'd learned my craft by making amateur films. The most successful of these, a religious fantasy, was seen by Huw Wheldon, the editor of *Monitor*, who, fortunately for me, was on the lookout for a director to replace John Schlesinger, who had just spread his wings to fly off to the world of feature films. Rather against his better judgement, Huw Wheldon took me on approval and painstakingly taught me how to make films on a great variety of subjects, all connected with the arts.

It was a laborious process but a very rewarding one. Between us we turned the boring run-of-the-mill-Post-Office type documentary into a kaleidoscopic trip of the senses which attempted to communicate the intentions of the artists and the spirit of their creations – a tall order which did not always succeed. But nothing ventured, nothing gained and the experimental work that Wheldon pioneered with myself and other enthusiasts working on the programme (such as Melvyn Bragg, Humphrey Burton, David Jones, Tony Palmer, old Uncle Tom Cobbleigh and all) certainly bore fruit, as a glance at most arts programmes of today will testify.

By the time I left the BBC in 1971, I'd made something in the region of 38 films ranging from straightforward cinematic essays on subjects ranging from *The Guitar Craze* to *The Dance of the Seven Veils*, a comic-strip on the life of Richard Strauss. This last was a biting political satire that offended everyone from Mary Whitehouse to the Houses of Parliament, who hauled Huw Wheldon up on the carpet to explain why such a piece of pornography had been allowed to pollute the airwaves. He defended the film and my right to express my beliefs fearlessly, but that did not stop Auntie putting the boot in a week later by setting up a group of pundits condemning me and extolling the virtues of a man who, in my opinion, was a Nazi and an egomaniac to boot.

It was my swansong. I did not make another film for the Beeb for the next 21 years. But after *Your Honour I Object*, which caused quite a stir when it was shown on BBC 2, I had the ear of Alan Yentob and began to batter it – fairly gently as it happened because he was reasonably receptive to my ideas. One of these was a visualisation of Edward Elgar's *Dream of Gerontius*; another was Ken Russell's dream of making a film on Bohuslav Martinu – who was as obscure to British audiences as Elgar was familiar. These two composers had something in common in that they were first appreciated in foreign countries. In Elgar's case it was Germany and with the Czech composer it was America, where Martinu spent many years in exile during and after the last war. When I enthused to Alan about Martinu's musical interests such as jazz, ants, aeroplanes, surrealism and dream-girls, he showed considerable interest. And when I mentioned that the 100th anniversary of his birth was coming up, he commissioned me to write a treatment.

After a trip to Martinu's birthplace at the top of a tower 60 miles from Prague, this was duly accomplished. A few weeks later I was given the go-ahead to write the script and make the film. From then on I was answerable to Dennis Marks, the Head of Music at BBC 2, who in turn produced an Executive Producer, in the form of Diana Lashmore, to keep an eye on me. And apart from being extremely supportive, they both kept very much out of my hair.

So what had changed in the intervening years? Well, very little so far. As in the past I was given a completely free hand to realise *The Mystery of Dr Martinu* exactly as I conceived it. No one interfered, no one censored the sex scenes. In this regard this was an advance, for Huw Wheldon had occasionally banned a few scenes he personally found offensive in a couple of my *Monitor* films. 'That homosexual sequence will have to go, old boy; I'd have to explain to my 85-year-old mother-in-law the meaning of the word lesbian, and I'm not going to do that at her time of life.'

But the biggest difference was the increased budget and the fact that I made the film with my own production company, Dreamgrange. This meant that I was free to choose exactly who I wanted to help me make the film. This was often not the case in the old days, when I was allocated my cameraman and designers etc. Most of the time I was lucky, but there were occasions when a particular individual was not my first choice. In this instance, my resourceful and energetic young producer, Maureen Murray, was not only responsible for day-to-day production matters, but was also instrumental in helping set up the co-production funding necessary to make the film.

As was occasionally the case in the past, I shot some of my material at the BBC Ealing Studios. Without question these were the best maintained sound stages in Britain and they were available at a very reasonable price. Tragedy! One day when I was busy filming a black-haired boy bonking a statue, the shattering news came through that the studios were to be closed down. For a moment I experienced a pang of regret. The walls that had seen the birth of the Ealing Comedies and many memorable BBC productions would soon come tumbling down: another nail in the coffin of the British film industry. Oh well, no time for nostalgia – the sort of freewheeling improvisatory style of film-making I've practised man and boy for 30 years never relied on studio production in the first place.

February 24, 1992: Leslie Woodhead

Message in a neon bottle

I arrived late at the BBC. After 28 years in the incomparable haven of Granada, and two years freelancing, I dropped anchor at the BBC, Kensington House, in autumn

1991. I stepped ashore in rough weather, with forecasts of worse to come – job cuts, drastic reorganisation, low morale. There were even those ancient BBC mariners who predicted darkly that the arrival of an alarming creature, identified by some as 'the al-Birtross', would soon make ghosts of the entire crew.

I got lucky. The pink neon bottle bobbing towards me from the *Arena* titles suggested that the natives were friendly. There were, of course, the curious dislocations of a strange country: the sense of inhabiting a BBC system as vast and unknowable as Stalin's Kremlin, where the talk is of 'strands' and 'streams' and the canteen gossip dissects slivers of influence and power too subtle for a newcomer from the cruder infightings of ITV.

There were those gloomy staff bars which always gave me the weird impression that I'd wandered into a set for one of my own Polish drama-documentaries. There was also an arcane system for settling expenses. But I felt strangely at home. For days I wondered why. Then I got it. That *Arena* office, with its zany graphics, cast-off guitar and the big photograph of Van Morrison slouching with Bob Dylan – it was Granada in the 1960s.

During my early years at Granada, Hugh Greene's BBC appeared a charmed place, glittering like the America of my childhood – vast, full of goodies, over there. Over the years, I saw some of my most talented colleagues, from Jeremy Isaacs to Jonathan Powell, cross the divide and prosper. (My old researcher John Birt has also done quite well.) In the 1970s and 1980s the BBC continued to look like an eccentric promised land. As a maker of ITV documentaries, I envied the seemingly endless range of documentary slots and strands and series. Most enviably, spared the rival claims of Pedigree Chum and Pepsodent in their airtime, BBC programmes seemed blissfully unaware that a TV hour should be 52 minutes and 30 seconds.

So how has the real BBC matched up with my long-matured fantasy? One documentary vagrant's experience may be a slender basis for taking the pulse of an institution which still employs more than 20,000 people. But I can report that the Beeb still works wonderfully when it comes to the business of making programmes.

The Incredible Case of Comrade Rockstar, my film for *Arena*, involved hauling BBC crews from Berlin to Moscow and from Denver to Hollywood in pursuit of an American cowboy called Dean Reed who became the biggest pop star the Communist world has ever known. He died mysteriously behind the Berlin Wall in 1986. I've appreciated those BBC crews who seem to have been crafted by Rolls Royce. Back in the cutting-room, I've relished the support systems that appear able to deliver anything overnight, no fuss, no re-shoots. And I haven't met a single BBC accountant.

Most miraculously, when I suggested my one hour film seemed to work best at 90 minutes, the BBC said OK. For someone grown wearily familiar with the ghettoising of ITV documentaries to the wastes beyond *News at Ten*, the offer of a slot at 9pm, all 89 minutes and 15 seconds of it, has the quality of a mirage.

It was more than a decade ago when Jeremy Isaacs, then an ITV programme controller, insisted during his MacTaggart lecture that the health of the BBC was of vital interest to anyone who cares about British television. In the 1990s, the patient is giving cause for concern. My experience suggests that the limbs are in good shape, but it is apparent that the heartbeat is increasingly uncertain. Now that the free market vandals have had their way with ITV – and David Plowright's dismaying departure from Granada suggests that there may be worse to come – the BBC seems to be preparing itself for its own dose of Year Zero. In corridors and canteens, I heard much of study groups and review bodies and policy probes. I didn't hear so much about programmes.

'I'm not surprised you've enjoyed working for *Arena*,' a senior BBC man said to me the other day. 'It's just about the last of its kind.' Amid the anguishing over the licence fee and politicians and ratings, I'd suggest one important message may be drifting by under-noticed: the one about programmes, the message in the pink neon bottle.

January 23, 1992: Derek Malcolm

Taking another shot at Kennedy

There are few half measures where Oliver Stone is concerned. For him, the screen is not for compromise. In *JFK* (Empire, Trocadero etc, 15) the youngest ever President of the United States is assumed to be the ultimate hero, destroyed by the serried ranks of those for whom a liberal chief executive, who made Washington into an approximation of Camelot, was too much too soon.

The film, three hours and a little more, thus becomes both a tribute to a martyr and a thunderingly polemical thriller – a diatribe against the dying of the light, that swallows the conspiracy theories of New Orleans district attorney Jim Garrison wholesale and then adds a few of its own.

It is in no way a balanced piece of work and it strains credulity to breaking point and well beyond. But you still come out of its long battle with fact and fiction admiring its daring, its tension and its sheer unadulterated chutzpah.

Uneven as it is, *JFK* at least persuades you that the Warren Report was as badly flawed as any of the contrary propositions in the film. Stone's version of events works

on the general principle of there being no smoke without
fire. It is almost but not quite history as gossip.

Can one possibly believe that even LBJ was implicated?
At one point the former Vice-President says to a suspicious
looking group of power brokers: 'I've given you Vietnam.
What are you going to do for me?' But can one possibly
disbelieve that the bullets that hit Kennedy and Governor
Connally came from more than one sharpshooter and
more than one gun? At the conclusion of the film, you
have to face the fact that a conspiracy of some sort,
orchestrated by powerful special interests, was involved.

But who exactly was it? Johnson himself thought it was
the Mob, with whom Kennedy certainly had dealings
before and during his narrowly victorious election campaign. Stone thinks it was everyone under the sun who
simply couldn't stand the man – LBJ, the Mafia, the CIA, the
military-industrial complex and quite possibly Uncle Tom
Cobbleigh as well.

This, though, is a film rather than a piece of history and,
as such, you have to prepare for the fact that there are
times during it when you have to know your onions about
an event which took place before the substantial part of
the movie's likely audience were born. And well as the
subsidiary cast play, the intricacies that fill the screen after
the initial excitements of the assassination of JFK (Steve
Reed) and Oswald (Britain's Gary Oldman) not only
passed my full understanding but seem pretty boring into
the bargain.

There was a moment about a third of the way through
when this critic would have given a substantial sum to be
relieved of his duties. Fortunately that feeling goes on the
entrance of Donald Sutherland's Mr X who explains to
Kevin Costner's hitherto curiously lacklustre Garrison
exactly what is what and who is who. Thereafter the film
perks up considerably as if suddenly discovering its real
raison d'être.

Admittedly we have to put up, presumably for box

office purposes, with Sissy Spacek's tearful Liz Garrison doing the usual Hollywood bit of the wife asking an obsessed husband whether work or family comes first (and then gritting her teeth and becoming the splendid little woman behind her hero).

But the long Clay Shaw trial scene, which uses some of Garrison's own words and rather more of those of the screen-writers (Stone and Zachary Sklar), is fascinating and gives the director a chance to redress the balance a bit by having the spectators openly laugh at Garrison's more absurd propositions. And at the end of this slightly ponderous but still frequently exciting epic, it is perfectly possible to salute a major American film, flawed but still mind-boggling.

Costner delivers his big set scenes like a star trying to be an actor rather than an actor trying to be a star and Stone's work hereabouts is full of the almost operatic intensity that is so often his signature.

Elsewhere, the newsreel footage is used sparingly in favour of grainy and frequently highly skilled reconstructions and Robert Richardson's dramatic cinematography moves a good few mountains. If the film lacks balance, it doesn't lack either visual conviction or an appropriate sense of horror that the full story has never been told.

Oldman and Sutherland are reliably good in Costner's support, with the familiar faces of Ed Asner, Jack Lemmon, Vincent D'Onofrio, Joe Pesci, Walter Matthau, Tommy Lee Jones and John Candy producing cameos of some watchability.

It is the kind of cinematic odyssey that does manage to work on the mind as well as the emotions and which, through sheer persistence, wins more battles than it loses. Only the nagging doubt about what Kennedy really represented prevents it triumphing against the odds.

When all is said and done, *JFK* conjures up a curious picture of the director himself, as a man naïve enough to believe that Kennedy would have prevented the necessity of him making either *Platoon* or *Born on the Fourth of July* by successfully scuttling from Vietnam, and who ends his film with a burst of tub-thumping patriotism that would have made the grunts in Vietnam instantly reach for their pot pouches.

It's a film that seems to mirror its director's faults and virtues exactly. But at a time when most American movies seem to be made by a clever computer, that is not necessarily a bad thing. What it will do for the Kennedy myth is another matter altogether. That story continues.

January 31, 1992: Derek Malcolm

Sticks and Stone

Oliver Stone, audaciously rewriting American history in a series of controversial films, is not a man to be trifled with. He's like a dog with a bone, and he won't let go. Particularly as far as *JFK* is concerned.

'I don't think I'm paranoid,' he said quietly when I met him in a Hamburg hotel. 'But I ought to be. They tried twice to kill my film – once before I started shooting and again when the film came out. But I owe a great debt to the American public. It was they who prevented a fiasco. Right across the age spectrum, they're going to see it in droves.'

That day, the early, very favourable returns came in from Germany, and Stone had just been awarded a Golden Globe as best director. He had a right to be in a good mood. But, he says, he also has the right to be very angry at the way the American media has treated him, accusing him not only of bias but of downright lies.

He admits nothing, and he thinks that time will eventually show that President Kennedy was killed not by one man acting alone but by a two-tier conspiracy that involved one set of people organising the assassination, and another set covering up for them.

'It could have been disastrous for me and the film. The *New York Times* had 20 pieces against the film, *Newsweek* had a cover George Orwell would have been proud of – you can't trust this movie – and a lot of all this happened before it was actually made. We had the first script stolen from our offices and sent to almost every American newspaper. It was analysed, the ending was given away and my conclusions were discussed and ridiculed both before and while I was making the film. Have you ever heard of an instance like that before? A powerful man like Dan Rather even interrupted two newscasts to editorialise about the movie before he had seen it. This film could have died. We were that close.

'Quite a bit was below the belt, because they've been misrepresenting what the film says. They said that Mr X doesn't even exist. Well, he does exist. He's based on Col. Fletcher Prouty, who served in the Pentagon from 1963 as chief of special operations for the general staff, liaising with the CIA.

'The worst form of ridicule has been the claim that I say 5,000 people were involved and, if so, how could such a conspiracy be kept secret? Of course, we never suggest that 5,000 people were involved. What the film says is that there was a limited conspiracy to kill the president, and a second, wider conspiracy to cover it up. The cover-up was largely out of embarrassment because of the likely international effect. And I believe Lyndon Johnson and J. Edgar Hoover were part of it.

'The thing is that I've invaded a lot of the turf that's only supposed to be inhabited by the politicians and so-called "experts". They screwed up the case and they know they did, and we uncover at least three dozen discrepancies that they didn't investigate. They seem to have spent a million words attacking me instead of admitting it.

'How, for instance, did Oswald get a job at the book

depository only a few weeks before, at a spot overlooking the place where Kennedy's car was to slow to 11mph? Even the House felt the Warren Commission had done a lousy job there. Why didn't the press investigate that in depth? The answer is that they were lazy and scared. They preferred to conform rather than accuse their own government of perfidy. But the fact is that, with this film, I feel the people are behind me. They may not be as dumb as some people believe.'

Stone feels strongly that Kennedy would have manoeuvred his way out of Vietnam. He says the new book, *JFK in Vietnam* by John Newman, supports that view.

'Basically, what we now know is that between 1961 and 1963, Kennedy had a no-combat troop policy in Cuba, which they wanted him to invade, in Laos, and in Vietnam. He did send 16,000 "advisers" in response to the pressures he was under, but he'd decided by 1963 that, if he won a second term, he would pull out altogether by 1965. He knew he couldn't do it before that. He told that to a number of people, including Senator Mike Mansfield, who confirmed it to me on the phone the other day, and also to Wayne Morris and Tip O'Neill.

'He was making public statements that were hawklike about the domino principle, but that was because he could not publicise what he wanted to do in the face of the threat from Goldwater and the right. He did what a lot of politicians do. He feinted one way and intended to go the other.

'He said clearly that if the American public would not support an invasion of Cuba 90 miles away, they would certainly not support an invasion of Vietnam 9,000 miles away. Also, he was a man who had the ability to change. After the Bay of Pigs and Cuba, he didn't have to prove himself as macho like Johnson had to over in Vietnam.

'I think that, if he'd lived, the cold war would have ended in the seventies and the era of Reagan and Gorbachev would have been brought forward by over 20 years. Trillions of dollars would thus have been saved, and quite a lot of lives.

'But he was rocking the boat, and he paid for it with his life. And I think Robert Kennedy and Martin Luther King were killed for that same reason. The three most progressive figures in the sixties were apparently gunned down by single lone nuts, all of them under highly suspicious forensic circumstances. Can you honestly say you believe that?'

August 14, 1991: Imogen Stubbs

Sex action

My first 'public' kiss was when I played Mary in the Nativity play. I reacted as though a rabid dog had tried to climb down my throat, Joseph requested a transfer to the goat department and I realised, for the first time, that kissing someone you hardly knew – and with good grace – was an essential part of an actor's job.

At RADA we learnt all the theatrical disciplines – how to be a penguin, what to do with a splashyplosive, how to sing the 'Dambusters Theme' in harmony – but they never taught us how to do kissing or sex on stage or screen. This is a big gap in the cv when you are a young actress. Most roles for such women centre on these activities; they often have little else to define them. And this lack of technical expertise means that the first time you have to act some sex – and the 20th time – are equally embarrassing and undignified.

It starts with rehearsals. While the script says, 'They embrace passionately,' the actors give each other a cursory peck. The director responds with something like, 'That's going to be electric – when your hips stop being at right angles to each other.' Eventually one actor will pluck up the courage to give the scene some credibility, while the director keeps his eyes glued to the script and the rest of the cast stand around murmuring, 'I told you she fancied him.'

One of the actors may seize upon this splendid opportunity to stick his tongue legitimately down the throat of the other, meeting any protest with, 'It's not you, you know. You're an actress, a character.'

Bed scenes are even worse. Directors tend to believe nakedness lends credibility, but what this really means is the actor wears boxer shorts, while the actress's breasts are on show. This desire for 'reality' results in paralysingly self-conscious actors imitating love scenes from other films as their only source of protection. Like many actresses, I think these things are best left to the imagination. What was wrong with, 'Bedroom door closes – cut to sunrise in the suburbs'?

The first naked scene I did on film was playing a character who thinks she is pregnant and is looking at herself in a mirror in a darkened room. It was not meant to be sexy (there was no notion of seduction) – and, after all, we see ourselves in a naked state every day – but I felt violated. I burst into tears every time I thought of my family watching the scene.

Another time I had to stroke an actor's groin in a film. Even though I was going out with him at the time, I was so mortified that on 'Action!' I squeezed my eyes shut, held my breath and my hand became a frenzied rolling-pin. Finally I blacked out.

Directors are often coy when dealing with a euphemism like 'Big Heat'. 'Nothing granny can't see' becomes a 'closed set' (with dozens of new technicians and producers suddenly appearing) and no direction. 'OK, you two, in your own time. Go with the flow. I'll trust you to follow your instincts and we'll just keep the camera rolling. Warm enough?'

Embarrassed dressers shuffle forward to remove the dressing gowns and someone bawls 'Action!' This is followed by a ghastly silence. You start kissing tentatively, then necking and finally the dreaded 'simulated hump'. By which point, united by the degrading lunacy of it all, you crash teeth or get the giggles or fall out of shot. And still no one calls 'Cut!'

You overhear the director whispering what sounds like, 'Frame it to avoid her cellulite' – though he later claims it was, 'Her beautiful frame is devoid of light' – then, 'Well, that's warmed things up a bit. The next take will be gangbusters. Oh, and I didn't say "Cut" because they seemed to be enjoying themselves so much. Ha, ha, ha! And . . . action!'

At which point the actress bursts into tears and has to be dragged off to have her bags covered up again, while the actor pulls the director aside for a man's talk, which is picked up by the sound guy, to the amusement of the crew.

In the end the director realises some choreography is called for. So the scene becomes, 'You put your hand on her breast, then nibble her left ear. Try to keep that tongue out of sight – the camera's picking up yellow fur on it. Then I'll call, "Knee up, knee down" for a bit, and we'll call it a day.'

Acting sex has provided me with some fascinating challenges, though. I once had a clause in my contract that stated not 'No nudity' but 'No pinky bits'. This entailed a lot of sticking plaster and in the end the scene was cut.

Another memorable occasion was a night shoot near Eastbourne. A pond had been emptied, covered with a plastic sheet, then filled with fresh water. The plastic was only removed at the last moment. We had to run naked down a hill and into the floodlit pond (which had been covered in dry ice), embrace and sink under the water. When we surfaced my fellow actor was covered in dead worms and woodlice, all the insect life that had been killed by the plastic sheet. Seeing this, we shrieked and fled, and the next day the local paper ran a story reporting that elderly motorists had been shocked to see a luminous spaceship land in the downs and two Martians scuttle out of it, making eerie noises.

Perhaps the only constructive thing you learn from this area of acting is what you don't want to do in real life. Now I know that I don't want to make love on a wet sand dune in Norfolk in January. Nor on a pile of untreated sheepskins. Nor during a thunderstorm in a swimming-pool filled with electric cables. I don't want to kiss someone the same way 22 times, until my lips look as though I'd got them stuck in a bottle of Cherry Cola.

Writing this – that each time I play a love scene feels like the first time – I'm conscious that in a not-too-distant future, I might be writing about the last time. Inevitably I will reach the age at which actresses get to play mother, spinster and very-depressed-indeed roles. And, of course, are no longer eligible for sex scenes.

July 11, 1991: Derek Malcolm

The woman who dares

'My life is splayed out for the world to see,' Madonna told the *Advocate*, the American gay and lesbian news magazine shortly before appearing, amid almost unprecedented scenes of hysteria, at the Cannes Festival this year. 'They already compare me to Adolf Hitler and Saddam Hussein.'

The quote is almost as mind-boggling as the reception accorded to her at the festival. Hitler? Saddam? This little woman, to whom one highly respectable British paper sent a young man with a large basket of flowers, to stand outside the exclusive front entrance of the Hotel Du Cap, Antibes in a desperate, and ultimately unavailing, attempt to obtain a brief audience?

But the bald words, no doubt accurately written down by the interviewer, do not do justice to her sense of irony, which is rather more pronounced than that of your average Hollywood superstar. Nor to the fact that she is likely to laugh both at herself and at the showbiz circus that surrounds her from morning to night. Yet she does appear to be trapped inside this cocoon of hyperbole, and whoever it was who said that she was like someone standing on top of a tall building, with the crowd in the street below shouting 'Jump, jump!', seemed to sum up her situation with telling accuracy.

It is true that she has, shrewdly and with great persistence, made the bed that she is now lying in. Even so, what one doesn't expect, when meeting her (without, alas, the flowers), is the awareness she displays of her circumstances and the frankness with which she speaks about them.

It was noticeable at the disco party organised for her at Cannes that the superstar who was accused of hiring a bevy of cloth-eared thugs to protect her on a London visit not so long ago sat with more orthodox friends at a table near the dancers while Eddie Murphy, the rage of Harlem, stood in the background surrounded by heavies with shades on. Her frankness in interviews, which allows for a rather touching and not totally calculated vulnerability as well as a fairly full-blown narcissism, is neatly displayed in *Truth or Dare: In Bed with Madonna*, the documentary made round her Blonde Ambition tour which was the cause of the hubbub at Cannes.

In it, she appears self-obsessed, maternal, beautiful, plain, extraordinary and just plain ordinary in quick succession – aware of the camera but not actually playing to it and urging a reluctant Warren Beatty to join her because 'the light's good here, don't worry'.

She clearly sees herself as having a considerable need to be loved and admired, and also wanting to nurture those around her, like the mother she never had long enough for it to count. She adds that her dancers, mostly gay, took advantage of the fact on the Blonde Ambition tour, and her well-known penchant for surrounding herself with men who don't want her seems as much an insurance policy as an identification with them, despite the talk of libidinous bisexuality, often encouraged by herself, and later to be denied with statements such as 'People think I'm fucking all the time, but I'd rather read a good book.'

'I only realised what a little mother I was when I saw the film,' she says, 'and it gave me quite a shock. People keep on saying that we faked a lot of it. Warren thought I faked the whole thing. But actually most of the time, probably 95 per cent of it, I would have done the same thing whether the cameras had been running or not.

'I told Alek [Keshishian, the young director of *Truth or Dare*] that he'd have to stand up to me, because I was going to tell him to push off all the time. And he had the balls to do that, which is why the movie is more interesting than it would otherwise have been. I usually get my own way on these matters, but I didn't on this occasion, and I'm glad. The film embarrasses me a little at times, but if it was going to be any good, it would have to, don't you think?'

Thinking is difficult when faced with this attractive but not conventionally beautiful woman who answers questions very directly and, if they are stupid, doesn't hesitate to say so.

Typical reporter's question: 'How big is Warren Beatty's dick?' Answer: 'I haven't measured it. Why don't you ask him?'

She doesn't so much drop her guard as appear not to

bother with it at all on other occasions. Doubtless it is all a bit of a performance, tailored to the occasion. But she does appear – and it's the only word that springs readily to mind, however feeble – nicer than one would expect from so immensely ambitious and sharp a generator of instant publicity. One need not be surprised that she is no bimbo with a series of male Svengalis orchestrating her career.

It may have been a carefully manufactured showbiz personality, but it now fits her like a glove and it was undoubtedly manufactured by herself. You don't get the sense that she's saying what she ought to say – like the stars of the Hollywood that doesn't really comprehend what she is about at all. She's playing a game which she generally wins: 'No, I'm not appalled by myself. Are you appalled by yourself, or just a bit defensive like everybody else?'

'Yes,' she says, when asked about the prayer meetings before each show on the tour, 'I am religious. They were sincere, at least as far as I was concerned. Anything could happen at these shows, anything could go wrong. We were about to be thrown out in Toronto [for simulating masturbation on stage]. If you believe in something other than fate, you need to ask for some sort of a blessing.

'The thing is that I'm a true believer, but a sceptic as far as the church is concerned. Not really a good Catholic girl. I just think the church has filled so many people with a lot of terrible fears and repressions, and if I do any good at all, it's to loosen things up.

'It's not that I'm trying to build a bridge between sex and religion. It's just that the Catholic Church insists on separating the two and they always have, and it's bullshit. It's just a way of controlling people. That's why they freak out when they see me dressed in a corset with a crucifix hanging around my neck.

'As a matter of fact, the pussy-stroking business on stage wasn't actually intended to be masturbation. But if people think it is, why should I care? I don't think masturbation is a mortal sin. If it was, millions would fry, wouldn't they? And if it's out in the open in my show, then perhaps the kids who watch will lose any fear of it they have. You have to remember that we've just come out of a very reactionary and repressive phase in America – it's a non-card-carrying liberal Democrat talking now – and I'm getting the flak from people I mostly don't respect at all. In fact, if I wasn't criticised by them, I'd be mortified. They are trying to influence the people I play to, and so am I in a completely different direction. I don't know how much I can do, but I might as well try.

'All the things I find shocking, they don't find so at all. Like poverty, exploitation and conventional morality, which actually makes people accept these things. If they are shocked by me, they can go to hell. I don't owe them anything.

'I'm always trying to challenge the accepted way of behaving, the "right" way of running your life, and other people's. No, I don't know what my father thinks about it all. He's very straight and traditional because he grew up in that very macho Italian-American world. And the fact that I accept gays so easily probably makes him as uncomfortable as the fact that my brother Christopher is gay. He keeps a lot inside. But he is what he is and you can't change him now.

'I dearly love him but sometimes he can be very naïve. You know, when he wanted to come to the show, I gave him some alternative dates and he said: "Which nights have you got tickets for?" So I said, look, I run this show. You can come whenever you like, you can sit wherever you like. Honestly. It will be OK. We can dump some of the celebrities in the front rows. No worry. But he couldn't quite accept it. His little girl running things, I suppose . . .

'When we got to Europe a lot of the flak dropped away, except in Italy where it was orchestrated by the Vatican. No one was very shocked at all. Not even in Spain. But in America we've still got this stupid residue of false values.

There are some things you do and some things you never do. I break the rules. So I'm some kind of monster. They don't feel that way in Europe. They are too sophisticated there to fall for all that crap. Except the Vatican and the British press. The Vatican thought that all the religious imagery and symbolism in the show was sacrilegious. So they influenced part of the Italian press to try to put the kids off coming. It didn't succeed but it hurt me because I'm basically Italian. It was like a slap in the face and I felt unwelcome and misunderstood. Apart from anything else, it was completely sexist.'

She says that the song in the show that has always attracted most criticism is 'Like a Virgin', probably because of its ambiguity. But for her it is only the most obvious part of the proceedings – the point where the fact that the whole evening can be taken on different levels can be best illustrated. Those levels, she adds, include irony and humour. And what her critics don't get, or don't like, is the outright humour. They get uneasy when a show is funny and serious at the same time. She says passion and religion bleed into each other and that it is perfectly possible to be sexy and religious at the same time. Not all saints are eunuchs. And people who aren't in touch with their own sexuality are likely not to be in touch with a lot of other things as well. 'Like a Virgin' is intrinsically about this and the hypocrisy it creates – 'Catholicism has beautiful rituals but often the messages are not so lovely.'

As for the British popular press, its rituals are not so impressive and its message matches them in sleaze. 'Why are they so awful? Honestly I used to love coming to Britain. I'd go round all the museums and galleries and to cinemas like the ICA and have a great time. Nobody much bothered me. But now, it's hell. I can't do anything without that mob surrounding me. If I talk to them, they twist the words; if I don't, they get me for not doing so. You can't believe to what lengths they go. But what I want

to know is – do they believe what they're writing themselves, or do they just have to write it?

'It's true that if you're a star, you can't expect privacy.
You have to accept a lot of things, and even welcome them
and use them to your advantage if you can. But that lot just
tear you apart. They sort of hate you. And I can't accept
that. It annoys me to the extent that I absolutely can't ever
go to London. Maybe that's what they want, but I have fans
in Britain too, and they should know why I don't go there
any more.'

Doing the Blonde Ambition tour was a different matter.
It lasted six months and she lost count of the number of
shows it involved. 'I often woke up in the morning and
didn't know where I was at first. Once I had to call room
service to check out the language. I think some of that
comes over in the film, so it's not a fake. It's the real me in
there. That doesn't necessarily mean that I'm always being
spontaneous, but it's really me not being spontaneous!

'When I played the "Truth or Dare" game, however (in
which scene she shows how to fellate a man, with a bottle
as a model), I was being spontaneous. It's a great way to
break the ice at dinner parties, you know . . .

'We had a dinner after the showing of the film at Cannes
and I played it with Dino de Laurentiis and all these very
straight business people in suits. It loosened things up
alright. Dino had to kiss Luc Besson [the French director],
for instance. I had to kiss Luc's wife. I enjoyed it, but then
everyone knows I'm as perverse as hell. I don't know
whether he did.

'A lot of those people were from the film world, and
that's where I want to be at this point in my career. I want
to act in movies, and I want to direct. As a matter of fact I
think it is probably easier for me, surprisingly enough, to
be behind the cameras than in front of them.

'But one person I would play for is Pedro Almodovar
[the Spanish director of *Women on the Verge of a Nervous
Breakdown*]. And he says he's writing a movie for me. I

hope it comes off because he's very talented and a free spirit like me. They tell me he's going through a bour-geois period now after all his commercial success, but I hope he gets over it in time for me. I love all his films, particularly the early ones, which are the most radical and anarchic. It's the kind of rude stuff I identify with.

'The most difficult thing for me in our film was not the process of making it but afterwards, trying to think of how much trouble I would be in with Warren, because he was the only one who wouldn't sign a release form. He asked me to take him out altogether but I said no, because he was there, he knew the camera was on and I had told him not to come around if he didn't want to be included. But he's fine now. He just was very frightened because, you know, he's a control freak and he's not like me at all. He doesn't want anybody to know anything about him. He didn't want to look silly or stupid or something. But he got quite a few favourable reviews and people said he looked pretty good, so he stopped worrying. He's the voice of sanity in the movie if you like.

'Of course, Kevin Costner didn't sign a release either but there were notices posted up everywhere saying that if you walk into certain rooms you will have the camera there, so he knew the score.

'No, I wasn't angry when he called the show "neat", just irritated. Because if that's all it is, I've failed. So I made my feelings clear. He probably wasn't too thrilled about it, but he's got seven Oscars now so why should he care?

'As for the bit about Sean [Penn], it was there because somebody asked me the question – who was the love of my life? And I said, quite truthfully, that he was. It's very sad for me to think that my marriage to him didn't work and that now he's with someone else. But I'm not devas-tated and paralysed by it – I know everyone would like to think that I am. But I'm not. I still love him, and I probably always will. But I have to get on with my life.

'As to that life, well, perhaps my father was right when

he said that I was growing up on stage. And in a way I'm confronting him about a lot of issues through this movie and, though it may be painful in the beginning, in the end it's very growth-provoking for us both. I think he'll understand, given time.

'Actually, he hasn't seen the movie yet. He lives in Michigan and I didn't want to put him through all the insanity of the Los Angeles premiere. So I'll probably set up a private screening for him. It's going to be like going to group therapy or something. He's going to be confronting one of my brothers' alcoholism and Christopher's homosexuality as it were in open court, though for me there's no judgment involved whatsoever. I've got quite a big family and we are all insane in one way and another. But I think he's already come to terms with most of it, and he'll survive this OK.

'Yes, I think I'd have been a very different person if my mother hadn't died when I was so young. But you survive these things, and now I would like to marry and have children of my own – oh, six or seven of them. I'm cast as a very aggressive person but I'm also pretty maternal too, as you can see in the film. But first, I have to find a man and that's more difficult than you might suppose.

'He'll have to be pretty strong and he'll have to know that there are disadvantages. Anyone with me gets their private life gone over. It isn't nice and it isn't easy. But it's part of the game. I've chosen to play it but I can't expect too many others to want to.

'Besides, how do I find a man who likes me for myself? If you are in my position, you trust, but you are often let down.

'Yes, I'm afraid of growing old without this wish being fulfilled, but also because I'm a very physical person – I love to run and dance and I'm full of energy and I hate to think that a day will come when I can't do it. But that's life. You grow up. You become more tolerant of yourself and other people. I'm more patient now – not much more, but a bit. I want some hair left when I'm 80, whether it's blonde or not.'

Nancy Banks-Smith

The other side of the tube

January 3, 1992

It is an astonishing moment in **The Master Blackmailer** (Granada) when Dame Gwen Ffrangcon-Davies appears, encrusted in black jet and sporting a rather insouciant widow's cap. She will be 101 on January 27.

She leaned her chin on her hand with the index finger running up her cheek. It was a slender, flowing gesture and she must have used this, or something very like this, for Juliet:

> *See! how she leans her cheek upon her hand.*
> *O! that I were a glove upon that hand*
> *That I might touch that cheek.*

She was the greatest Juliet of her generation, playing her for the first time as a childlike girl. It came naturally. All her gestures and intonations are light and youthful. When I heard her speak some Juliet on radio recently, her delivery was rippling, fluent, joyful. It sounded as if they were her own words and, here and there, they were. She can barely see and hear any more so she remembers. I thought it was some astonishing new actress and stood still . . . on one leg . . . listening. Afraid to put the other foot down as though a bird had flown in the room and started singing. As a girl this woman saw Irving's Shylock, played with Ellen Terry's collection of dolls. It was like seeing Shelley.

She hadn't acted for more than 20 years when June Wyndham Davies, producer of *The Master Blackmailer* by Conan Doyle, Granada's Christmas goody, asked her to play the small part of a dowager who hired Holmes. She was delighted. Travelled to Manchester from Essex. Drank champagne with Robert Hardy, the master blackmailer in question. The first take was all over the place. She watched Jeremy Brett's lips and took her cue from that. The second went like a song.

There is a certain playfulness about her performance which suggests she is, perhaps, too young for the part.

The film itself is a gorgeous business. Thickly buttered not to say jammed with mist and mirrors, greenery and tapestry, reflections of reflections. And a group of girls like a Fragonard on the grass. *The Master Blackmailer*, Charles Augustus Milverton, lives in Hampstead in premises of unparalleled grandeur with his own rain forest, which suggests that business is encouragingly brisk. As Sherlock Holmes remarked there are hundreds in this great city who turn white at his name.

I can't help feeling a twinge of pity for blackmailers, who must have fallen on hard times. Charles Augustus had only to accuse a viscount of a moment of indiscretion with an actress (Jeremy Brett and Edward Hardwicke took this disclosure with admirable seriousness) to make his brother shoot a footman in the face. Not, as you might imagine, the foot.

The details of this noble imbroglio are a little fuzzy in my mind. I can't imagine what I could accuse a viscount of nowadays that would cause a footman a moment's concern. There should probably be a Society for the Alleviation of Distressed Blackmailers. All clustered together in sheltered housing, piping about how they once put the wind up Lady Whatsit.

Jeremy Paul, who expanded the story, Chris Truelove,

who designed it, and Peter Hammond, who directed, beautifully conceal the fact that there is no story there at all. *The Master Blackmailer* is melodrama with knobs on. The sum total of Holmes's contribution is to become engaged to the Milverton housemaid and burgle the Milverton house to very little purpose. I do hope Dame Gwen wasn't paying him too much for all this. While Holmes and Watson are shut in a cupboard, Milverton is despatched by the Miss Otis of her day, who shoots him six times, crying ringingly, 'Vile creature! I will free the world of a poisonous thing.' Robert Hardy succumbs at some length with much poisonous writhing.

There is something about the content of the story which says red revolution to me. The rich and aristocratic are riddled with folly and hypocrisy and get away with murder. The incriminating evidence is eagerly supplied by their valets and maids. Holmes's own treatment of the kitchen maid has to receive a high romantic gloss to pass muster today. I probably read too much into it but I doubt if 1903 was a very good year.

I recommend the sight of Nickolas Grace looking like a malevolent flatfish on a dish. All eye. And a suffocatingly erotic cabaret scene with Simon Fogg singing to a cavalry colonel. George V said: 'I thought men like that shot themselves.' In this film they did.

Gwen Ffrangcon-Davies died on her 101st birthday.

January 9, 1992
Call me old-fashioned, Monica, but I had my doubts about Dr Jobinet, an old Swiss goat with a goatee, the moment he began testing Krystal Carrington's motor reflexes: 'Look directly at me and undo the upper two buttons of your blouse. Beautiful! Beautiful!' And he slavered copiously into his stethoscope.

Krystal, of course, Suspected Nothing. It is very important in a soap heroine that, if the family doctor grows fangs and bays at the moon, she should suspect nothing. Krystal is an exceptionally strapping woman with the animation of a large fridge freezer. Above the snowline of her throat, all is tundra. Also she can't spell. For six years Krystal has regularly got it in the neck from a small but vivid villainess called Alexis.

Now at last in **Dynasty: The Reunion** (BBC 1) Krystal has a role tailored to her talents. For three years she has been comatose in Dr Jobinet's mountain greenery and has now come out of her coma. Though you'll have to take my word for it. She Suspects Nothing but Dr Jobinet has, in fact, *hypnotised* her: 'Mrs Carrington has been scientifically triggered to kill Mr Carrington the next time they make love. Which should be anytime now.'

And Krystal, looking glazed, began to undo the buttons on her rather ample nightie.

At this heart-stopping point, with its unexpected overtones of Eskimo Nell, *Dynasty* broke off and we all went to bed. Mr and Mrs Carrington included. Oh, heavens, Monica, how can you sleep? Even as I speak Krystal may be scientifically triggered.

We must reassure ourselves with the thought that there are two-and-a-half more hours of this stuff to come, that no soap star ever dies, they only go on a world cruise, and that John Forsythe, who plays Blake Carrington, is 74 at the end of this month and may well drop off before the second button.

Happy birthday. Assuming, of course, that you . . . Well, hurrying on ↓ . .

The last series of *Dynasty* ended in mid-air. As far as I remember Adam Carrington hit Dex Dexter, who cannoned into Alexis Carrington Colby Dexter who, top heavy with surnames, fell head first off a balcony. I do have this strong image of two little legs suspended in space like a sparrow dropping off the twig. You suspect the script-writers thought there would be another series. ABC thought otherwise.

The Reunion, a last round-up of the Carringtons, offers

a somewhat cynical explanation of Alexis's survival: 'They say she managed to turn in mid-air so she could land on top of Dex Dexter. He didn't fare all that well.'

Suffice to say Dex makes no further appearance in *Dynasty* while Alexis, in a small towel and excellent spirits, is restored to perfect health by a personable masseur with a ponytail. Adam Carrington also survived but with a new face.

No, you do not recognise Adam Carrington, Monica. What you recognise is a resemblance to Leonard Sachs, who used to hammer away with such vim in *The Good Old Days*. The new Adam is his son, Robin.

The plot froths at the mouth. If it were a dog, you would shoot it. It trades on American fears that foreigners, the Japanese in particular, are taking over. Blake seems to be completely off his head: 'A mysterious international consortium is plotting to buy up America!' But he's not as mad as the man who is plotting to buy up America: 'I am going to be the most powerful lunatic the world has ever seen since Bonaparte!'

Only Blake and his four brave boys can save America. The plot, the acting, the four brave boys reminded me of something. It was a while before I could put my finger on it. *Thunderbirds*.

If *Dynasty* has any value it is Joan Collins, who proved that humour and style, rubbed briskly together, can burst into fame. She was getting on for 50 when she swept into a court-room scene in *Dynasty* and kick-started the stalled series. I have nothing but admiration for a woman who refused to accept a character called Caresse.

And who, when pronouncing *Dynasty* or in any other context, refused to say die.

January 28, 1992
The luxury, 'the object of no practical use', is always a desert-island castaway's most revealing choice. John Major chose to take the Oval cricket ground. Off air, as **Arena**

(BBC 2) showed, there was animated debate about the usefulness of cricket, if any, among the women running the show.

Sue Lawley, the interviewer: 'Should we allow him to get away with that?' Janet Lee, the producer: 'Caroline says it's of practical use.' (Caroline Millington is Head of Magazine Programmes, Radio.) Lawley with an almost audible snort: 'Not very practical, to play cricket!'

The prime minister shuffled his papers composedly and drank his Highland Spring. Much to his surprise, they let him have the Oval. 'I thought you'd tell me that was cheating. I had a fall back.' 'Oh, do you want to do it again?' 'Oh, no!' quoth he. 'If I can get away with that, that's fine.'

It was a handy lesson in politics. Speak with what passion you can command on behalf of Plan A ('It will be lovely. The sun will shine, the grass will grow and the pitch will be beautiful and I will be able to bat and bowl to my heart's content') but have Plan B up your sleeve. And don't tell them what that is.

I fancy a fresh egg as my luxury. You can't call an egg animate. I would contest that interpretation through every court in the land, which, with any luck, would delay my departure to the desert island by several years. A peacock's egg would be nice. Edith Sitwell, a dauntingly plain child, used to walk in the grounds with her arm round a peacock's neck. Or an ostrich or a duck-billed platypus. Sitting on the egg would pass a month or so in happy anticipation and then there's decorating the nursery and choosing the name . . .

It is unfortunate that almost anything you get out of an egg is either half-witted or liable to take your leg off at the knee. I draw the line at an alligator. As Dorothy Parker's cleaner said on finding one in the bath: 'I cannot work in a house where there are alligators. I would have told you this before but I didn't suppose the question would ever come up.'

That is exactly the sort of question that tends to come up

on *Desert Island Discs*. Is it a *nice* island? Are you sure? As someone said, 'A desert island is like dying. No one minds going if they can come back.' This, I was surprised to discover, was me. I reviewed this *Arena* 10 years ago.

Fortunately, like the Venus fly trap, TV critics have a retentive memory of 40 seconds. I was charmed to re-discover what a funny, touching programme Antony Wall's 10-year-old *Arena* was. (The John Major item was tacked on recently.) And cheered to notice that I was right first time.

There *are* odd overtones about this island. They give it a resonance beyond the dolly blue bag waves, the plastic palm and the well worn seagull. Clutching a few memories and a precious possession, guests go with reluctance, leaving all living things behind.

When Roy Plomley leaped out of bed crying 'Eureka!' it was November, the fire had gone out in his bed-sit and we were losing the war. It is amazing what attraction desert islands have under such circumstances. It sounded like heaven. As parrots flew across John Major's Oval, it looked like heaven.

February 21, 1992
Any gossip columnist in the early sixties knew Lord Moynihan. If the upper classes ever flagged in their efforts to create a public nuisance and a blasted racket, Tony was always there to take up the slack. I was a gossip columnist on the *Daily Herald*, a chastening experience I can tell you. I have been thrown out of some of the best places in the land and my hat after me. The friends of the *Daily Herald* were not, in general, good gossip column copy. Boilermakers and Amalgamated Metal Bashers rarely ran away with a polo player with no visible means of support but his jock strap.

The top drawer, that was the ticket. That's where the nobs and the knickers were. Seeking frivolous or scandalous copy among the nobs and debs, I leaned on the kind-hearted and the irredeemably rackety and I remember both rather fondly.

Moynihan was then, as later, large and loud. His soul wore a bookie's suit and a brown bowler. He was managing a pop group at the time with young Lord Wharncliffe on the drums. Even against the background of Wharncliffe's banging, Moynihan was loud. Oo, he was awful, you almost liked him.

'He must have qualified as one of the biggest shits of all time,' a business associate, his scarf pulled up and his hat pulled down, told Denis Tuohy on *This Week* (Thames). 'He put his friends up front to do his nefarious deals and then he ran away and left them to face the music.' This may be the only verifiably truthful comment in the whole programme.

The entertaining thing about a hereditary system is that you never know what you are going to get out of the bran tub and, whatever it is, you can't throw it back. Who could have deduced Lord Moynihan from his solid ancestry or matched him up with his microscopic half-brother, Colin Moynihan?

Nothing, however, prepared us for the next Lord Moynihan. 'The Little Lord Moynihan Mystery' considered the competing claims of three-year-old Andrew and one-year-old Daniel, Moynihan's sons by his fourth and fifth wives. Editha and Jinna are good-looking local girls, who hauled themselves out of Manila's worst slum by working in Moynihan's brothels. *This Week* cut from the lords in red velvet, to the ladies in the red light district and set it to music. Come the worst there's a musical in it.

At the prospect of approaching death Moynihan started to believe in the Lords. He acknowledged Daniel as his heir and violently repudiated the elder boy, Andrew, even announcing the child's death in *The Times*. He didn't believe Andrew was his son and he had a sample of DNA taken to protect Daniel's claim. His brother-in-law and

trustee, Charles Vance, challenged the fourth Lady Moynihan to check Andrew's DNA against this.

No doubt to his surprise, she agreed and Tuohy brought
the blood samples back but now the trustees of the
Moynihan estate refused to allow a comparison. Messrs
Donne, Mileham and Haddock were dismissive: 'Not, with
respect, for Thames TV.' The phrase 'with respect' from a
lawyer is always a slap in the face with a haddock.

A remarkable point about the report was the number of
women who were prepared to give Tuohy phials of their
blood. I mean, I've nothing against the man but he can
whistle for mine. Moynihan's second wife, Shirin, a
former belly dancer who lives in Italy, gave a sample of
blood and so did their daughter Miranda, who lives in a
tower block in London. If you subtract Shirin's DNA from
Miranda's you are left with Lord Moynihan's and this can
be matched with Andrew's DNA. Do you follow me? That's
a relief.

You can't say it wasn't nail-biting stuff. As Thursday
unrolled, *This Week* waited for the result of the DNA
digital typing test, an experimental technique which can
take only 48 hours. It was quick but it was not conclusive.
They are now reverting to a full DNA test, which takes two
weeks. A wise child might be keeping his fingers crossed
that Lord Moynihan is not his father.

April 17, 1992
But I've met this woman . . . At the time I was making a
perfunctory attempt to learn Indian cookery but life is too
short to stuff mushrooms and it was always a doomed
endeavour. Anyway, there she sat in a shining white sari
and a shining white room looking cool as a mountain
stream. Advertising was the word that came to mind. I
understood she was a model. I had no idea she was an
angel. What! In Maida Vale?

Angel of Bengal is a title she seems to have given herself
since she became a spiritual leader. Bangladesh would be

more accurate but Bengal sounds more romantic. In Bangladesh palm trees were reflected inverted in still water, a butterfly fluttered like a leaf falling upwards and the morning mist moved to show her standing perfectly still, modelling a sari.

Anna Raphael's 'Angel of Bengal' (*True Stories*, Channel 4) was exhilaratingly comic and then quite painful as if someone who was tickling you had, suddenly, stabbed.

The comedy tended to be in Palm Beach, where she is a socialite, and the sorrow in Bangladesh, where she is a spiritual leader. I strongly recommend the section where she haggles for a prize for her Palm Beach charity ball. She is a heavenly being. He is a Jewish jeweller called Joe. One watched this evenly matched contest with the liveliest interest.

'I want,' she said spiritually, 'a really sensational prize.'

He said briskly that business was bad: 'Look out on the street! It's dead!'

'Perhaps we could use your name? You wouldn't want it attached to a watch. You'd want something a little more . . .'

'Not necessarily,' he said firmly.

'. . . spectacular,' she went on as if deaf in one ear. She tapped a glass case containing a $20,000 necklace sharply with her long nail. 'This is really nice but that . . .' She flicked the nail dismissively at the watch he offered. 'All the photographers will be there. Just think of the picture on the cover of a magazine.'

'What magazine?' he said quickly.

'I think a watch doesn't have quite the impact . . .' she said driftily, as if he hadn't spoken.

Reflected in a glitter of mirrors, the Baroness Thea von Theilheimer Shenkman, her mother, said: 'She adores Bangladesh. She put in an irritation system,' and you could well believe it. If Paul McGann in *The Gospels* (BBC 1) looks like an angel who has eaten a lot of yeast, she looks like an angel who has had a few facelifts. No muscle of her beautiful white face, jewelled with bright-blue contact lenses, moved. Except when she was laughing at the villagers of Ramsala behind her hand.

In Ramsala the cream cows dip their innocent noses in water drawn by buckets. This is the village where her charity, Food Relief International, has bored three wells and built a clinic. But the wells don't work because the villagers can't afford electricity and the clinic is only used for her Hare Krishna classes. When a villager touchingly tried to intercede with her 'Holy Mother, if only I could explain to you this pain in my heart. Holy Mother, please listen,' she didn't understand because she doesn't talk Bangla. However, her close companion, Razzaque Khan, bawls Bangla fluently. 'He curses us and calls our children bastards,' said the villager. Razzaque Khan translated, rather to his own advantage, and laughed. She smiled into her hand.

The Angel tends to glide around with her eyes closed having, one must suppose, inner light and no legs. Personally, I liked the bit where she tripped.

May 15, 1992
Ponders End is a name on the front of London buses you never catch. Like Desire, it is a destination with great romantic resonance unless you live there. Who was Ponder? Was he, as his name suggests, a *ruminative* man? An early Briton often to be seen standing in the middle of the road, lost in thought? And was his end anything to do with this distracted habit?

In Ponders End there is something very like an Anglo-Saxon village, a scatter of haphazard huts among intensely cultivated little patches of earth. This is the Ponders End and District Smallholders Association. It is prey to raids from neighbouring vandals or, perhaps, Vikings. As Doris, whose fruit cake mows down the competition at the annual show, said, 'We had them three times in five weeks. They left all the sherry and took all the spirits. Then they

took the organ and came back a few days later and took
the stool.' You see, with some effort of the imagination,
sozzled Vikings singing hymns around the organ.

Vegetable Plots (Channel 4), produced and directed by
Taghi Amirani, was an indomitable little pastoral.

The autumn show is a demonstration of vegetable love,
vaster than empires. Onions that look as if the Kremlin
had come to Ponders End and pupped. A pumpkin that
took two men to carry it. 'Stay there!' said Tony. 'Don't
move!' said Tommy as if it might suddenly rise on its vast
haunches like a Sumo wrestler and attack. Pale parsnips
like stalactites, forests of celery, leeks with belligerent
whiskers and brassicas as big as magnetic mines. Bill's
cabbages seemed on the point of explosion. He trundled
them in on a wheelbarrow, which squealed in protest.
Like grandfather's clock they were too big for the bench
so he stood them on the floor. They peered out from
beneath the bench with bulging, deep green eyes fringed
with vast lashes.

After the judging, the camera tracked Bill's implausibly
casual approach, glancing at this man's parsnips, that
man's potatoes. Then he saw his own cabbage with a first
prize card on it. 'Cor, blimey!' he shouted. 'I've done it,
man! Bloody great, man! Oh, you beauty!' and he fell on
his knees and kissed it. Posing for the winner's photo, only
his shining eyes showing over his cabbage, he said simply:
'It's the first time I've been recognised.' Bill is black and
works for London Transport.

The gardeners thought we were looking at their veg-
etables when we were really looking at them. These were
prize-winning people.

Charlie has one leg. He had the other off when he was
eight. He didn't elaborate on this. These things happen.
He was taking geranium cuttings and talking about his
wife, Florence. Florence was far more disabled than he.
She had, according to Charlie, masteroids (*sic*) and facial
burns and hip replacements. 'And, when she was 40, they

put her in a place where they train 'em and they asked her what she'd like to be and she said "I like needlework." And she had only one arm.' Charlie's eyes began to glow. 'She could needle. She could take bits and pieces. She'd look at your wife and say . . . so many yards . . . I'll give you three fittings . . . and it'll fit you like a glove.'

He met her when he pruned her apple tree. 'One day she said "Would you marry me?" I looked at her – oh, well – if I can't make somebody happy. So we got married and I was 13 years with her and she was quite a nice girl. Oh, yes. She'd 'ave a little tiff then, all of a sudden, "Want a cup of tea, darling?" She could take all the stuff out of the oven with one arm better'n I could. I grew to love her.'

And did Flo love Charlie? 'Oh, yes. She said to her friends in the firm, "It's the best part of my life." So I said, "Well, I've pleased somebody in my life." '

The short and simple annals of the poor are not particularly short and rather obscure if you haven't got your teeth in, but don't they take your breath away?

The Vikings struck again and again. They burned and burgled. Doris said, 'Oh, the sods! Excuse me. Leave that bit out.' The allotment holders rebuilt their smouldering clubhouse and held their prize-giving. The winners cradled their cups in the crooks of their arms like twins. You knew and liked them all. Tony, Dave and his young son, Charlie, Bill and Maureen, whose hut is furnished with a three-piece suite and antimacassars. When they burned it, she rebuilt it. Their names are engraved on the cup of life.

Adieu

December 16, 1991: John Samuel

The voice of linseed oil on willow

John Arlott, who died on Saturday aged 77, was born in the Old Cemetery Lodge, Basingstoke. He never thought he would make old bones, but not for this reason. His beloved father, Jack, had no especial love of cricket, although later on his son delighted to recall that when cricket began to seek better playing surfaces it found them in the graveyards.

His mother Nelly, stuffing Liberal tracts into envelopes long into the night, was his induction into radicalism, so often at odds with his Hampshire traditionalism. 'The bastards are closing the Watercress Line forever . . .'

It was sometimes hard to find the right thing to say. His instant emotion was the actor-manager's: theatrical cordite. As you scrambled for response the philosopher took over. Often you could wish you were an audience of millions instead of one. The mildest remark about an honest Dao enjoyed in an Algarve beach café could draw a withering response: 'The most evil colonial power the world has known.'

The MCC were to reel under a similar onslaught on the matter of South Africa. One visit in 1947 persuaded Arlott of the rightness of multi-racialism and the wrongness of apartheid. It was typical of him to find a place for Basil D'Oliveira in English cricket after the South African had written to him in desperation.

Cyril Connolly had offered a similar generosity and recognition to the young Arlott, then a police sergeant in Southampton. His poems in *Horizon* and elsewhere, collected in book form in 1944 and 1945, led to his appointment by the BBC as a staff producer and then an instructor in broadcasting technique. As head of poetry in the early days of the Third Programme he grew to know Dylan Thomas, Roy Campbell and the postwar generation of poets and writers. They influenced him for a lifetime, though he would sometimes grump, 'I write like a copper, dun I?'

Sport, and especially cricket, projected him into a much wider domain, though it came about over the dead bodies of some BBC stuffed shirts who thought his Hampshire burr 'vulgar'. Arlott knew plenty about pusillanimity and meanness in high places.

At best it was a snobbery which wholly overlooked his timing, eye and exactitude of judgment and imagery. Throughout the land listeners could *feel* the lethal pace of Lindwall or Miller running in to bowl at Hutton, Washbrook or Compton in that Ashes summer of 1948. Arlott's punctuation remains as evocative as the smell of linseed oil on willow. His voice was heard wherever on the earth cricket is played. Small boys swaying on the branches of trees overlooking Bridgetown, Kingston and Port-of-Spain sought to imitate him. But to others who knew nothing of cricket he sounded like home and no one could match his poetic gift for the right image. Asif Mahmood reminded him of Groucho Marx pursuing a pretty waitress. The

South African Van de Buyl, bowling for Middlesex, was like a younger Lord Longford, 'though not nearly so tolerant'.

Nostalgia and sentiment helped him to his living but the road accident which cost him his son Jimmy at the age of 21 all but destroyed his religious faith. The hurt never left the depth of his eyes and each day of his life he knotted a black tie. A second son, Tim, to his great pride became a television executive. Valerie, his second wife, bore him a third son, Robert, a difficult birth presaging troubles which eventually cost her her life in her forties. It was a deeply unhappy time. The BBC had turned from county commentaries to one-liners. A presenter who gabbled the Hampshire score switched to Arlott at Bournemouth for an update. 'You've given it,' said Arlott. 'Back to the studio.'

Test match broadcasting and his writing helped bind many personal wounds. In the 1950s he wrote soccer for the *Guardian* as 'Silchester'. Only the last-minute availability of 'Old International' – Donny Davies, his soccer senior – saved him from the Manchester United catastrophe at Munich airport. To his grief, Donny's widow could not find it in her heart to speak to him again.

For a while he was active in politics, twice standing as a Liberal. He described himself as a passionate Liberal, not a radical one. In 1970 he refused to broadcast the proposed South African tour. Persisting with the tour, he said, was a social, political and cricketing error. It brought him abuse from the Tory press and suspension from *Twenty Questions*. It was an issue on which he never bent. When he filled in a South African immigration questionnaire in 1947 he wrote 'Human' in the space marked 'Race'. He lived to see South Africa and the sports pages bend instead.

After writing for the *Observer* and *The Times* he returned to the *Guardian* as cricket and, subsequently, wine correspondent in the late sixties. For a dozen years it was a vintage period in all respects. His books ranged from his early verses to *English Cheeses of the South and West* (1956), *Jack Hobbs: A Profile of the Master* (1981) and *Arlott on Wine*.

Lunch at the Old Sun, his temporal and spiritual home at Alresford in eastern Hampshire, would usually end with the lamplighter. Libation began in a vast library-living room, often the bottle a newly discovered chateau or domaine, gleefully introduced with the latest ripe tale.

Much that was important in Arlott's life was in this room, lined with first editions. John Piper, John Betjeman, Hardy, Osbert Lancaster, Hogarth, Cobbett, Kingsley Amis, and so much more. The aquatints, the country house topographies, the ship's glass . . . No Arlott journey of the middle years was without a chart of second-hand book shops.

On the last day of the Centenary Test of 1980, Arlott signed off as a commentator: '. . . and Boycott pushes this away between silly-point and slip; picked up by Mallett at short third man; that's the end of the over; it's 69 for two, nine runs off the over, Boycott 28, 15 Gower, 69 for two, after Trevor Bailey it'll be Henry Blofeld.'

A swig of claret, then, as the sweat ran he took a handkerchief to mop his brow. The Lord's public address announced that Arlott had finished his final stint. The huge crowd spontaneously broke into applause. Boycott dropped his bat to clap. Lillee waved a fisted salute. The players applauded. Arlott took another gulp and walked out of regular broadcasting forever.

His decision to retire to Alderney with his third wife, Pat, was never easy. The family had spent warm and happy holidays in the fifties on this seagirt rock, one mile by three, a fortress over the centuries, now beckoning him with a fine house, the Vines.

At the last he could not bring himself to sign the exchange contract. In that frozen moment his adviser said, 'C'mon, you bloody fool. Sign it and sell it if you must. You can't lose.' Sign he did, giving up his past at the Old Sun.

Next day he broke out in a savage rash, but the move began to Alderney and the last comfortable, well-solaced years. He'd auctioned his wine cellar and chuckled at the £28,000 it made. 'Only the big money stuff I'd choke if I drank . . .'

He was honoured with a life membership – of Somerset. His best book, he once said, was of Maurice Tate (1951). He was a proud, caring president of the Professional Cricketers' Association, especially during the difficult Packer years, the implications of which he read better than any. Asked once how he would like to be remembered, he said, 'for producing *Under Milk Wood* and getting Basil D'Oliveira a cricketing job in England.'

Leslie Thomas John Arlott, born February 25, 1914; died December 14, 1991.

December 16, 1991: Frank Keating

Like Uncle Tom Cobbleigh reading Neville Cardus to the Indians

On June 11, 1947, from the terrace of a small villa in the sweltering Appenines, Dylan Thomas put down his bottle and picked up his pen to reply to a letter from his erstwhile BBC wireless producer in the talks department:

'My dear John, Thank you for writing. It was very good to hear from you. Though I hear your voice every day: from Trent Bridge at the moment. You're not only the best cricket commentator – far and away that; but the best sports commentator I've heard ever: exact, enthusiastic, prejudiced, amazingly visual, authoritative, and friendly. A great pleasure to listen to you . . .'

Later that month Dylan wrote to another English friend, Margaret Taylor: 'I hear John Arlott's voice all the week, describing the cricket matches. He sounds like Uncle Tom Cobbleigh reading Neville Cardus to the Indians . . .'

He was to continue to do so for another 33 years. On the last day of the Centenary Test at Lord's in 1980, Arlott signed off, handed over to the next commentator without frills, stood up, and with scarcely a glance at the field below him, turned, took a large slug of the red wine in his glass, mopped his brow with a red-spotted hankie, and walked away, embarrassed by the three cheers of farewell which sounded for him round the famous stadium.

John liked cricketers more than cricket. Once, when he was young, he asked: 'Is there, I wonder, anywhere in the world such a human, generous, unenvious, shop-talking, enthusiastic, mellow, craft-versed community as English cricket professionals?' Not long ago, he thought about that, and then said: 'Of all the cricketers I have known in my time, I have come across only four bad ones. Four bastards. But only four in thousands.'

He was touchingly proud when he was elected life president of the Cricketers' Association, the pros' trade union. Proud, too, of his part in helping Basil D'Oliveira, the Cape Coloured, to escape the manacles of apartheid and make a new life as an England cricketer. The young man had bombarded John with letters from Cape Town: 'Courteous, sincere, anxious, still hoping: the oblong air mail envelopes with the green ink handwriting became familiar.'

After D'Oliveira had indeed played for England – and when the South African government in its embarrassed pique refused him entry with his new England colleagues – Arlott spoke at the Cambridge Union against the motion, 'That politics should not intrude on sporting contacts.'

Seconding the minister of sport, Denis Howell, Arlott's was a mesmerising denouncement of the motion (over-turned dramatically by 334 votes to 160) proposed by Ted Dexter and Wilf Wooller. 'It is political commitment and political belief that can make a man think that his opponents' views are so obnoxious that he will abstain from playing any game with him as a protest against what the other man believes . . .' John said. 'Any man's political commitment, if it is deep enough, is his personal philosophy and it governs his way of life, it governs his belief, and it governs the people with whom he is prepared to mix.'

His generosity to the twittering tyros in his trade was legendary: immense, warm, uncomplicated, totally unenvious of youth. Once, in these pages, I displayed a cross-patch flippancy about the pointlessness of writing on sport. By return, kindly admonishment (hand-written in black ink, and full of the dashes and colons which were, of course, his natural broadcaster's sole punctuation marks):

'It is clear that sports writing is not – or should not be – important in the pattern of literary life: just as sport is not – or should not be – important in the shape of world history: the fact remains that many unimportant – and important – people retain a deeply romantic and nostalgic feeling for the sports, and the great sportsmen, of their childhood, and abiding interests and loyalties in the sporting events of today.'

In the 1970s when he was the *Guardian*'s cricket writer, the unparalleled joy was to travel often with him: to the Test matches sometimes and, less fraught, around his beloved county shires. Carrying the typewriter, cork-screwing the bottles, nipping across to the county stores for more pâté or another hunk of Cheshire. Five hundred words of waffle after tea made it cheap at the price.

Among John's many books, one of his favourite was

English Cheeses of the South and West. 'The English are too humble to claim, and the rest of the world too loth to discover,' he wrote, 'that British cheeses are the finest in the world. Clean, rich, subtle, strong, of fine variety, they are a half-forgotten, but still great, catalogue – Cheshire, Blue Cheshire, Lancashire, Caerphilly, Wensleydale, Blue Vinny . . .' He listed them all, before coming down to his mood for that particular day: 'I shall today ask for a Gloucester. With it I will take, if I may, a 1934 Chambertin, a wine as big as a house, a drink to put the imagination of five Shakespeares into one jobbing journalist.'

The voice, the cricket, the books, the pictures; the moist tearfulness when he talked of his beloved Thomas Hardy heroes (which he so associated with, not forgetting the heroines); the desperate love of his family and close friends; the always insisted 'accident' of his good fortune in life ('relished and relishable' as he would say): but I will remember most, I think, a day I spent in Alderney when he was still, just, in his great bullocky, bright-eyed prime.

We walked down from the Vines to collect the mail at the post office. 'I do love my post.' Then rolled on down towards the sea wall, via the pub and the morning's first bracer, a Fino sherry in tomato juice. Then another when we had settled ourselves in another hotel bar's conservatory, which gave us a spectacular view of the relentlessly angry waves snapping and fretting, and fizzing and dying.

Pat, good Pat, herself doting and doted on, was waiting with lunch back up the hill. But he called for one more mammoth pre-lunch bracer, watched some more gloriously savage white horses tilt again at the Becher's of the sea wall, and reflected softly in probably the most celebrated British voice after Churchill's: 'I'm not talking remotely about cricket, m'boy, when I tell you it ain't half a bloody old game, ain't it? It ain't half a bloody old game.'

He pondered on his words, shrugged, chuckled, and ordered two more of the same.

December 19, 1991: Richard Gott

Corker of a delivery

John Arlott's chief fear as the *Guardian*'s wine correspondent was that he might be sacked. A man of great achievement and enormous charm, he could also be extremely touchy and was notably lacking in self-confidence. Any change at the *Guardian*, he felt, was bound to affect him for the worse. He had come to believe that the £30 a week he was paid for writing about wine was all that lay between him and the poorhouse.

When I became the features editor, with the customary instruction to wield a new broom, the first note on my desk was an urgent invitation to lunch from our famous wine columnist, not at that moment my most pressing priority. I knew little about wine, and absolutely nothing about cricket. 'You must go,' my secretary whispered, 'but watch out for the drink.' The editor, who had earlier hired Arlott to give him something to do in the winter months when there was no cricket, gave a knowing look.

I arrived nervously the following lunchtime at the Tate Gallery restaurant, known in those days for its Rex Whistler décor, its astonishing wine cellar at benevolent prices, and the easy familiarity with arcane vintages of its manager. 'Don't worry, I'll be back by three,' I told my assistant.

John was waiting for me, clearly equally nervous. We sat down at a corner table, just the two of us. Two or three bottles of red had been selected and ordered that morning, and stood already opened. The white was waiting nicely chilled. I have, perhaps understandably, forgotten many of the details of the rest of the day, though I do recall that, starting with champagne, the equally inviting wine waitresses frequently brought fresh bottles for us to try, ordered by admirers across the crowded room. John was determined that his new editor should be left in no doubt about his continued suitability for the task of writing about wine, and to that end he had soon unlocked his erudition, his genius for autobiography, and (above all) his immense capacity for friendship.

Long before the end of the first bottle I had fallen into his clutches for ever, totally beguiled, like almost everyone who met him. In the Middle Ages, he would have been a wandering magician or a story-teller. In the 20th century it was entirely appropriate that he should have been a producer for the Third Programme and a cricket commentator. He was also a most outspoken radical. I doubt whether he would much like to be compared with J. B. Priestley, but he belonged to a similar historical strand in English life, present in all political parties and in none. He was both a genius and a showman, a radical intellectual with the common touch.

We drank, and he talked, all afternoon, and at about four o'clock, I staggered out to a telephone in the corridor to tell the office that I might be a little late. I thought I detected a slight snigger at the end of the line. Finally, about six, as the gallery itself was closing, we came out on to Millbank and said goodbye. The bill, which he paid, was considerably larger than his weekly stipend from the *Guardian*. I walked back along the Thames to Farringdon Road in a desperate and unsuccessful attempt to sober up.

Two days later, even before I had had time to renew his contract, there was another letter from John. Our lunch had been so successful – or perhaps he feared that it had been insufficiently successful – that he had decided to organise another one. It was to be at home in Hampshire that weekend, just for me and the wine wizard from the Tate Gallery and our companions.

We drove down to Alresford on a sunny Sunday. John proudly announced that he had sat up half the night scrubbing mussels. And there was the ever-hospitable and put-upon Pat presiding over a great table laid for six. At each place, a line of five different glasses stretched halfway across the table, an earnest of what was to come, an afternoon of serious drinking from his cellar, to which only Lord Peter Wimsey could do justice. He wanted to prove that he owned wine superior to that held in the Tate Gallery. We drove away late in the evening, incandescent with drink, having providently arranged to stay the night nearby.

Every man has his price, and mine was the friendship of John Arlott. The renewed contract was in the post on Monday morning, and the invitations never stopped coming.

Like many others, I was soon making improbable but regular pilgrimages to Alderney, for more good food and wine, and for ever more radical opinions. If John thought the rulers of the Hampshire County Cricket Club were fascists – and he did – his views on Mrs Thatcher were equally unprintable.

There was once a famous book called *The Strange Death of Liberal England*. In the character of John Arlott, Liberal England never died. It simply turned away from politics and was reincarnated elsewhere – in a man of great personal uncertainty who wrote beautifully about poetry, cricket, and wine.

December 9, 1991: Michael McNay

Live now pay later

Nothing anybody wrote about Jack Trevor Story was half as funny as the stuff Jack wrote about himself, and plenty of journalists tried. Story's very presence was enough to transmute life into comedy. And, like breathing mist on to a window, his characters came to life. Sometimes they even threatened to sue.

The one thing you could safely predict about Story is that he would remain broke all his life. A *Guardian* profile of him in 1970 said as much, and there was never any danger that he would disprove it. Anyone who could sell the sole rights in *The Trouble with Harry* to Alfred Hitchcock for £150 was destined for the bread line. That was one of Story's earlier and better known novels.

The title of another, also filmed, was *Live Now Pay Later*. It became a catchphrase for a style of life, but it was always Jack's personal motto. When he was discharged from his second bankruptcy, he strode from court beaming and saying: 'Thank Christ I can get into debt again now. I'm going to find myself one of these marvellous credit cards.'

Despite the one-liners, and the publicity grabbing statements designed to send himself up as well as the whole celebrity industry, Story never thought of himself as a funny man. He simply thought life was funny, and that everyone around him was funny, even his loved ones; and the occasional loved one was apt to up sticks and leave after a year or two of being parodied in print. Maggie, the character to whom Jack devoted his Saturday column in the *Guardian* in the early 1970s, had a huge following of readers who assumed she was an invention. She wasn't. She was a sensible (and, it goes without saying where Jack was concerned) bonny Scottish lass who finally protected her privacy by fleeing abroad.

Jack's column became an elegy for his lost love, and Maggie rang one day and said her employers in Brussels were threatening to sue Story and the *Guardian* for libel. I took the call and assured her, touching wood as I did so, that there were no legal grounds. But after that I did begin to wonder about intrusion into private grief.

Fleet Street mythology is that people get fired when they are on holiday. In Jack Story's case, he got fired while *I* was on holiday: he was my signing and I was a fan as well as his editor, so my immediate boss waited for me to be away before wielding the axe, an act of butchery which, I never refrained from pointing out to the culprit, brought an unprecedented shoal of letters from mortified readers. Jack thought his executioner was right and I was wrong. But he was still receiving letters about the column 20 years later.

Jack Trevor Story started life as a butcher's boy in Cambridge. He sold his first story to John o' London's when he was working as an electronics engineer with Marconi. Soon afterwards, he joined the Sexton Blake Library and wrote 30 pulp paperbacks. This taught him the quick way into a narrative, an accomplishment he never lost. One of his later stories starts: 'Beryl had been with the firm for 15 years when the elder partner asked her to take her knickers off.' The approach may lack subtlety, but it wants for nothing in pace.

And it was a wonderfully agile style: he shot the rapids of his own stream of consciousness. He had an acute eye for the starched daintiness of middle-class manners, like Orton but without the vicious streak. His own models were George Orwell, the novelist rather than the essayist, and William Saroyan and James Thurber. He had Fielding's robust love of life, but he often wrote of death, as though it were some kind of social gaffe.

Milton Keynes corporation found a farmhouse for him to live in when he became Arts Council writer-in-residence in the late seventies. He never moved out. There weren't many places he could afford to move to; his 40 novels and hundreds of short stories brought him an annual income of around £2,000.

Sad really; but then Jack Trevor Story never thought so.
Jack Trevor Story, born 1917, died December 7, 1991.